3

Sociology as Disenchantment

Sociology as Disenchantment
The Evolution of the Work of
Georges Gurvitch

by

Richard Swedberg

HUMANITIES PRESS
ATLANTIC HIGHLANDS, N.J.

First published in 1982 in the United States of America by Humanities Press Inc., Atlantic Highlands, N.J. 07716

Library of Congress Cataloging in Publication Data

Swedberg, Richard.
   Sociology as disenchantment.

   Bibliography: p.
   1. Gurvitch, Georges, 1894-1965.   2. Sociology.   3. Social classes.
   4. Communism and society.   I. Title.
HM22.F8G859   301'.01   82-931
ISBN 0-391-02397-7   AACR2

Manufactured in the United States of America

Dedicated to DRS

Contents

INTRODUCTION   1

CHAPTER ONE
The Problems of the Russian Revolution   5

CHAPTER TWO
Fichte and the Dialectics of Idealism   20

CHAPTER THREE
The Revival of Juristic Socialism   35

CHAPTER FOUR
Sociology and the Impasse of the Liberal Bourgeoisie   51

CHAPTER FIVE
North American Sociology and the Triumph of Bourgeois Hegemony   69

CHAPTER SIX
The Task of Sociology in Post-War France (1945-1952)   88

CHAPTER SEVEN
Sociology and Socialism (1953-1965)   115

AFTERWORD   146

NOTES   151

BIBLIOGRAPHY
Works by Georges Gurvitch   185

INDEX   196

ACKNOWLEDGEMENTS

This book is dedicated to Deborah R. Swedberg, to whom I owe my largest debt. I also received help from Meshy Reinfeld and my parents, Hans and Dagmar Swedberg. Many people kindly let me interview them: Dr. Kagan at International Universities Press, Henri Lefebvre, Talcott Parsons, Stephen Schaefer, and Anthony Giddens. There were also many people who generously answered my written questions about Gurvitch: Theodore Abel, Phillip Bosserman, Daniel Guérin, Yvon Bourdet, Tom Bottomore, Myrtle Korenbaum, Wilbert E. Moore and many others. Larry Nichols at Boston College helped me with Gurvitch's writings in Russian. Four people in particular have helped me to appreciate social theory: Seymour Leventman, Severyn Bruyn and Tonia Aminoff at Boston College and Terry Freiberg at Boston University. A special thanks also to the gracious publisher of Humanities Press, Simon Silverman.

the parts into the whole."[9] The whole, according to Goldmann, here equals the class; consequently, the author's work has to be seen as an integral part of a class. The privileged position that the notion of class occupies in the Goldmannian scheme is, of course, no novelty; Marx and Engels saw class as the principal subject of history. *The Communist Manifesto* opens with the statement that "The history of all hitherto existing society is the history of class struggles," and this "history of all hitherto existing society" naturally includes the history of people's consciousness as manifested, for instance, in analyses of society.

The reason for attaching such importance to class, as opposed to other groups, is that only classes are able to transform society in its entirety. And only a class is able, as part of this total transformation, to develop a fundamentally novel vision of the relations between people and nature. The importance of groups such as the nation, i.e. what is called "the national tradition," is minor in comparison, apart from the important fact that the class struggle develops unevenly in different countries. To look at what is specifically "French," for instance, in the works of Lucien Lévy-Bruhl and of Marcel Mauss does not especially help one to understand or explain them. Groups such as the family and the friendship circle, which the biographical method so exclusively focuses on, always express themselves within the dialectics of class and class society.

Another group to which the sociology of knowledge has lately turned its attention is the professional group's most common institutional setting, the university. Terry Nichols Clark's *Prophets and Patrons: The French University and the Emergence of the Social Sciences* (1973) illustrates the fallacies of this approach.[10] The decline of Durkheimian sociology after World War I, according to Clark, is mainly attributable to the fact that French sociology was so poorly institutionalized at the time. This fact is valuable if one is measuring the importance of a sociological school in purely academic terms, as Clark indeed does. However, if one takes into consideration that classical bourgeois sociology ignored the class struggle as well as imperialism, it becomes clearer why it failed when confronted with World War I and the Russian Revolution. The objective significance of an intellectual work cannot be adequately grasped through a sociological analysis of the intellectual profession unless it is firmly placed within the dialectics of the capitalist division of labor. "*The occupation assumes an independent existence owing to division of labor,*" Marx noted, adding that this leads to "illusion regarding the connection between [the] craft and reality."[11]

The same argument must be levelled against those who have tried to unlock the secrets of social theory with the concept of role. A role is always played out within the dialectics of the class struggle. By itself, the role concept can in no way disclose "the social role of the man of knowledge" (Znaniecki).[12]

A useful model for a Marxist sociology of knowledge is provided by Goldmann in *The Hidden God*. According to the author, one must first lay bare the internal structure of the work in question, which in this case is the writings of Pascal and Racine. This structure is then "inserted" in a larger whole, in this case the Jansenist movement, which according to Goldmann "explains" the work. The Jansenist movement is in its turn inserted in the next larger whole, the class of the *noblesse de robe,* an aristocratized bourgeoisie which can be explained by examining the structure of the declining feudal society. There are many problems with an analysis of this kind, and it is difficult to apply it in all its rigor to someone like Gurvitch who lived in Russia, France and the United States. However, the general scheme — the successive insertion of an author's work into larger wholes, such as social movements, class, and class society — is very useful because it is so straightforward and of simple design. In addition, *The Hidden God* contains many practical hints on how to proceed in an analysis of this type. One has, the author says, to "oscillate" throughout the research between the parts and the whole. An "outer structure," for instance, only requires study up to the point that it explains the genesis of the "inner structure" of the work.

Goldmann's most important contribution to modern Marxist thought undoubtedly lies in his creating this "three-step" model for the analysis of social thought. There are, however, drawbacks to Goldmann's method. The most significant of these is perhaps Goldmann's tendency to overemphasize the creativity of social class at the expense of its structural determination by the mode of production and its specific place in history. In the study of Gurvitch's work that follows, which is inspired by Goldmann, I have tried to counteract this tendency. If I have succeeded, the potential as well as the limits of Goldmann's analysis will emerge with clarity in the ensuing pages.

1 The Problems of the Russian Revolution

The basic assumption in the analysis of Gurvitch's work which will be undertaken here is that "the history of social theory is the history of class struggle." This means that the basic actor in theory, as in history in general, is the class and not the individual. Several important methodological consequences follow from this which require explanation. First, one overcomes the abstract character that theory inevitably has as long as it is seen as the product of a single individual. Problems such as "Freedom of the Will," "the nature of the Absolute," and so on, immediately become practical problems when analyzed on the level of class. For the class, as opposed to the individual, all theoretical problems are practical problems.

A second consequence of using class rather than the individual as the point of departure is that it enables theory to disclose its essentially *strategic* nature. A class is always faced with a variety of concrete problems which are determined, in the last hand, by the mode of production itself. A class is engaged in a permanent struggle against other classes, a struggle which can end in victory, compromise, retreat, or extinction, depending on the conjuncture of historical circumstances. Theory is the elementary conceptualization of this struggle. Theory is moreover the formulation of the concrete strategy to be chosen in a concrete situation: whether to attack, seek a reconciliation with another class, acknowledge a defeat, and so on. Theory, from a Marxist perspective, is therefore fundamentally practical and strategic in nature. It always represents an effort to solve class problems. A sharp distinction between "infrastructure" and "superstructure" is not possible from this perspective because, in the process of the class struggle, one cannot separate the strategy from the struggle. The strategy is inherent in the struggle, just as thought is inherent in human action.

The tendency of class thought to mask its intentions is a secondary consideration. It is naturally to the advantage of a class, especially to a ruling class, that its actions are misunderstood. The primary task, however, is always

5

an attempt to solve the basic problems a class faces directly. For example, the fundamental problem of the bourgeoisie is the extraction of surplus value from labor. In order to solve this problem, the various bourgeoisies are forced to tackle the problem of separating labor from the means of production, of getting the workers to work in the factories, and, finally, of making them consume what they themselves produce at a higher price than they are paid in wages. For each of these basic problems the bourgeoisies will develop a multitude of strategies depending on the concrete circumstances.

An interpretation of the notion of ideology along these lines is quite compatible with Marx's use of it. To Marx, ideology is derivative in nature, not because it is a mere reflection of "the economic basis," but because it denies the inherently practical nature of thought and hence gives rise to illusions that the basic social problems can be solved outside the class struggle. German philosophy, law and religion are seen by Marx as ideological, not because they are mental products *per se*, but because they fail to express the real forces behind history. The Marxist position is to de-ideologize or de-spiritualize the various strategies of the classes in order to bring the class struggle into the open. The more important strategies of a class in capitalist society are centered around the direct extraction of surplus value, but of course they are not exclusively concerned with this. Ideology is not a distortion of truth, as Mannheim's interpretation of Marx suggests.[1] It is thought denying its part in praxis, i.e., thought which denies the existence of class struggle.

The more difficult the problem a class faces, the more solutions will be proposed. Some of these will be totally utopian, serving, perhaps inadvertently, to install illusions in the opponent. Others might be more realistic, and even used with some measure of success before they are abandoned. The strategies that are ultimately adopted, however, become the most celebrated and become part of the "world vision" of the class. Successful and long-lasting class strategies — such as the theories of a Hobbes or a Rousseau — are naturally surrounded by enormous prestige and are viewed as genial. There is nothing, however, which suggests that less successful strategies are less genial despite Lucien Goldmann's assertions to the contrary.[2] Utopian thought, for instance, catches the imagination just because of its refusal to compromise with reality. This is a flaw in Goldmann's theory. A more important point is that the notion of "class strategy" as opposed to Goldmann's "world vision" can better take into account the struggles that always exist within a class. A fraction of a class, even if it partakes of a fundamental "world vision," often fights against other groups within the class. It has its own distinct methods of dealing with the problems that confront the class as a whole. Within one group it is possible to discern a variety of different strategies.

These general observations about the strategic nature of theory and about its place in praxis provide the theoretical basis for the analysis of Gurvitch in

INTRODUCTION

This study sets itself two intimately related tasks – to assess the importance of Georges Gurvitch's work and to outline a methodology which makes this assessment possible. The fundamental unity of these two tasks has specific theoretical implications, and these first pages will be devoted to a brief discussion of them. For theoretical guidance I have drawn upon the Marxist tradition and especially on the works of Lucien Goldmann.

There are two perspectives which I find crucial to avoid in a study of this type, the first being the history of ideas approach and the second the biographical approach. The basic premise of the former is that ideas can be explained and understood through their own immanent development. Most histories of sociological thought follow this model, among them, Timasheff's *Sociological Theory* (1955), Martindale's *The Nature and Types of Sociological Thought* (1960) and Sorokin's *Sociological Theories of Today* (1966).[1] From a Marxist perspective this is an inadmissable procedure. Marx himself clearly elaborated this point and his critique of Hegel in the 1840's centered on it: "Hegel makes man the *man of self-consciousness* instead of making self-consciousness the *self-consciousness of man,* i.e., of man living also in a real objective world and determined by that world" *(The Holy Family).*[2] In short, the question of idealism versus materialism is raised in the Marxist critique of the history of ideas approach. Idealism, according to Engels' classical definition in *Feuerbach,* in this context means the primacy of the spirit, while materialism means the primacy of the objective reality. Ideas, consequently, do not follow upon ideas but rather, in Engels' view, they are part of the totality of people's acts. These acts are in a dialectical relation to nature, and it is the totalities of acts which follow upon each other, not simply the ideas within the totalities.

A similar attention to totality is necessary when one discusses the "intellectual influences" on a particular author. Instead of looking at the author's bibliography to determine his/her influences, one should try to discover why the author was attracted to certain "influences" over others. Goldmann notes:

What are commonly called 'influences' have no *explanatory value.* They constitute rather a given problem for the researcher to explain.

There are always a large number of influences which could have an impact on an author; what has to be explained is why only a few of these or just really one did have an impact, and also why the reception of the works which did exercise this influence took place with a certain number of distortions in the influenced mind. But these are questions whose *answers are situated on the side of the work of the author that is being studied* and not — as is usually thought — on the side of the work which is supposed to have influenced it.[3]

There are equivalent dangers in the biographical approach. It seems easier to tackle and understand one author than it does to understand, for instance, a whole movement of thought. "Since we are larger than little things," Pascal writes in *Pensées,* "we think ourselves capable of grasping them. But nevertheless, we need just as much capacity for the Nothing as for the All."[4] The temptation of this approach is to reduce the objective significance of the work to a personal drama. Arthur Mitzman's study of Weber in *The Iron Cage* (1970), despite its many virtues, is an example of this.[5] If the footnote is the appropriate symbol for the history of ideas approach, the anecdote is the mark of the biography. The objective importance of the work tends to get lost in myriads of trivia.

Goldmann has noted that an author's inferior works are often the ones that lend themselves most easily to explanation through his/her life story.[6] This is certainly true of contemporary sociology wherein the spirit of "publish or perish" encourages professional contacts between sociologists to appear as the key to their theories. Mullins' *Theories and Theory Groups in Contemporary American Sociology* (1973) is a case in point.[7] It contains minute details of the careers of hundreds of sociologists. Contrary to this, however, is the fact that the more important works always stand by themselves. Little can be added to *Suicide* or *The Protestant Ethic,* for instance, by detailing their authors' everyday lives. The fact that Durkheim had a close friend who committed suicide and that one of Weber's grandfathers was a protestant capitalist adds nothing to the objective significance of these works. If, as Lukács has said, the monographic method is the best way to obscure the horizons of a problem, the biography is the best way to preclude understanding the objective significance of an author's work.[8]

Historical materialism, on the other hand, furnishes a distinct method for understanding the objective significance of a work. This method views the work as a constituent part of the class struggle, i.e., of the dialectical unfolding of society. In this context, Goldmann, in *The Hidden God* (1955), which I consider to be the most important post-war study in the sociology of knowledge, says: "We can separate the essential [in an author's work] from the accidental only by integrating the individual elements into the overall pattern, by fitting this work. As theoretical propositions they are to a large extent inspired by Lucien Goldmann, but they also represent an independent attempt to further develop his ideas. As we have seen, the analysis of an author's work, according to Goldmann, consists of laying bare its internal structure, of "inserting" this structure into a larger whole, such as a social movement, and finally, of "inserting" this second structure into the class structure of the society in question. This method can be applied to Gurvitch's work with some minor modification. Instead of using Goldmann's concept of "internal structure," it is more precise to conceive of an author's work in terms of the basic problems with which it is concerned. The notion of problem is preferable in this context because it directly establishes the work as part of a more general praxis. Faced with one or more problems, the work also proposes more or less realistic solutions which always imply, on the level of class, definite strategies.

There are many difficulties involved in establishing the exact problem that an author is confronting in a work. The work may present the problem as very minor or as already solved; the problem might be analyzed on a level distinctly divorced from praxis, and so on. Some of these difficulties are present in Gurvitch's work which is profoundly idealistic in nature. Especially hard to deal with is the first, and most decisive, period of his intellectual development — roughly the ten years before Gurvitch, who was born in Tzarist Russia in 1894, left the U.S.S.R. in 1920. Only two of the writings Gurvitch produced during this time — a short work on Prokopovich (1915) and another one on Rousseau (1917) — are known today. Both were minor works, soon to be superseded by Gurvitch's works in the 1920's and 1930's. However, we are lucky enough to have a brief intellectual autobiography, written by Gurvitch in his later life, as a source of information about this early period. The autobiography is an article about twenty pages in length entitled "My Intellectual Itinerary" and published in 1958.[3] It covers in detail the time between what Gurvitch calls "the awakening of my mind" in 1910, and his departure in 1920. Together with the work on Rousseau, this article constitutes the major source of material on the 1910-1920 period of Gurvitch's production.

"My Intellectual Itinerary" describes how Gurvitch, from the tender age of fourteen, read the Marxists who were then in vogue in Russia: Kautsky, Plekhanov and Lenin. What first impressed him in these writers was their emphasis on "rigorous determinism." It bothered him, however, that there seemed to be no room for independent action. "Why then," he asked, "the constant appeals to the revolutionary will...?"[4] Some time later, Gurvitch tackled *Capital* itself and after that Hegel's *Logic*. Now increasingly disturbed by the strong determinism he found in both these authors, Gurvitch read Hegel's *Philosophy of Right* and was instantly repelled by the deification of the Prussian state he discovered in it. At the age of seventeen, he announced his "complete break with Marxism and Hegelianism."[5]

Seeking an answer to what had bothered him in Hegel especially, Gurvitch started to read Stirner, Proudhon and Kierkegaard with interest. These thinkers, in his mind, had broken with the "necessitarianism" of Hegel and Marx.[6] He was also impressed by Kant and the neo-Kantians, especially by their attacks on all forms of "dogmatism," including what he called "the spiritualism of Hegel and the materialism of Marx."[7] Gurvitch studied the neo-Kantians very intensely in Germany during the summers of 1912-1914. Soon, however, he reacted against the lack of rebellious spirit in the neo-Kantian movement as well as against the emphasis on essences. It was at this point that Gurvitch discovered Henri Bergson's *Matter and Memory* and *Creative Evolution.* These works were a revelation to Gurvitch. He felt that he was being led back to "a realism that was free from determinism."[8] But there were also elements in Bergson that worried Gurvitch, notably his spiritualism and individualism. Before World War I, which completes what Gurvitch considered to be the first part of his intellectual development, he attended Emil Lask's lectures in Heidelberg and was very impressed by Lask's attempt "to go beyond idealism...within neo-Kantianism."[9]

The second part of Gurvitch's intellectual development covers the years between 1915-1920, during which time he studied law at the University of Petrograd. In these years "realism" maintained its powerful influence on him and for a while even led him to the "intuitionism" of Lossky and Frank and the great Russian slavophile thinkers. However, realizing that he was coming dangerously close to mysticism, Gurvitch withdrew and redefined his epistemological positions with the help of Fichte.

In social philosophy, Gurvitch attempted to find a position which was both "anti-individualist" and "anti-statist" at the same time.[10] The works of Saint-Simon, Fichte and Proudhon provided some clues for the solution to this problem. He also read Rousseau in this context, but found him to be an "enigma" because he could alternatively be considered a "state socialist," an "anarchist," or an "individualist."[11] Gurvitch decided to write a study of Rousseau focused on the notion of "general will," which he viewed as Rousseau's solution to the problem of the "social contract" between the state and the individual. In it, Gurvitch defended some of the contradictions present in Rousseau's work, but denounced Rousseau's attempt to solve all theoretical problems using the concept of "individual reason."[12]

Of all the thinkers, it was Proudhon who made the strongest impression on Gurvitch during the war years. Gurvitch later recalled: "[Proudhon's] notion that what is social cannot, without the risk of being alienated, be projected outside of the participants either as a superior subject or as an exterior object, his deep-seated social pluralism seeking to balance the multiple groups, his negative dialectics, his demonstration of the relativity of any social prediction, his theory of human creation having precedence over predetermined progress, all filled me with joy."[13] Gurvitch's interest in Proudhon during these years had definite political implications for him:

> From the point of view of social theory I was very much of a Proudhonian and a syndicalist at the time of the two Russian revolutions in February and November 1917....This, by the way, combined itself rather well with the rising factory committees and their tendency to elect representatives not only to the politically competent "central committees" but also to the "administrative committees" in various companies.[14]

The direct experience of the Russian Revolution, Gurvitch writes in his autobiography, was very influential on his later work, especially in sociology. He traces some of his basic thoughts back to the years 1917-1920, such as the idea that social reality can be conceptualized in terms of different strata which are in contradiction with each other; the idea that the group is a microcosm of forms of sociality and that society itself is a macrocosm of different groups; the idea that "social law" emerges spontaneously and outside of the state apparatus; and the idea that collective planning is possible on the basis of "a pluralist economic democracy" and of "federalist ownership."[15] Summarizing his intellectual development, Gurvitch writes: "My philosophical and sociological thinking . . . has often been breathless, going from one extreme to the other, lost in the inextricable webs of contradictory systems which I inevitably dismissed . . . only to start weaving my web again."[16]

An intellectual autobiography of this type does not facilitate a meaningful analysis of an author's work. From the information Gurvitch gives, it can be established that he was a Proudhonist with sympathies for Bergson, the neo-Kantians, etc., between 1910-1920, but his article lends no insight into the "internal structure" of his work. However, if the information is rearranged according to the type of basic problems Gurvitch was struggling with at that time, a more coherent picture emerges.

If one examines Gurvitch's relation to the Marxists around the turn of the century, it becomes clear that he had a very ambivalent attitude toward their notion of "determinism," toward the existence of what he terms "implacable laws of history."[17] He also reacted against the emphasis on "determinism" he found in Marx, and Hegel was likewise rejected because of his "necessitarianism." Stirner and Kierkegaard he appreciated, precisely because they, in Gurvitch's opinion, "ruined necessitarianism."[18] Gurvitch was attracted to Kant's critical method with its promise to unveil all "dogmatisms," but left the neo-Kantians as soon as he realized their hidden strain of "complete obedience."[19] Bergson's writings had such a direct impact on Gurvitch because they showed the possibilities of "a realism which was free from necessitarianism."[20] Finally, one of the qualities that impressed Gurvitch in Proudhon was "his demonstration of the relativity of any social prediction."[21]

There are many reasons for the clear opposition to any form of "determinism" that is revealed in Gurvitch's autobiography. Referring to the authors who presided over the "awakening of [his] mind," i.e., Kautsky, Plekhanov and Lenin, Gurvitch wrote:

> I was very much impressed by their belief in a rigorous determinism, as revealed by the "implacable laws of history" — a determinism which would have "economic determinism," their favorite theme, as its basis; but all the while I had my doubts. If ultimately economics determines the direction that society and history are to take, I asked myself: where does its own determinism come from? Economics is, after all, a human activity, production, a struggle to control nature and to secure a better share in its distribution, and, in particular a class struggle. And if all this profusion of effort, of human energy, can be considered as determined, why the constant appeals to the revolutionary will in order to precipitate the course of events?[22]

Evidently, Gurvitch saw a contradiction between what he called "the constant appeals to the revolutionary will" and the "implacable laws of history." Therefore, it becomes understandable why he appreciated Proudhon's "theory of human creation having precedence over predetermined progress."[23] Clearly, the problem of *determinism versus voluntarism* was one of Gurvitch's main concerns in the 1910-1920 period of his development.

Gurvitch's difficulty with the idea of determinism does not stem from the fact that he was an individualist. It is true that Stirner's *The Ego and His Own* played an important role in his intellectual development. But his predominant attraction to this book was not its emphasis on radical individualism *per se* but rather Stirner's attacks on Hegel. He also rejected the "latent individualism" of Bergson as well as Rousseau's emphasis on "the universality of individual reason."[24] Gurvitch quite correctly defined his own position in 1915-1920 as "anti-individualist."[25]

Gurvitch's resistance to the notion of determinism is actually more connected with his critique of the state. Describing why, at the age of seventeen, he felt such a tremendous "indignation" reading Hegel's *Philosophy of Right,* Gurvitch wrote, "it confirmed my worst apprehensions regarding the practical results of deterministic necessitarianism."[26] The "practical results" of Hegel's reasoning were the establishment of an authoritarian state. Between 1915-1920 Gurvitch was very concerned with finding an "anti-statist" position, and he read through the works of Grotius, Fichte, Proudhon and others for theoretical guidance. He embraced Proudhon's idea that groups become alienated when they become hierarchical, and he was also very interested in Proudhon's notion about "deep-seated social pluralism seeking to balance the multiple groups [in society]."[27] During the revolution, Gurvitch said he realized "the possibility of collectivistic planning outside of state control...based on a pluralist economic democracy and federalist ownership."[28]

Gurvitch's second great concern was to find a position which could encompass "anti-individualis[m]" and "anti-statis[m]" at the same time, a position which could bring together the interests of the group and the individual harmoniously with neither having predominance over the other. This important theoretical problem can be labelled as *the individual versus the collective.*

The problems with which Gurvitch was struggling during these years have left their marks on all his major works. "When I left my country of birth in 1920," he writes, "I took with me, as my only baggage, the outlines for three books: one on 'Fichte,' another on the 'Idea of Social Law,' and the third on 'Scales of Strata of Social Reality.' "[29] These are the works we know as *Fichtes System der Konkreten Ethik* (1924), *L'Idée du Droit Social* (1932), and *Essais de Sociologie* (1938). The contradictions between the individual and the collective, on the one hand, and between determinism and voluntarism, on the other, form the core of these works. The terms in which these contradictions are conceptualized vary according to the field—whether the work is in law, philosophy, or sociology—as well as according to the terminology in use at different times in different countries. In general, there is also a tendency for the conflict between the individual and the collective to be more consciously conceptualized and elaborated, in Gurvitch's work, than is his concern with voluntarism versus determinism.

An illustration of some of these points can be seen in Gurvitch's only writing of any significance before 1920, *Rousseau and the Declaration of Rights: The Notion of the Inalienable Rights of the Individual in Rousseau's Political Doctrine.* This work, little more than a hundred pages long, was written in 1916 and published the next year in Petrograd.[30] As mentioned earlier, Gurvitch's first impression of Rousseau was that he was an "enigma" in that he could be considered an "individualist," an "anarchist," or a "state socialist" simultaneously. But after having worked through Rousseau's arguments, Gurvitch came to the conclusion that these categories were not necessarily mutually exclusive. Using an individualistic framework, Rousseau had ended up with a statist position, an enterprise which Gurvitch termed a complete "failure."[31] However, Gurvitch felt that Rousseau had located and tried to solve an extremely important problem in his work, and therefore Gurvitch devoted most of his analysis to "defending the contradictions which Rousseau was being accused of and trying to bring out the depth of his dialectics."[32]

The basic difficulty Rousseau had attempted to work out, as Gurvitch saw it, was the contradiction between "liberty" and "equality."[33] "Liberty" was considered to be a quality inherent in each individual, an inalienable individual right. "To renounce one's freedom," Rousseau had argued, "was to renounce one's quality as a human being."[34] "Equality" meant the equivalence of all human beings in this aspect. The problem was to prevent the freedom of all from degenerating into the tyranny of the few. Somehow, a regulating body had to be introduced which could defend the interests of all without alienating them in the process.

Rousseau's solution to the antagonism between the liberty of the individual and the equality of all was his notion of "general will." If the general will expressed the deepest convictions of each individual citizen, there would be no conflict between the individual and his/her collective representation. But if the state did not represent the "general will" of the people, it would not express the interests of the individual, who would then have the right to oppose it. This argument, as is well known, is very ambiguous and has led to a variety of different interpretations. Gurvitch's reading of Rousseau on this question is quite original. Basing his analysis on the first draft of *The Social Contract,* as well as on some minor articles by Rousseau, Gurvitch advanced the thesis that Rousseau's notion of "general will" was an attempt to solve the contradiction between "liberty" and "equality" through philosophy of law.[35] Gurvitch's argument was subtle. Rousseau, he claimed, conceived of the "general will" as a "synthesis" between equality and liberty.[36] The "general will" itself, according to Gurvitch, was nothing but Rousseau's version of natural law: each individual, by associating in society, would give up his/her "instinctive natural law" (*"droit naturel instinctif"*) for a "natural law of reason" (*"droit naturel raisonné"*), or in other words, for the "general will."[37] More precisely, a developed sense of justice *("droit naturel raisonné"),* as opposed to the primitive, pre-social sense of justice (*"droit naturel instinctif"*), would be the only base upon which an egalitarian society could be constructed. If the existing laws did not express the interests of the individual, it would become a "hierarchical" society which our individual sense of justice would forbid us to accept.[38]

This interpretation, which views law as the key to the problem of "equality" versus "liberty," constituted the important part of Gurvitch's analysis of Rousseau, and it was to remain a major theme in his writings for the next twenty years. On the negative side, Gurvitch claimed that Rousseau was a statist, and had consequently failed to find a successful synthesis of "liberty" and "equality" on the organizational level. Such an organization, however, Gurvitch was to discover himself in the form of the *soviets* (workers' councils) which appeared everywhere in Russia the very same year that his book on Rousseau was published.

In a very complex way, both of Gurvitch's main concerns are present in his interpretation of Rousseau. The conflict between the individual and the collective is present in the opposition between "liberty" and "equality" and achieves resolution, in Gurvitch's analysis, through "law." It also underlies Gurvitch's critique of Rousseau's statism. The problem of determinism versus voluntarism is not confronted squarely. However, it is present in Gurvitch's idealistic appeal to law as a solution to the problem of social equality, and it also underlies his utopian construction of a non-hierarchical society. These last two points will be discussed in more detail later.

As noted above, the second step in the analysis of a work, according to Lucien Goldmann, consists of "inserting" its internal structure into a larger structure. The term "insertion" is not a particularly happy one. Goldmann uses it, however, to indicate that thought must be seen as internal to social action, viz., that it is absurd to view the relation between thought and society as an external one. In the language of the modified terminology established earlier, the second part of the analysis of a work consists of the conceptualization of its "basic problems" on the collective level. In this stage of the analysis, the theoretical problem is shown to be a distinctly practical one, a problem for a whole class or for one of its fractions.

Using this method, it can be postulated that the basic issues with which Gurvitch was concerned in the years between 1910-1920 were aspects of the major problems confronting the Russian *intelligentsia*, a fraction of the bourgeois class which played a very important ideological role before 1917. The intelligentsia substituted for a revolutionary bourgeoisie which had never existed in Russia. Its basic problems stemmed from the fact that it had its objective class roots in a bourgeoisie that it rejected on ideological grounds. Instead, the intelligentsia looked initially to the peasants, and later the workers, to be agents of revolutionary change. This position was contradictory, and represented the dialectic of "determinism" versus "voluntarism" in the ideological debate. Very briefly, the intelligentsia's two major projects were voluntaristic to the core: originally it wished to stop capitalism with the help of the peasants ("populism") and then later it hoped to bring about a socialist revolution — not just a bourgeois one — with the backing of the workers. Another contradiction in the position of the intelligentsia was that it was being undermined gradually by the growth of the bourgeoisie with its need for its own "organic intellectuals" (Gramsci).[39] As a result, the conflict between the intelligentsia's revolutionary project ("collectivism") and its historical function to prepare the bourgeoisie for power ("individualism") became much sharper. Both of these contradictions were intertwined in highly complex ways, and their ideological expressions, which for the moment have been given in a crude and schematic outline, were also very complex.

Before the intelligentsia's position can be analyzed in more detail, a brief presentation of the whole Russian class structure is necessary. The nineteenth century was a period of transition from feudalism to capitalism and has been documented by Lenin in *The Development of Capitalism in Russia* (1899). During this transition, two basic contradictions overlapped and intensified each other: in feudal society, the conflict between the aristocracy and the peasants; and in capitalist society, the conflict between the bourgeoisie and the workers. Consequently, a weak bourgeoisie could waver between supporting the aristocracy and attacking it. The peasant classes, if united with the proletariat, could become an anti-capitalistic force, or they could simply attack the landed aristocracy, etc.

The most striking feature in Russian society in the nineteenth century was the successful survival of feudalism. While most European countries long since had abolished serfdom, it was to remain in Russia until 1861. The political hegemony of the landed aristocracy lasted even longer; it was not until after the revolution of 1905 that the bourgeoisie achieved something similar to parliamentary representation (*duma*). However, the aristocracy was not strong and independent. It had been crushed by earlier tzars, and had a tradition of servility to the state.[40] In 1861, it was allotted a huge amount in redemption pay and started to invest in industry. During the remainder of the century, the aristocracy sold more and more of its land.[41] With its economic base rapidly declining, it was a class on its way out.

The majority of the Russian people belonged to the peasant classes. In 1917, for instance, ninety percent of the population was still peasant.[42] The Orthodox Church, which preached submission and resignation, had a powerful grip on the minds of the people.[43] The peasants seldom revolted, but when they did—as in the Jacqueries under Stenka Razin and Pugachev—it was with tremendous force and violence. 1861 was a year in which the peasants lost a vast amount of land which was traditionally theirs. The peasants were set "free" by being cleared off the land.[44] Even though the authorities tried to safeguard the village community (*mir*) in the reform law of 1861, it was slowly dissolved by capitalism. According to Lenin's *The Development of Capitalism in Russia,* the peasants were polarized in the 1890's into a "peasant bourgeoisie" and a "rural proletariat."[45] When the peasants supported the Revolution of 1905, the regime decided that the *mir* had to be destroyed because it kept alive the old belief that peasants had rights to the land they worked. The dissolution of the *mir* was accomplished with the Stolypin Reform (1906-1910), which encouraged the formation of a wealthy class of peasants (*kulaks*). According to Lenin, this new agrarian reform constituted "a second landowner purge of the land."[46] The peasants consequently entered the 1917 Revolution impoverished, embittered and internally polarized. The Social-Democratic Party, while realizing the revolutionary potential of the poor peasants, did not establish an organic link with them.

The weakness of the bourgeoisie was related to the strength of the feudal system in Russia. In Europe, the transition from feudalism to capitalism had proceeded gradually. The capitalist system had first found a stronghold in the cities, slowly dissolving traditional social and economic relations in the countryside.[47] However, in Russia the bourgeoisie never succeeded in capturing the cities, and with them, political, economic and legal autonomy.[48] The bourgeoisie was, from the beginning, a weak and splintered class living in the shadow of the Russian feudal state upon which it was dependent. It totally lacked the democratic tradition of the classic Western bourgeoisie. When in 1861 the serfs were transformed into "free labor," the bourgeoisie was so weak that it was incapable of launching Russia on the road to industrialization without the help of the state and international capital.[49] It was not until the 1890's that the industrialization process really began, and even then, it was financed by so much foreign capital that Russia was soon reduced to a state of semi-colonial dependency.[50] Up until 1905, the bourgeoisie, despite its fundamental compromise with the feudal state, opposed the political hegemony of the landed aristocracy. The Revolution of 1905 changed this; the bourgeoisie was frightened by the strength that the proletariat and the peasants exhibited in the revolt, and turned against them. In this sense, 1905 in Russia was equivalent to 1848 in Europe. The Revolution of 1905 assured the bourgeoisie some constitutional rights with which it was largely content. During the remaining years before the fall of tzarism in early 1917, the bourgeoisie tried to develop a more progressive type of political alliance with the aristocracy, such as the "bourgeois monarchy" (Stolypin).[51] When it entered the Revolution of 1917, the Russian bourgeoisie was a weak class, lacking the ideological strength to gather "the people" behind it as the French bourgeoisie had done in the 1790's.

Unlike the bourgeoisie, the proletariat was strong. Before the Reform in 1861, the proletariat was practically non-existent, but by the 1890's the workers had become a powerful force in the class struggle. The Russian Social-Democratic Party was also formed during this decade.[52] The strength of the proletariat grew out of a bitter struggle with the Russian capitalists, who submitted the workers to the classical horrors of child-labor, extremely long working hours, etc.[53] The militancy of the workers, was also affected by the extreme concentration of industry in Russia. According to Lyashchenko, 53.5 percent of the workers in 1910 could be found in companies with more than five hundred workers,[54] a higher percentage than in any European country. Nevertheless, the workers constituted a very small percentage of the population, and they had little experience with open democracy. The soviets created in 1905 were crushed within weeks, and the workers did not support the brand of unions that were permitted after the 1905 Revolution. Though the extremely combative Social-Democratic Party was behind the workers, it was unable to reach the masses before the 1917 Revolution. Thus, the small Russian working class entered the Revolution of 1917 with a high degree of militancy and little political experience.

The position of the intelligentsia, as has already been mentioned, was highly contradictory.[55] On the one hand, it was the ideological avant-garde of the bourgeoisie, and on the other, it was extremely critical of the bourgeoisie. In addition, the intelligentsia's increasing success at undermining feudalism increased the pressure on it to become integrated into the bourgeoisie.

The intelligentsia made its first appearance in the 1830's and 1840's and included people like Herzen, Bakunin and Belinsky. It set as its goal the destruction of the feudal system, especially the state and the church. On the basis of their common mission, analogies between the early Russian intelligentsia and the French *philosophes* have been drawn. Bakunin, for instance, called Herzen "our Voltaire."[56] However, the intelligentsia was structurally much closer to the German idealists. Both groups were extremely isolated and blocked from any realization of their goals. The Russian intelligentsia, especially in the 1830's, identified strongly with the works of German idealism. But there were also fundamental differences between the two: in the early nineteenth century the German bourgeoisie was preparing for its eventual confrontation with the nobility in 1848, but there was no parallel movement of this kind in Russia at this time. For this reason, the Russian intelligentsia was also attracted to the French utopians, whose moralistic critique of the bourgeoisie served as an inspiration for the intelligentsia's own disillusion with the bourgeoisie.

Hence, the intelligentsia was isolated and increasingly felt the need to find support outside the bourgeoisie. Since the working class was practically nonexistent, it concentrated its energies on the peasants. Between 1850-1880, the radical intelligentsia built a distinct ideology around their choice — "populism."[57] The tenets of populism stated that it would be possible for Russia to avoid capitalism by building socialism directly on the existing communal institutions of the peasants. The first problem would be to carry out a successful revolution against the feudal aristocracy. A variety of strategies for the accomplishment of this task emerged in populism: the intelligentsia would have to lead the peasants (Tkachev); the intelligentsia would first have to prepare and educate the peasants (Lavrov); the intelligentsia would have to live with the people, gain their confidence and become one of them ("Go to the People," 1873-1874); the intelligentsia would have to set off a "spark" to which peasants would immediately rise because of their "instinct" for revolution (Bakunin). All of these strategies failed.

In the 1890's, with the emergence of the proletariat, the radical intelligentsia shifted its attention from the peasants to the workers. The question as to how a revolution might be sparked was especially hard in this new situation. Should there be a bourgeois-democratic revolution first, and then later a socialist one (Plekhanov)? Could the bourgeois revolution be immediately turned into a socialist one (Trotsky)? Could the peasants and the workers carry out a revolution tomorrow (the anarchists)? The relation between the Russian intelligentsia and the masses was formulated with exceptional clarity at this time because of the intelligentsia's long-standing isolation from the masses. For example, Lenin claimed in *What is to be Done?* (1902) that socialism is a creation of the bourgeois intelligentsia and must be brought to the working class from the outside by a socialist party. Other thinkers put more faith in the workers' capacities to create their own organizations, such as the soviets, and these thinkers ignored the role of a political party (Gurvitch).

The first major problem of the intelligentsia concerned its relations with the proletariat and the growing bourgeoisie. The difficulty consisted in the fact that the intelligentsia had to fight for some of the goals of the bourgeoisie, such as legal equality, at the same time as it fought for the goals of socialism. The result was a growing pressure on the intelligentsia to become integrated as "organic intellectuals" in bourgeois society, i.e., as intellectuals who are necessary to the functioning of capitalism. This pull on the intelligentsia became very clear in the 1860's. The "nihilists," who appeared at this time, emphasized the cultivation of one's own personality, and endorsed practicality — the "useful," as in the natural sciences — as opposed to the idealistic theories of the earlier intelligentsia. Tkachev articulated the problem with singular clarity. Capitalism, Tkachev wrote, would approach the intelligentsia in the following manner:

> 'I need you,' it says, 'and I will not feed you if you do nothing. Your "ideal principles" do not correspond to the interests which I have created for you. But this does not matter to me. For the development of my principles, I need agricultural foremen, technicians, industrialists, doctors, lawyers, etc. To each one of them I am prepared to give full freedom in the sphere of his own specialty and nothing more. You must help me. Develop industry and trade, rationalize agriculture, teach the people to read, found banks, hospitals, build railways, etc. And for all this I will do what I can to make your work not too hard. I will create conditions that correspond to your character, and I will give you a feeling of satisfaction with your work and so do away with your melancholy. Those are my conditions.'[58]

The great reforms of the 1860's — such as the introduction of limited self-government in the rural districts (*zemstvos*) and the establishment of a judiciary — were signs of this development. The expansion of the educational system, which had begun under Alexander I, was another. At the turn of the century, the radical intelligentsia constituted an increasingly small percentage of the intellectuals. A variety of professional organizations were formed and liberalism was growing. This tendency was reinforced after 1905 when the Kadet party and the Octobrists were formed. In 1909, *Vekhi,* the famous work which attacked the radical intelligentsia, appeared. In 1917, as in 1905, many intellectuals left the socialist party.[59]

On a theoretical level, the intelligentsia's problematic place in Russian society can be conceptualized in terms of the fight between determinism and voluntarism and of the individual versus the collective. The populists were extremely voluntaristic in their belief that Russia could avoid capitalism, while the Marxists were more deterministic, stressing that Russia needed a bourgeois revolution first. The Marxists did have a voluntaristic side, however. Lenin, for instance, decided quite early that only the proletariat and the poor peasants could be trusted to carry out a revolution — even a bourgeois-democratic one. From the very beginning, the Russian intelligentsia was against *laissez-faire* individualism and claimed that if the classical bourgeois values — "egalité, liberté, fraternité" — were to be realized, they had to be instituted on the mass level, not just for a minority of people. The populists took a similar but accentuated position. In general, they placed a very high value on the individual, but saw the collective as the best place for the individual to develop. Shelgunov, a critic, said, "We, the intelligentsia, are the representative of individualism; the people is the representative of the collective." By merging with the people, the two values, he claimed, would be reconciled.[60] The Marxists de-emphasized "the role of the individual in history" (Plekhanov) but were equally opposed to the "fatalistic" view that the individual didn't matter.[61] The closer the revolution came, the more the opinions on this question became polarized within the intelligentsia. The socialists stressed the importance of the collective over the individual while *Vekhi*, for instance, proclaimed the priority of the individual.

When the Russian Revolution of 1917 broke out, these contradictions, which the intelligentsia embodied, were heightened rather than diminished. The socialist parties initially thought that the Revolution was bourgeois-democratic and that it would be impossible to proceed immediately to a socialist stage. This was a belief shared by the Bolshevik Party until Lenin's famous "April Theses," after which they decided to try to break the deadlock in the Revolution and proceed directly to the socialist stage. That the Russian Revolution would have ended with a victory for the counter-revolutionary forces without the resolute action of the Bolshevik Party is evident. Whether the Russian Revolution became a socialist revolution in the classical sense of the word, however, is more questionable. The working class, it must be remembered, was an extreme minority. Paul Mattick has labeled the Revolution "semi-bourgeois, semi-proletarian"; the exact class nature of the Revolution is still an open question.[62]

Gurvitch was personally active in the Revolution. As early as 1910, he had been a prominent member of the Social-Democratic Party in Riga.[63] During the Revolution of 1917 he was in Petrograd, the very center of action. He was a member of a left-wing student association and took an active part in the formation of workers' councils in the Putiloff factories.[64] The impact of the Revolution on Gurvitch's thought can only be understood when placed in the background just described. The basic contradictions in the intelligentsia became open and vital questions for the whole of Russian society in 1917-1920. Was it possible to accelerate the bourgeois state of the revolutionary process and proceed directly to socialism? Was it possible, through an enormous collective effort, to reconcile the liberty of the individual with social equality? The basic problems taken up in Gurvitch's early work were, in many ways, the basic problems of the Russian Revolution itself.

2 Fichte and the Dialectics of Idealism

When he left the Soviet Union in 1920, Gurvitch brought with him the outlines of three books: one on law, one on sociology and one on Fichte. The first one he chose to work on while living in Prague during the early 1920's was the Fichte material. In 1922, he published a thin volume entitled *Die Einheit der Fichteschen Philosophie* which was later incorporated in a slightly modified form, in *Fichtes System der Konkreten Ethik* (1924).[1] The order in which Gurvitch chose to complete his projects from Russia — after the Fichte book he finished *L'Idée du Droit Social,* and then he turned to sociology — was directly related to the concrete problems of the time. Fichte, for instance, was a very apt topic in the early 1920's because of the strong utopian feeling in revolutionary circles at that time. *L'Idée du Droit Social,* written during the latter half of the 1920's, represented Gurvitch's effort to come to terms with the increasing stabilization of the capitalist world which, according to the Comintern, had already begun by 1924.[2] Finally, Gurvitch's studies on sociology in the 1930's and 1940's were strongly influenced by the rise and success of Fascism all over Europe.

Fichtes System der Konkreten Ethik deals primarily with questions of ethics and epistemology. Originally, Gurvitch had intended to devote a volume to Fichte's social philosophy as well, but this book never materialized.[3] *Fichtes System der Konkreten Ethik* is a complex work, and there are many difficulties involved in a Marxist interpretation. The main question to be answered, consequently, is to what extent the theoretical propositions in the preceding chapter are applicable also to ethics and epistemology, i.e., whether these can be adequately conceptualized as part of a class's praxis.

The first step in a Marxist analysis of epistemology must be to re-establish the direct connection — the "umbilical cord," to use an image from *The German Ideology* — between the basis of knowledge and human praxis.[4] The individualistic approach is incapable of dealing with problems of epistemology. From the individual's point of view, "categories" of thought tend to appear as

20

unchangeable and eternal; they are seen as general conditions of human knowledge rather than as inherent to a specific praxis. However, when the class instead of the individual is the basic reference point, it becomes impossible to maintain the strict separation between the "forms" and "contents" of human thought. The class has to effectively orient itself to other classes and to nature in order to survive, and it necessarily develops a specific epistemology in the course of this process. At the collective level, it is indeed artificial to separate the "form" from the "content" of human thought, just as it is nonsensical to separate "values" from "facts."[5] Form and content are inseparably united in the continued existence of the class. Consequently, different epistemologies answer to different modes of production as well as to different classes. An epistemology is accepted when it helps to solve the fundamental problems of class encounters; it is seen as dogmatic and as an obstacle to be overcome when it fails to be of use to a class.[6]

When viewed from this perspective, developed by Marx at the time of the first clashes between the proletariat and the bourgeoisie in the 1830's and 1840's, the "understanding of the world" and the "changing of the world" become complementary aspects of the same process. Therefore, concepts such as "innate ideas" and "a prioris" represent mystifications, i.e., the ideologization of the fact that the fundamentals of human knowledge are actually posited in the class struggle.[7] Consequently, in the Marxist view, the question of epistemology is a thoroughly political one which cannot be answered outside of the class struggle. In short, epistemology is part of the class struggle. It expresses a specific class strategy, or, conversely, it tries to discredit the strategies of other classes. The imposition of its epistemology on the other classes, from the perspective developed here is an important part of a particular class's struggle for hegemonic control.

However, the general analysis of epistemology becomes extremely complex when the focus is on a specific historical conjuncture. As the class struggle develops differently and unevenly in different countries, the epistemology of a class develops unevenly as well. Lucien Goldmann, for instance, discusses the difference in epistemological strategy between the British and the German bourgeoisie at the time of Kant:

> Only a class already in power such as the English bourgeoisie at this time could permit itself to answer the fundamental question of the connections between the elements which constitute the universe with the assertion that those connections are not *necessary a priori* but that they are nonetheless established *in fact* by habit, association of ideas, and so on. One can only have recourse to a fact if that fact is already actual and universally acknowledged. This was impossible in countries where those connections were only to be awaited, or even merely wished for, in the future.

On the continent, and particularly in Germany, where the birth of the bourgeois was still problematic and in any case projected for a distant future, to assert that the freedom of the individual could not guarantee the realization of a harmonious and *necessary* connection, that there exist a *priori* laws of thought and action which would *necessarily* assure harmony between reasonable and free individuals, must have appeared a heresy, or at any rate a dangerous skepticism, casting doubt upon the most sacred values. It was only much later — in France a little before the Revolution, and in western Europe generally in the second half of the nineteenth century — when the bourgeoisie had *already* achieved political ascendency, that despite all the contrary traditions continental thought could feel a growing sympathy for empiricism and this could become the dominant current of thought...[8]

It is always the "concrete analysis of the concrete situation" (Lenin) that counts.[9] Within a class itself, several different factions which have their own separate epistemological strategies can be distinguished. In *The Hidden God,* for instance, Goldmann focuses on the espistemology, among other things, of the *noblesse de robe.*

The Marxist approach to ethics is also quite distinct. Lenin stated, "We repudiate all morality that is taken outside of human, class concepts."[10] Morality is not seen as an individual question as Kant conceived it — the lone individual in front of the categorical imperative. The subject of morality is the "we" of a class, and in the same way the epistemology is inseparable from class praxis, ethics is equally inseparable. The transition of a class from being in-itself to being for-itself is as much a question of ethics as of knowledge — or more precisely, it is a question of the organization of values and knowledge of a class when it is confronted with practical problems in praxis. The Marxist notion of class consciousness, as that of praxis, goes beyond the formal distinction between "fact" and "value;" only through solidarity can a class effectively unite and withstand the attacks from another, more dominant class. All morality is therefore class morality as opposed to "really human morality." Marx and Engels claimed:

A really human morality which transcends class antagonisms and their legacies in thought becomes possible only at a stage of society which has not only overcome class contradictions but has even forgotten them in practical life.[11]

The conception of morality in terms of class strategy is in accordance with the socialist tradition. In his analysis of the Rights of Man, Marx illustrated how these rights were of direct strategic use for the bourgeoisie.[12] They helped to separate labor from the means of production and to ally the various classes behind the bourgeoisie in its fight against the nobility. However, when confronted with new fundamental problems — such as coming to terms with the emergent proletariat — the bourgeoisie changed its strategy, embracing some of the values of the declining aristocracy (i.e., the idea of organic unity) in order to maintain its dominance.

In order to lay bare the class strategy in Gurvitch's two studies of Fichte, it is necessary to present their content. *Die Einheit des Fichteschen Philosophie* deals exclusively with Fichte's epistemology. It differs in some minor details from *Fichtes System der Konkreten Ethik:* it is shorter, and it contains no discussion of the relationship between transcendentalism and the doctrine of ideal-realism.[13]

The first task Gurvitch set himself was to establish the unity of Fichte's *Wissenschaftslehre.*[14] According to Gurvitch, Fichte himself always viewed his works in theoretical philosophy as elaborations of the same basic theme. Consequently, Gurvitch argued, Schelling and several historians of philosophy who followed him were wrong in their view that Fichte, at a certain point of his development, drastically changed his philosophy. Gurvitch affirmed that definite changes could indeed be found in Fichte's theoretical philosophy, but they stemmed from an inner contradiction in Fichte's basic thought, from its "spontaneous immanent development" as Gurvitch phrased it.[15] Following Rickert and Lask's well-known works on Fichte, Gurvitch claimed that one could distinguish three different phrases in Fichte's thought instead of the usual two. Nonetheless, all three of these phases shared the same basic "transcendentalism."

It was Gurvitch's compatriot Wisscheslawzeff who, in a work entitled *Fichte's Ethics* (1914), had been the first to see transcendentalism as the underlying theme in Fichte's work.[16] For his understanding of transcendentalism, however, Gurvitch relied heavily on Rickert. Rickert had characterized transcendentalism as a doctrine according to which the attainment of knowledge was a never-ending task. All answers that knowledge could give were necessarily provisional since, within knowledge itself, there was always a tension, an aspiration toward something else. The very meaning of "trans," according to Rickert, encompassed the unsolvable dualism between "the one" and "the other." Gurvitch, however, felt it necessary to advance beyond Rickert's position. He argued that merely emphasizing the infinite task of knowledge would leave transcendentalism suspended in mid-air. Transcendentalism had to be taken to its logical conclusion, i.e., to some form of ideal-realism in Gurvitch's opinion. For Gurvitch "trans" also meant to go beyond knowledge itself and to establish contact with that which is independent of knowledge. Transcendentalism therefore led to a metaphysics of knowledge, in which it was crucial—and Gurvitch stressed this point—that neither "the one" nor "the other" was elevated into an Absolute. To turn empirical life itself into an Absolute would lead to a superficial *Lebensphilosophie*, and to turn logical contents into an Absolute would end in an equally shallow *panlogism*. Both approaches would be incapable of grasping the transcendental tension of knowledge, for the attainment of which a truly transcendental ideal-realism was necessary, Gurvitch argued. In transcendental ideal-realism the Absolute would be conceptualized as separated by a *hiatus irrationalis* from both the realm of the Logos and from the unknown "X" by which the Logos is surrounded. Reason, Gurvitch continued, would attempt to penetrate the "X" or the "thing-in-itself," but since this is an infinite task, neither force could ever dominate the other. The ideal-realistic theory of knowledge, Gurvitch claimed, constituted the core of Fichte's theoretical philosophy. During the three phases of Fichte's *Wissenschaftslehre,* different aspects of his metaphysics of knowledge were emphasized—the "X," or Logos or both—but the fundamental basis of Fichte's conception always remained the same.

Fichte, in his earliest works, had a very strong tendency to rely exclusively on reason and dialectics for the understanding of the world.[17] This tendency, Gurvitch argued, eliminated the "thing-in-itself" and reduced the task of knowledge to an empty building of categories. In many aspects, according to Gurvitch, Fichte's early philosophy was similar to Hegel's. Both thinkers had, in effect, turned reason into an Absolute under which reality was crushed. The result was dogmatism and a false conception of dialectic, in which the synthesis suppressed the thesis and the antithesis rather than reconciling and balancing them. Even when Fichte, with his notion of the active "I," tried to give his first philosophical system a non-contemplative character, it ended paradoxically in panlogism anyway. The "absolute I" was often improperly separated from reason. In *Grundlage* (1794), which was Fichte's main work of this period, the "absolute I" was openly depicted as an idea. However, despite the shortcomings inherent in Fichte's overreliance on reason at this point, it would be wrong to claim with Lask that his *Wissenschaftslehre* was totally rationalistic. Instead, Gurvitch argued, it was clear that Fichte had tried to counteract the predominance of the Logos with the "X." Opposite to the "I," Fichte posited the "not-I," and the "absolute I" was principally separated from the other "I's," as it should be in the ideal-realistic doctrine of negative theology. Hence, Gurvitch concluded, Fichte's earliest works contained the fundamental transcendental ideas even if they were obscured by a strong tendency toward rationalism.

Fichte's second period consisted of the works he wrote at the time of the *Atheismusstreit,* which took place at the end of the 1790's.[18] Through his attack on a very dogmatic and rationalistic concept of God, Fichte now began to exaggerate the second element in transcendentalism, the "X." According to ideal-realism, the "X," or "life," i.e., the material of knowledge, was basically irrational. It could not be known through dialectics and categories, i.e., through reason, but only through intuition. Life itself was elevated into an Absolute, and logical thinking was seen as something that could only obscure a true knowledge of life. It was important to capture the stream of life in its immediacy without presuppositions of any kind. In its essential character, Gurvitch argued, this phase of Fichte's thought amounted to a *Lebensphilosophie* which could lead in a variety of directions, such as empiricism, nominalism or phenomenology. Fichte, however, had rejected all these alternatives and had given his romantic-irrational *Lebensphilosophie* a religious quality by making faith the sole criterion of knowledge. "The sphere of our knowledge is determined by our heart," Fichte wrote.[19] According to Gurvitch, Fichte's epistemology during these years, just as in his first period, represented an attempt to work out the difficulties inherent in transcendentalism. If there had been somewhat of a neo-Kantian danger in Fichte's earliest works, it had now become phenomenological. But that Fichte had nevertheless remained faithful to the fundamentals of transcendentalism in this second period could be easily verified, Gurvitch argued, by Rickert's *Fichtes Atheismusstreit* (1899), in which the analogies between Fichte's theory of knowledge and that of the neo-Kantians were clearly drawn.

Fichte's third period, according to Gurvitch, represented the culmination of his theoretical philosophy.[20] In works such as the *Wissenschaftslehre* of 1804, Fichte successfully avoided both the "Scylla of Panlogism" and the "Charybdis of Irrationalism."[21] In the writings from this time, which roughly covered the years from 1801 to Fichte's death in 1814, ideal-realism achieved its fullest expression. Fichte finally firmly separated the Absolute from the Logos as well as from the "X," and this separation solved the problems with which Fichte had been struggling up to the present. As a result of his efforts, Fichte came to see that truth was no longer dependent on the "I" (subjective idealism) but on the Absolute (objective idealism).

Fichte's epistemology during his last years, according to Gurvitch, was built on a very interesting synthesis of dialectic and intuition. To reach the logical essences, intuition — *Erschauen der Wesenheiten* in Husserl's terminology — was absolutely necessary. Mere reasoning was powerless when confronted with the trans-rationality of the pure essences. However, the exclusive reliance on intuition in theoretical philosophy would be a grave mistake, similar to that of modern phenomenology, which was purely descriptive. Dialectic was also indispensable for constructing the general system of categories with which Logos always confronted the "X." In Fichte's opinion, Gurvitch noted, this general system had to be an open system which was ever ready to confront the irrational, empirical multitude. A closed system such as Hegel's, Gurvitch added, would only lead to panlogism, in which the infinite richness of reality would be suppressed in an arbitrary way. Hegel, who in *Glauben und Wissen* (1802) had said that for Fichte "the absolute is above reason," was in Gurvitch's opinion perfectly correct.[22]

Though Gurvitch's study of Fichte's epistemology was extraordinarily rich and penetrating, it was not intended to be more than an introduction to the study of Fichte's ethics.[23] As mentioned, changes in Fichte's epistemology had often been observed, but his ethical system had escaped this attention. However, Gurvitch claimed, on the basis of his analysis of the unity and periodization of Fichte's *Wissenschaftslehre,* that Fichte's moral doctrine also displayed a certain internal coherence which had evolved in three distinct stages. Gurvitch again traced the basic unity of Fichte's work, this time his ethics, to transcendental ideal-realism. However, Gurvitch did not stress so much the infinitude of the moral task as the autonomy of the moral realm. The Spirit (*Geist*) or ethical purity, Gurvitch argued, had to be separated from the Absolute, as well as from Logos, by an unsurpassable abyss. If this separation was not effected, morality would lose its autonomous stature and become either panlogistic moralism or moralistic irrationalism. According to Gurvitch, this process had indeed occurred in the first two stages of the development of Fichte's moral doctrine. Only in his third period did Fichte manage to overcome his mistakes and to lay the foundation for a truly ideal-realistic ethics.

In his earliest works, Fichte stressed the irrational character of moral activity.[24] The "I" was the subject of all moral acts and was conceptualized as pure alogical activity. This alogical character was true of the "absolute I," as well as of the "theoretical I" and the "practical I." Fichte's moral doctrine, Gurvitch pointed out, was very individualistic at this stage. In his last works dating from the 1790's, however, Fichte approached the postulation of an objective moral order with his notion of man's pure instinct. A sharp line was drawn between ordinary consciousness and moral consciousness in Fichte's early work, Gurvitch continued. Moral consciousness was depicted as totally irrational, and was only realizable in the moral act itself; it embodied the immediate knowledge of one's having acted in a moral way. The notion of will, eminently irrational also, was very close to moral consciousness. Nevertheless, Gurvitch claimed that Fichte's moral doctrine of these years could best be described as panlogistic moralism. To describe Fichte's ethics as panlogistic at this time might seem paradoxical, but given the predominance of the "practical I," Fichte's moral doctrine could only result in a logical system in which the irrationality of the moral act had been eliminated. Morality had been choked, as Gurvitch expressed it, in the chains of a logical system.

In the works dating from the *Atheismusstreit,* Fichte exaggerated the irrational "X," according to Gurvitch, at the expense of Logos.[25] The sharp distinctions between Logos and the Spirit, on the one hand, and between these two entities and the Absolute on the other, were now totally abandoned. Fichte presented reality as an irrational stream of life in which the Absolute, the Spirit and Logos all fused with each other. During this period, according to Gurvitch, Fichte's ethics became a pantheistically colored *Lebensphilosophie.* Logical thinking, Logos, was viewed as a hindrance to the full understanding of life and was replaced by belief. The activistic element in Fichte's ethics, which was very strong in the early 1790's, now became threatened by mysticism and an emphasis on contemplation. Morality itself was more or less dissolved into a romantic type of religion. The only positive quality in Fichte's ethics from these years, Gurvitch claimed, was that Fichte, under the influence of the Romantics, introduced the notion of Spirit into his moral system. In Gurvitch's opinion, this constituted an important attempt to go beyond the subjective idealism of the "I" and to establish an objective moral order.

In his last works, Fichte overcame his earlier difficulties and laid the foundations for what Gurvitch called the doctrine of pure moral spiritualism.[26] Fichte did not live long enough to completely formulate his final moral system, so Gurvitch was faced with the difficult task of trying to reconstruct it. He based his reconstruction especially on the *Sittenlehre* of 1812, but he also relied on some of his own interpolations of Fichte's original manuscripts at the Prussian Library in Berlin. According to Gurvitch, in Fichte's final period, Logos was conceptualized as transobjective, as a static system situated opposite to the Spirit. It was, however, Fichte's notion of the Spirit in the last period which, in Gurvitch's opinion, constituted Fichte's main contribution to practical philosophy. Fichte described the Spirit alternately as pure moral activity or as pure irrational freedom. He considered the Spirit to be ideal reality and, as Gurvitch pointed out, in this sense Fichte was definitely a Platonist. Fichte had now overcome Kant's individualistic moral doctrine, founded on the single person and not on the existence of the objective realm of the Spirit. The "I," however, still played a very important role in Fichte's work. Only the individual, through the exercise of his will in the moral act itself, could reach the transsubjective realm of the Spirit. In the spiritual realm, the metaphysical "I's" were grouped into a true community (*Gemeinschaft*) which was qualitatively distinct from the single "I's." According to Gurvitch, this doctrine of pure moral spiritualism represented a tremendous achievement in moral philosophy by Fichte, which had remained unsurpassed in richness and penetration.

The last part of Gurvitch's book on Fichte was devoted to Fichte's effort to go beyond moral formalism and to develop a concrete ethics.[27] This problem, as Gurvitch saw it, could equally be formulated in terms of the question of the exact connection between the ideal realm of the Spirit and the moral act of the individual. Gurvitch here stressed Fichte's opposition to Kant's philosophy which in many aspects was the epitome of ethical formalism. The categorical imperative had been conceived by Kant as an abstract law using the model of the natural sciences, and to Fichte it disregarded the unique individuality of the moral act. Kant had also neglected the ideal of eternal values being concretized in social reality, and in Fichte's mind this raised additional difficulties in his moral philosophy. Fichte posed the Spirit against Kant's categorical imperative. It was concrete as opposed to abstract, unique as opposed to general, and unconditional as opposed to relative. In the Spirit's two lower regions — ideals and values — its degree of purity was not the same. Gurvitch now proposed to analyze how Fichte dealt with the Spirit in his three phases of thinking in order to reconstruct Fichte's struggle against ethical formalism.

Fichte had great difficulty fighting ethical formalism effectively in his early works because of the general panlogism of his thought.[28] He did not conceptualize the moral realm as unique and irrational, but as a law, i.e., as something general and logical. Hence, morality, at this point in his thought, dissolved into reason and became a kind of moral *Logonomie,* to use an expression Gurvitch borrowed from Scheler's *Der Formalismus in der Ethik und die materielle Wertethik* (1913-1916). Fichte's analysis of the empirical realm in his early works was more successful, according to Gurvitch. Especially in the *Sittenlehre* of 1798, Fichte came very close to an understanding of the process of concretization between the higher and the lower realms of reality. The "X," or the "not-I" in moral matters, was quite correctly, according to Gurvitch, depicted by Fichte as unique, as illogical and as concrete. Fichte, however, did not succeed in establishing the exact nature of the link between the realm of the pure Spirit and empirical reality. In order for him to do so, Gurvitch argued, he would have had to develop an adequate conception of the relationship between the finite and the infinite. He would also have had to realize that values and ideals were part of both the spiritual realm and empirical reality, and that they represented a kind of connection between the two realms.

During the *Atheismusstreit* Fichte succeeded in going beyond moral formalism, according to Gurvitch.[29] He began to correctly understand moral action as value-filled human behavior, as behavior which strove toward and reached the realm of moral values. But Fichte's victory, according to Gurvitch, was also his defeat. He reached the solution to the problem of ethical formalism through a mystical and monistic *Lebensphilosophie* in which the autonomy of the moral realm was sacrificed. The limits between the various realms were totally dissolved in the process: the Absolute, the Spirit, Logos and empirical reality all blended in the mystical stream of life.

In his last works, Fichte most successfully overcame ethical formalism by elaborating an ethics fundamentally different from Kant's.[30] As opposed to the forbidding and negative character of Kant's categorical imperative, Fichte's "concrete ethics" was positive and voluntary. Fichte considered that each person had a unique moral capacity. To become conscious of this capacity and to use it to the fullest constituted man's moral vocation. Fichte constantly stressed the importance of acting morally and of not reducing morality to an abstract doctrine. Fichte's ethics was also positive in the sense that it was a social ethics: only in society were moral acts possible. Each individual had a different moral task to carry out in life. This did not mean that people had to conflict with each other in society. All moral acts, Fichte explained, were directed toward an ideal situated beyond empirical reality and which served an inspirational purpose. The ideal was depicted as an organic whole in which each individual was equally indispensable, and this organic whole could also serve as a model for societal organization. Gurvitch found Fichte's synthesis of the group and the individual so interesting that he promised in the last lines of *Fichtes System* to devote his next work to it.

Fichte's new ethics presupposed a new moral metaphysics.[31] The notion of the Spirit was at the center of this new system. Fichte described it as pure transsubjective creativity; it was totally irrational and was situated beyond reality. In a lower form, the Spirit appeared as the system of ideals, which mediated between the extratemporal world of the pure spiritual stream and the empirical world. Values, the embodiment of the ideal in the empirical sphere, constituted the lowest form of the Spirit. Such was Gurvitch's interpolation of Fichte's new moral metaphysics.

A difficult question to answer is whether Gurvitch's analysis represents a close rendering or a free interpretation of Fichte's thought. It can be argued that this is a false issue: Fichte and Gurvitch, the one belonging to the German idealists and the other to the Russian intelligentsia, faced the same problems through structural affinity. However, while their stuctural affinity is indeed present on a general level, a line must be drawn between Gurvitch's and Fichte's ideas of knowledge and morality, although an analysis of these ideas reveals that Fichte and Gurvitch agreed to a remarkable degree on most epistemological and ethical issues. Both saw the dangers of irrationalism and panlogism; both chose to conceptualize reality in terms of Logos, the Spirit and so on. That their affinity is close can be seen in some of Gurvitch's later works, such as *Les Tendances Actuelles de la Philosophie Allemande* (1930) and *Morale Théorique et Science des Moeurs* (1937), in which Gurvitch presented his own philosophical system.[32] It does not necessarily follow, however, that Gurvitch simply read his own thoughts into Fichte's work, even though this occasionally happened.[33] To establish this assumption a very methodical comparison between Fichte's work and Gurvitch's analysis would have to be done, as Lossky has correctly pointed out.[34] It should also be remembered that Gurvitch was generally more interested in developing a

theory of the evolution of Fichte's thought than in blindly following it.[35] For
the purpose of analysis of Gurvitch's thought, it is sufficient to know that Gurvitch generally agreed with what can be assumed to be Fichte's thought. The
few occasions when Gurvitch differed from Fichte are clearly recognizable.[36]

The fundamental problem with which Gurvitch struggled was how to
avoid what he called the "Scylla of Panlogism" and the "Charybdis of Irrationalism."[37] That this question was a strong concern of Gurvitch's, as well as
of Fichte's, can be confirmed by reference to Gurvitch's *Les Tendances Actuelles de la Philosophie Allemande.* "The Scylla of Panlogism" symbolized
for Gurvitch the peril involved in letting philosophy become a mere product of
reason. In epistemology, this process would lead to an empty play of dialectics, and to the construction of an arbitrary system of categories which totally
lacked contact with empirical reality. More dangerously, panlogism also implied absolutism for Gurvitch. Hegelian dialectic, in Gurvitch's thinking,
falsely suppressed the thesis and antithesis in order to let the synthesis reign
supremely. All diversity, all opposition was crushed under the weight of absolute reason. The same fate would be destined for ethics if reason became the
leading principle. The richness and individuality of human morality would
disappear in the abstract categories of the moral system, and ethical formalism
would inevitably follow.

If one steered free of panlogism, there was instead the danger of the
"Charybdis of Irrationalism," i.e., the danger of overemphasizing the world
outside the subjective mind, the unknown "X." In philosophy, this could lead
to a variety of doctrines such as empiricism, *Lebensphilosophie* or pantheism,
all of which are basically contemplative. Reason and dialectic would be replaced
by intuition. The systematic construction of categories would be replaced by a
scattered, if penetrating, knowledge of unconnected parts of reality. In
morality, formalism would be vanquished, but mysticism would appear instead and contemplation would supplant moral activism.

Gurvitch's solution to the problem of panlogism and irrationalism was a
form of reconciliation between the two forces, an attempt to go beyond the
mistakes of both by balancing them against each other. This solution is illustrated in Gurvitch's metaphysical system: the Absolute stands above Logos,
as well as the Spirit, without destroying either of them, but it also refuses
crossing of the *hiatus irrationalis* by the Spirit and the Logos in order to prevent either one from becoming an Absolute itself. According to Gurvitch's
scheme, only the combined efforts of intuition and dialectic can insure a true
knowledge of reality. In addition, the two main elements in Gurvitch's moral
doctrine are the synthesis of activism and irrationalism on the one hand, and
of the group and the individual on the other.

As already suggested, Gurvitch's thought in general grew out of the contradictory position of the Russian intelligentsia. Upon closer inspection this

situation is true of his epistemology and ethics as well. What Gurvitch called "panlogism" was the expression of the old intelligentsia, which was separated from the masses and instead sought solace in the metaphysical systems of Hegel and the young Fichte. "Irrationalism," on the other hand, was the ideology of the new emerging intelligentsia, which was increasingly being integrated into capitalism.

The polarization in the Russian intelligentsia before the October Revolution was expressed through its several intellectual currents. The intelligentsia's small radical wing, which was already a minority in the 1870's, was organized into the revolutionary parties, the most important of which was the Social-Democratic Party.[38] Many members of the radical intelligentsia had left German idealism far behind, as illustrated by the works of Plekhanov and Lenin.[39] However, an increasing majority of intellectuals rejected the revolutionary alternative. They had long ago discarded German idealism, replacing it in the 1860's with various forms of positivism.[40] In the 1890's, positivism began to be sharply criticized by neo-Kantianism, which had rapidly become popular in bourgeois philosophical circles.[41] After the 1905 Revolution, idealist doctrines of various shades swept the field. "Intuition" became the slogan for the new philosophy, and it provided the epistemological basis for the very important works by Lossky, Frank and Petrazhitsky which now appeared.[42] Many Russian students — among them Gurvitch — went to Germany and brought back the latest works by Rickert, Lask and others.[43] A Russian section of the neo-Kantian journal *Logos* was established in 1911.[44] Metaphysics and religion flowered in bourgeois intellectual circles, and there was a renewed interest in slavophile thought.

The fight between the bourgeois and radical camps in philosophy was pointed. The bourgeoisie claimed that the "intelligentsia" was only interested in fighting against autocracy and not in pursuing truth *per se*. In addition, Struve claimed in *Patriotica* (1905) that the intelligentsia lacked religious feeling. He accused the intelligentsia of having little faith in individualism and of turning equality into a "fetish."[45] The sharpest attack against the old radical tradition within the intelligentsia came in 1909 in the work entitled *Vekhi (Signposts)*, which ran through several editions rapidly. *Vekhi* claimed that the "intelligentsia" had no respect for law and order, that it had elevated the people into a god-like power, and that it was not interested in becoming responsible in political matters. A whole new orientation of thought was necessary for the survival of intellectual life, *Vekhi* argued. True change in the world would only be possible through religion, and all forms of materialism would have to be rejected. First and foremost, one had to recognize "the practical primacy of spiritual life over the external forms of society..."[46]

The various ideological attacks on the radical intelligentsia scored their victims. Many revolutionaries — Gurvitch was one — rallied to the new idealism in the areas of epistemology and ethics. Some moved from Marxism to Liberalism and joined one of the bourgeois parties. In general, the new idealism in philosophy had a demoralizing effect on the radical intellectuals.[47] But the left retaliated. Lenin's ideas are especially interesting in this regard, because they were the most consistently revolutionary. According to Lenin, epistemology was a *"partisan* science" and an expression of the on-going class struggle.[48] The renewed interest in idealism, as he saw it, represented an attack of the bourgeoisie on historical materialism. This assertion did not imply that idealism-liberalism was totally reactionary in Russia. Rather, Lenin saw that the liberal-idealist position contained progressive as well as backward elements. Lenin's explanation for this mixture of elements was that the liberals *"have* to play at democracy to win the support of the masses but at the same time they are deeply anti-democratic, deeply hostile to the movement of the masses..."[49] After 1905, the liberal bourgeoisie, according to Lenin, increasingly sided with the reactionary element. *Vekhi,* to which Lenin attached a great deal of importance, was an expression of this movement to the right. *Vekhi* represented, as Lenin put it, "a whole social trend," and constituted "a most significant landmark on the road of Russian Cadetism and Russian liberalism in general towards *a complete break* with the Russian liberation movement, with all its main aims and fundamental traditions."[50] Lenin pointed to the thinly disguised individualism as well as to the fear of the masses that was evident in *Vekhi,* and he labelled it an *"encyclopaedia of liberal renegacy."*[51]

On the level of philosophy, Gurvitch expressed the class strategy of the progressive bourgeoisie, i.e., that part of the bourgeoisie which was still inflamed with the democratic ideals and which tried to unite the people under its ideological hegemony. Practically, this meant that Gurvitch searched for a kind of balance between the bourgeoisie, or liberalism, and the proletariat, or socialism, a balance which ultimately tipped in favor of the bourgeoisie. Gurvitch was not unaware of the political implications of his analysis of Fichte. Some years after the publication of *Fichtes System der Konkreten Ethik* he noted that "Fichte's thought tended in the direction of a synthesis between liberalism and socialism, toward an anti-individualistic liberalism and an antistate socialism."[52] The re-establishment of the relationship between Gurvitch's analysis of Fichte and the class struggle in Russia clearly reveals Gurvitch's position.

That Gurvitch did not accept all the positions of the *Vekhi* group is clear. Gurvitch's relation to religion was complicated, but there is no doubt that he rejected the mysticism of Lossky and Frank.[53] This is especially evident in Gurvitch's analysis of irrationalism in his book on Fichte. Gurvitch specifically reacted against the contemplative element in religion. The voluntaristic and activistic side in Gurvitch definitely separated him from the religious resignation that was spreading in intellectual circles.[54] The Absolute played a very minor role in Gurvitch's metaphysical system, in which its real function was to delimit the powers of Logos and the Spirit.[55] Finally, as Gurvitch himself pointed out, to rely exclusively on intuitive belief for a full understanding of reality was not enough; reason also had to play a role in this process.

On the other hand, Gurvitch accepted many of the basic elements of the new idealism. He borrowed heavily from Lossky's doctrine of "ideal-realism," and he was also influenced by the neo-Kantians. Most importantly, he accepted the notion of the primacy of the spirit and the bourgeois identification of positivism and historical materialism. One idea, very popular in the circles in which Lossky and Frank moved, was the notion of *sobornost,* i.e., of a religious communion in which the interests of the group and the individual were reconciled. Admittedly, this idea was in some aspects nothing but a subtle religious version of the old liberal belief that harmony will follow if everybody does as he pleases. But *sobornost* also had a progressive side—an acknowledgement of the importance of human community. Gurvitch was extremely attracted to the idea of *sobornost* and he made it the basis of his moral philosophy. Consequently, on one level Gurvitch was deeply influenced by the new idealism. However, what always distinguished him from philosophers like Lossky, Frank and Berdiaev was the revolutionary activism which permeated all of his work.

Upon closer study, it becomes clear that Gurvitch's voluntarism was concentrated in his most reactionary categories, such as the irrational Spirit and intuition. Conversely, his most progressive concepts, such as reason and the dialectic, were totally separated from freedom and activity. They were, at best, categories which he could not completely disallow. Hence Gurvitch's most revolutionary tendencies could only be expressed through his most reactionary categories. The methodological consequences of this fact are very serious, and they never stopped haunting Gurvitch's analyses.

Gurvitch's methodological impasse was rooted in the development of the class struggle in Tzarist Russia. The old intelligentsia had experienced no difficulty in understanding the revolutionary consequences of the young Fichte's disposal of the thing-in-itself, i.e., in the total triumph of Reason.[56] Nor did the old intelligentsia have any trouble in grasping the subversive character of dialectic. In Gurvitch's era, however, the situation had drastically changed. The bourgeois thinkers had more or less given up the radical dreams of their predecessors, and they had become incapable of seeing in Reason anything more than a simple category of mind.[57] Dialectic was no longer the "algebra of revolution" (Herzen) but merely the logic of philosophy.[58] Under these circumstances, bourgeois thought, in order to advance, turned to intuition or belief. Such was the nature of the tremendous attraction of irrationalism to bourgeois thinkers.

Similar philosophical tendencies to those of Russia prevailed in Europe at the turn of the century, as Georg Lukaćs has traced in his *Die Zerstörung der Vernuft.* The classical heritage of the French Revolution—Reason and historical dialectic—was under increasing attack by irrationalism in the form of neo-Kantianism and phenomenology. The antisocialist elements in European thought were, of course, much stronger than in Russian philosophy because of the protracted battles of over fifty years between the European bourgeoisie and the proletariat. Nietzsche's rabid anti-socialism is a case in point. The struggles in Europe made the young Russian bourgeoisie prematurely aware of the discovery of its European counterpart, namely that labor and capital were deadly enemies. Lenin, the best mind of the Russian Revolution, had been constantly stressing this fact. On the methodological level, Gurvitch's dilemma is clearly that he was a progressive bourgeois at a time when it was becoming increasingly difficult for the bourgeoisie to be progressive.

Gurvitch's choice of the old Fichte as his philosophical model illustrates his dilemma. Gurvitch was extremely drawn to—or, to use his own word, "seduced" by—Fichte's emphasis on will and action.[59] However, he could only respond to this emphasis when it was expressed in an irrational way, as in Fichte's last works. Gurvitch did not yet realize his methodological dilemma. His book on Fichte was primarily written during the years after the Russian Revolution, years which were characterized by extreme utopianism in revolutionary circles, and Gurvitch had sided with the socialists in the Revolution, not with the liberal bourgeoisie.[60] The basic philosophical currents which characterized these post-Revolution years were much the same as those expressed in Gurvitch's book on Fichte, i.e., activistic and utopian. Soon, however, the great revolutionary wave was to ebb in Russia and in Europe. It would be followed first by a brief period of capitalist stabilization and then by Fascism. Gurvitch, as will become increasingly evident, was methodologically ill-equipped to deal with the new developments in the European class struggle.

3 The Revival of Juristic Socialism

After his book on Fichte was completed, Gurvitch concentrated on the philosophy of law.[1] During the late 1920's and early 1930's, Gurvitch produced a series of important works in this field, the most famous of which is *L'Idée du Droit Social* (1932).[2] From a legal standpoint, the doctrine of social law is very interesting and merits more detailed discussion. However, in order to see the organic link between Gurvitch's book on Fichte and *L'Idée du Droit Social* on the one hand, and the link between *L'Idée du Droit Social* and Gurvitch's sociology on the other, it is imperative to examine the methodological aspects of Gurvitch's philosophy of law. For, in general, understanding the methodology of an author's work is a more decisive guide than is the academic field within which the work happens to fall.

To recapitulate, Gurvitch's book on Fichte had corresponded well to the revolutionary optimism of the early 1920's. However, the worldwide revolution that Gurvitch and many other socialists had hoped for did not materialize.[3] The revolutions in Hungary, Italy and Germany had all been defeated by the middle 1920's. Capitalism had not only successfully defended itself, it had also successfully smashed or split all the major working class organizations in Europe. Italy, where Fascism was already established in 1922, gave a foretaste of the brutal capabilities of the right-wing sections of the bourgeoisie. The time had come to change the revolutionary strategy, to go into a defensive position instead of continuing an offensive one. Stalin understood the need for a change in strategy far better than Trotsky did. His policy of "socialism in one country" was ultimately sounder than Trotsky's adherence to the notion of "permanent revolution."

The struggle over the right course of action for radicals to pursue was as bitterly fought on the level of philosophical methodology as in the political arena. Georg Lukács' own re-orientation of his thought illustrates the conflicts of the time. Because of his background in idealism, Lukács had been extremely receptive to revolutionary utopianism. *History and Class Consciousness*

35

(1923), as Lukács himself has admitted, is in many aspects still a pre-Marxist work.[4] However, from the middle 1920's onward, Lukács tried to go beyond "'left-wing' communism" (Lenin) and to adopt a more realistic approach to the dynamics of social reality. As the symbol of Utopian Socialism, Fichte was Lukács' chosen target.[5] Fichte's inclination, Lukács argued, had been more revolutionary than Hegel's, which explained the enormous attraction Fichte held for the Left-Hegelians, Lassalle, and others. Fichte had taken an essentially moralistic stance and had conceived the world as existing in a state of "total degradation." Hegel, on the other hand, had tried to bridge the distance between the world and the concept, and to reintegrate the subject and the object by historicizing the concept. Hegel, as Lukács well knew, ended by endorsing the Prussian state; but Hegel's famous "reconciliation" was not the point—in the 1840's Marx and Engels had corrected his methodology and freed it from its reactionary elements. The point for Lukács was that the Fichtean approach was incapable of dealing with reality because it disregarded economy as well as history and placed the philosopher outside society. Pointing to the "True Socialists" and Lassalle as examples, Lukács argued that Fichte's moralistic methodology led to reformism and opportunism because of its inability to encompass the dynamics of capitalist society.

It is clear that Gurvitch and Lukács shared the same feeling of revolutionary utopianism for a few years. Lukács, however, coming from a Marxist tradition, was able to re-orient his thinking to the changing conditions of the 1920's. But Gurvitch, as a Proudhonist, was handicapped by coming from a tradition very similar to Fichte's with its emphasis on morality and justice. Thus, Gurvitch's philosophical struggles in the late 1920's and the early 1930's stemmed from the increasing contradiction between his moralistic voluntarism and the changing reality.

Gurvitch's difficulty in coming to terms with the restoration of capitalism in the 1920's is as evident in his general doctrine of "social law" as in his methodology. Inconsistencies abound in Gurvitch's philosophy of law. For instance, Gurvitch embraced the reactionary ideas of Otto von Gierke while simultaneously advocating a fairly radical system of workers' councils.[6] The contradictions in Gurvitch's thought are not attributable to any scholarly deficiency—he was indeed a very able scholar—rather, they originate in Gurvitch's increasingly untenable class position in twentieth century society. That Gurvitch's philosophy of law produced a version of what is known in Marxism as "Juristic Socialism" is consistent with his class position.[7] Inherent in the notion of Juristic Socialism is the idea of class collaboration between the progressive part of the bourgeoisie and the proletariat, an idea which was progressive at the time of the bourgeois revolution in France (1789) and to some extent in Russia (1917), but which had lost its meaning by the 1920's.

Gurvitch's main works from this period are *L'Idée du Droit Social* (1932),

Le Temps Présent et L'Idée du Droit Social (1932), and *L'Expérience Juridique et la Philosophie Pluraliste du Droit* (1935).[8] In *L'Idée du Droit Social,* Gurvitch develops the notion of "social law" and traces its history. In *Le Temps Présent et L'Idée du Droit Social* "the victorious march of social law" in contemporary legal institutions is elaborated.[9] *L'Expérience Juridique et la Philosophie Pluraliste du Droit* outlines the methodological basis for Gurvitch's philosophy of law.

Each of these works illustrates different aspects of Gurvitch's philosophy of law. *L'Idée du Droit Social,* while trying to relate to the changing situation in the 1920's, shows how Gurvitch's analysis of law was indebted to his Russian background. *Le Temps Présent et L'Idée du Droit Social* exemplifies in a vivid way the political implications of Gurvitch's philosophy of law. And *L'Expérience Juridique et la Philosophie Pluraliste du Droit* illuminates the intimate connection between his political views and a specific methodology.

. *L'Idée du Droit Social* is in many aspects a very interesting work. Unfortunately, it has been disregarded in contemporary American sociology in which Gurvitch's name is primarily associated with *Twentieth Century Sociology* (1945) and, in a vague way, with some studies in general sociology and in the sociology of knowledge. The lack of American exposure to *L'Idée du Droit Social* is a pity because it is Gurvitch's most creative and thorough work. The idea of social law is "the living center of [Gurvitch's] thought," as Jean Duvignaud has written.[10] Academically, *L'Idée du Droit Social* is an impressive work, consisting of more than seven hundred pages of extremely well-documented material. It was successfully presented at the Sorbonne in 1932 as Gurvitch's primary doctoral thesis.[11] Gurvitch virtually put everything he knew into *L'Idée du Droit Social.*[12] More interestingly, perhaps, he also put everything he hoped for into the work, i.e., his ideal of a socialist society run by workers' councils. The result is a very complex and contradictory work.

There is some question about the translation of "droit social" into English. Gurvitch himself preferred the translation to be "social law."[13] "Droit," however, means "right" rather than "law," and therefore, "social right" would be a more literal translation. The problem with "social right," however, is that it does not convey the distinctly scientific-positivistic meaning that Gurvitch tried to give his notion of "droit social." Consequently, "social law" will be the translation used throughout the discussion of *L'Idée du Droit Social.*[14]

According to Gurvitch, the whole legal system in the western world was in need of change. Legal science, which had been modeled after Roman law, was no longer capable of guiding the administration of justice. All the basic postulates of Roman law were unfit for modern times, especially the postulate declaring that only the State could create law. The basic fault with Roman, and hence contemporary, law was its strong emphasis on individualism, according to Gurvitch. Law was always focused on the isolated individual and his conflicts with other individuals. The law's function was purely negative—to prevent harm to the individual. Law *per se* had become so identified with individualism, Gurvitch argued, that anti-individualism was nearly always combined with hostility to the very notion of law. The works of Saint-Simon, Bonald and Marx exemplify this hostility.

In order to combat the overemphasis on individualism in law, Gurvitch claimed that the notion of totality had to be introduced directly into the structure of law itself. Only then would one be able to construct a new type of law—social law as opposed to individual law—which would be able to solve the problems confronting legal science. Under social law, the "we" would replace the "I" as the point of reference. This "we" had to be conceptualized in accordance with what Gurvitch called "legal transpersonalism," i.e., the "we" constituted a synthesis between individualism and universalism. Gurvitch stressed that the whole must not be superior to its parts (as in universalism), or the parts superior to the whole (as in individualism). Social law was the law of communion. The very idea of social law, Gurvitch concluded, was very much in tune with contemporary legal science. It was especially close to the German notion of *Genossenschaftsrecht* (Gierke) and the French concept of *solidarité de droit* (Secrétan, Bourgeois).

Besides social law and individual law, Gurvitch described a third kind of law, which he called "law of subordination." This type of law Gurvitch characterized as a deformation and perversion of social law; it was social law co-opted by individual law and turned into oppressive law. An example of "law of subordination" would be the capitalist factory, in which the social law of the factory is perverted by the individual law of property.

Gurvitch minutely defined social law in his work.[15] The objective function of social law was to integrate the group through a communion between its members. This communion, depicted as the partial fusion of the individual members into a whole, could only occur if the members would actively participate in the task of the group. Social law answered to the feeling of the "we" in the group, and it was what Gurvitch called a law of integration as opposed to individual law which was simply a law of coordination. Individual law was expressed through the relations between "I," "he," "she," and "it." Gurvitch characterized social law as taking precedence over individual law, because he understood that individual law was essentially social in nature, requiring coordination to function.

In order to function properly, social law did not necessarily have to be coercive, Gurvitch continued. It could be coercive, but there was no inherent connection between law and force, between law and the state. Each active social group would by definition create its own law. This legal pluralism, of course, opposes the tendency in Roman law to see the state as the only group that can make law. It also implied a whole new concept of sovereignty. The state, Gurvitch asserted, should have the monopoly on force (political sovereignty), but not on law (absolute sovereignty). The state should be subordinate to law (legal sovereignty).

Gurvitch's basic premise in *L'Idée du Droit Social* was that law emerges spontaneously in each active group. In order for law to attain organizational expression, however, the organization had to be democratic and egalitarian. A hierarchical organization, Gurvitch wrote, would inevitably distort the underlying social law. Nevertheless, unorganized social law had primacy over any organization because of its richness and irrationality. All organizations, in Gurvitch's opinion, were mechanical in nature, and therefore they impoverished reality by rationalizing it.

Only in the realm of pure creative morality, Gurvitch argued, could harmony exist between individualism and universalism. In empirical reality, conflicts between the two were the rule. This condition, Gurvitch pointed out, did not imply that there is no connection between law and morality. Indeed, all law was based on what Gurvitch called "normative facts," i.e., facts penetrated by extratemporal values. The notion of normative facts, Gurvitch claimed, was close to Hauriou's notion of "institution," and law derived its basic authority from these facts. Social law, through sociality of communion in the empirical world, could partially realize transpersonal values, while individual law, through what Gurvitch called sociality of opposition, could only strive to embody personal values.

According to Gurvitch, it was possible to differentiate between varying types of social law by determining whether the group served a special or a general interest, or by ascertaining whether the group was subordinate to the state or *vice versa*.[16] The most crucial factor for distinguishing between types of social law was a group's relation to the state. An especially important type was what Gurvitch called pure social law, law which was equivalent or superior to the law of the state. International law is an example of a social law that is superior to the law of the national state. The law of the economic community — *"droit économique"* in Proudhon's terminology — was increasingly growing in importance, Gurvitch claimed, and he added that it might one day become as powerful as the law of the state. In that eventuality, the economic community would counterbalance the power of the political community. The Guild-Socialists and the Constructive Syndicalists (Jouhaux and others) were oriented in that direction, according to Gurvitch. In contrast to the Fascists and the Bolsheviks, they understood the critical importance of limiting the power of the state and of assigning law an autonomous place in socialist society. The essential task of legal science, Gurvitch concluded, should be to further develop the principles outlined in the French and American declarations of rights, and to make them truly effective by removing the outmoded individualistic elements.

Gurvitch's notion of social law was based on what he called legal ideal-realism.[17] Law itself, Gurvitch claimed, always represents an attempt to realize justice. Justice, in its turn, Gurvitch conceptualized as an intermediary between the moral realm and empirical reality. In the pure moral realm, there are no conflicts, in Gurvitch's view. However, in the realm of empirical reality there are constant struggles between personal and transpersonal values. The function of the law is to mediate these conflicts and to insure peace in society. In comparison to the realm of values, which Gurvitch described as irrational and individualistic, justice represents a more generalized and rational reality. Justice, in Gurvitch's expression, cools morality down. Nonetheless, justice is directly connected to the spiritual realm. It is founded on normative facts, i.e., on the extratemporal values which are partly realized in empirical reality. These normative facts are multilateral in nature, which means, according to Gurvitch, that claims and obligations fully correspond to each other. In Petrazhitsky's words, normative facts are "imperative-attributive." In the sphere of pure morality, on the other hand, obligations far surpass claims. Consequently, for Gurvitch, morality was more revolutionary than justice, whose first task is to insure social order.

Gurvitch applied the principles of legal ideal-realism to the question of the sources of the law as well. Normative facts, he wrote, constitute the primary sources of the law and can be apprehended directly through intuition. This Gurvitch called intuitive positive law. Normative facts can also be understood, though indirectly, through the usual legal procedures, such as written law and custom. Gurvitch labeled these standard legal procedures secondary sources and characterized them as formal positive law. For the sake of justice and stability in society, Gurvitch argued, formal positive law ought to take precedence over intuitive positive law. There are, however, moments when the two types of law sharply conflict with each other because formal positive law represents an outmoded legal reality. In these cases, Gurvitch thought that primacy should be given to intuitive positive law.

Gurvitch spent the main portion of L'Idée du Droit Social attempting to prove that there has been a viable but unknown tradition of pure social law in legal doctrine.[18] His method was to examine the way various legal theoreticians had dealt with the question of social law throughout history, but he disregarded the general systems the theoreticians had used to elaborate on their theories. The history of ideas, Gurvitch argued, should be oriented toward the history of intellectual problems and not to explaining the genesis of an idea.

Gurvitch's study led him to claim that the idea of social law could not have existed before the Renaissance. In Antiquity and in the Middle Ages the individual had been practically non-existent; therefore, there was no distinction between individual and social law at that time. The first signs of social law appeared after the Renaissance, more precisely in the school of natural social law (*jus sociale naturale*). Grotius was this school's most important theoretician, and he had made the original effort to synthesize the interests of the individual and of society in legal thought. Leibniz, Gurvitch wrote, continued Grotius' work. For Leibniz, *jus sociale* was the law of peace. The next major contribution to the idea of social law came from the Physiocrats. According to the Physiocrats, economic society produced its own spontaneous law. The Physiocrats also saw the opposition between state and society with great clarity.

Social law, as it was conceived before the French Revolution of 1789, was hierarchical in nature, according to Gurvitch. Rousseau and Kant, however, completely destroyed the idea of hierarchy and thereby resurrected the theme of human autonomy and creativity that had been characteristic of the Renaissance. Rousseau and Kant produced a rich heritage of legal thought, in Gurvitch's view. They had tried to synthesize freedom and equality into a government subordinate to law. But Gurvitch noted that Rousseau and Kant had eliminated the notion of totality from their systems, which he considered to be a serious setback in relation to the earlier theories of social law.

The notion of totality was re-introduced after the French Revolution in the works of Comte, the early socialists, and the Traditionalists (Bonald and de Maistre). Comte and the Traditionalists, however, were unable to conceive of a true synthesis between the individual and society. Their hostility to the individualism of the eighteenth century was primarily directed against the emphasis on human autonomy and creativity during that period. Gurvitch claimed that only the early socialists, such as Saint-Simon, Fourier and Louis Blanc, had successfully renewed and continued the tradition of Kant and Rousseau. In a progressive way, the early socialists saw beyond both atomistic individualism and oppressive statism. Nonetheless, their efforts resulted in various kinds of oppressive statism, according to Gurvitch, because they did not assign an autonomous place to law in their future societies. An example was Saint-Simon, who wanted to replace law with political economy as the basis of society and whose anti-individualistic liberalism was seriously threatened as a result. Gurvitch felt that Marx and Engels, who came from the Saint-Simonian tradition, made the same mistake and compounded it by glorifying the state.

The person who in Gurvitch's mind reunited socialism with respect for law was Proudhon with his notion of "droit économique." Proudhon, Gurvitch claimed, understood exceedingly well that a society without law results in authoritarianism. Proudhon attacked both individualism and collectivism and searched for a third alternative, in which justice would play the key role. In Proudhon's scheme, the state and economic society would counterbalance each other. The economy, as well as the state, would be permeated with law, and industrial democracy would complement political democracy. While realizing that Proudhon's legal sophistication was scant, Gurvitch nevertheless considered Proudhon to be the most important figure in the history of social law. Proudhon, Gurvitch claimed, had created the first crucial "synthesis between socialism and the idea of law."[19]

According to Gurvitch's researches, nineteenth century thought in Germany was generally considered to be dominated by Hegel. However, Gurvitch cited another, less noticed tradition—the Fichtean one. Fichte had succeeded in synthesizing individualism with universalism in the realm of morality (transpersonalism), though his philosophy of law remained very individualistic. But the thinkers following in the Fichtean tradition eventually began to join transpersonalism with social law. Krause's idea of *Gesellschaftsrecht* was one example of this change in thinking. The Historical School, which Gurvitch regarded as the right wing of the Fichtean tradition, was another. In addition, many of the mistakes made by Savigny and Puchta, Gurvitch argued, were rectified by the Germanists who played a quite significant role in the Revolution of 1848 and who constituted the German equivalent of the early French socialists. Another important figure in the Fichtean tradition, according to Gurvitch, was Otto von Gierke, who reintroduced the notion of ethical community into the science of law.

However, it was in France that the idea of social law had, in Gurvitch's estimation, reached its highest expression. After Proudhon, the Solidarists, such as Bourgeois and Fouillée, contributed the idea that solidarity based on justice represented the solution to social problems. Gurvitch felt that a true synthesis between individualism and universalism was implicit in the notion of solidarity. The Solidarists, however, were not very sophisticated in legal philosophy. It was not until the school of legal objectivism was created (Duguit, Hauriou and Saleilles) that the notion of social law achieved adequate legal expression. The problems of sovereignty and legal subjectivism, for example, were solved by the French legal objectivists to Gurvitch's satisfaction.

L'Idée du Droit Social was very well received in bourgeois academic circles. Louis Le Fur called it "a new step forward"[20] and Harold Laski wrote to Oliver Wendell Holmes that "it gives you a sense of legal philosophy changing to fit new needs which I find really exhilarating."[21] The consensus was that Gurvitch's work was extremely well documented and truly monumental in scope. There were some questions as to why Gurvitch had excluded the Middle Ages and Antiquity from his research. The negative criticism of the book, however, mainly concentrated on two points: whether Gurvitch's idea of social law was in fact just a new version of natural law, and whether Gurvitch had properly understood the relationship between law and the state.[22] Gurvitch's attack on natural law in *L'Idée* and his attempt to describe social law as purely positive did not impress his academic colleagues. His analysis of the state was also treated as dubious.[23] One reviewer, in *Archiv für Rechts-und Wirt-schaftsphilosophie,* wrote that Gurvitch had no true understanding of questions concerning power and the state. This, he claimed, was due to the influence of syndicalism on Gurvitch's thought.[24] Nicholas Timasheff, arguing somewhat in the same vein, pointed out that Gurvitch's philosophy of law constituted a kind of "legal anarchism."[25] Georges Aillet noted in passing that Gurvitch's emphasis on spontaneous, irrational law resulted in a "cult of irrationality."[26]

Some interesting points were raised by the discussion of *L'Idée du Droit Social* in bourgeois legal circles. The relation of social law to syndicalism was one, and Aillet's remark on the cult of irrationality in Gurvitch's work was another. However, these questions were never developed or elaborated upon. The criticism of *L'Idée* was very meager on the whole. What was missing was the more thorough and penetrating critique of Gurvitch's ideas on law that Marxism offers.[27]

According to the Marxist perspective, law — like morality and religion — is part of the superstructure. Two very important consequences follow from this view. First, law cannot by itself be "the true point of attack" for the working class.[28] "What we have to grapple with," Marx told the workers of the First International, "is the cause and not the effect — the economic basis, not its juridical superstructure."[29] Second, the legal superstructure changes with the economic basis: "The changes in the economic foundation lead sooner or later to the transformation of the whole immense superstructure" (Preface to *A Contribution to the Critique of Political Economy).*[30] Undoubtedly, Marx is referring to the change from one mode of production to another. However, his position is also valid for changes within one mode of production — for instance, for changes within capitalism itself.

The classical Marxist analysis of law related to *laissez-faire* capitalism. In "On the Jewish Question," Marx discussed the place of legal ideology at a stage of capitalism in which the state had played a subordinate role. His focus was on the Rights of Man.

Capitalism, however, underwent a decisive change at the turn of the century, whereby the "old" capitalism was, in Lenin's words, replaced by a "new" capitalism.[31] In the monopoly capitalism that emerged, the state's role was quite different and therefore legislation and the bourgeois notion of justice changed as well. There are many reasons why the state moved into a more dominant position, the two most blatant ones being the growth of imperialism and the need to check the growing strength of the working class.

It is possible to see the famous article on "Juristic Socialism" (1886) by Engels as an attempt to deal with the legal ideology of monopoly capitalism.[32] Engels did not explicitly point out a new stage of capitalism. But he was very concerned with the re-emergence, among many contemporary socialists, of the old utopian illusion that socialism could be constructed on the basis of a philosophy of law, and the re-emergence of this notion in socialist thought was caused by the change in the legal system that monopoly capitalism demanded. Engels reiterated that Marxism was built on political economy, not on a philosophy of law. No emphasis on "justice," he argued, could replace a scientific-economic analysis. He also stressed a point of great importance — law represented for the bourgeoisie what religion had been for the feudal system: a world view (*Weltanschauung*). In short, in the 1880's Engels reaffirmed the idea that law was still the most important bourgeois ideology; therefore socialists should not under any circumstances replace political economy with an illusionary philosophy of law, however "progressive." The only alternative to the "juristic *Weltanschauung*" of the bourgeoisie was the "materialist conception of history," Engels concluded.[33]

Marx and Engels had looked upon the utopian socialists and their juristic illusions with a certain benevolence in the *Manifesto,* but this tolerance is completely missing from Engels' article forty years later. The early utopians had been pre-Marxist, but the "late utopians" were, as a result of the development of the class struggle, anti-Marxist.[34] Engels attacked them accordingly.

To a certain extent Gurvitch can be considered to be one of these "late utopians." *L'Idée du Droit Social* is an outgrowth of the Russian class struggle and of the role legal ideology played for the bourgeoisie at the time of the Russian Revolution. For, as Gurvitch himself stated in "My Intellectual Itinerary," between 1915-1920 he searched for an ideological position that was both anti-individualistic and anti-statist: "Much later I recorded my findings of these researches in the main thesis of my Doctorate in Humanities: *L'Idée du Droit Social...*"[35]

Legal science was fairly backward in Russia because the bourgeoisie developed so slowly.[36] Absolutism had a much stronger hold than in the West and, as mentioned earlier, did not leave room for free cities in which the bourgeoisie could flower.[37] When the serfs were emancipated in 1861 and reforms followed over the next decades, capitalism and legal science finally began to develop. The general situation, however, was such that the reforms of the legal system were soon discontinued. The Russian bourgeoisie was complacent, but there were many unruly peasants, and there was discontent especially among the radical intelligentsia who were not satisfied with the few formal rights that the tzarist regime was willing to grant.[38] Hence, the bourgeoisie in Russia — which had historically allied itself with the working class and the peasants against the king in order to gain ascendancy — was forced into a contradictory position between the two. In the ideological sphere, the relationship of the Russian bourgeoisie to the masses was reflected in the increasing difficulty it had uniting the demands of "freedom" and "equality."

The bourgeoisie's relationship to the feudal class, which refused to share political power with the bourgeoisie until the Revolution, was expressed in the legal sphere in the discussion of the "State" versus "Society."[39] The extreme power of the Russian state undoubtedly also contributed to the popularity of the pluralist element in the liberal doctrine.[40]

The contradictory position of the bourgeoisie, as shown earlier, was clearly expressed in the shifts in the intelligentsia. These shifts occurred in relation to the development of the "juristic *Weltanschauung*" in Russia as well. The early intelligentsia had been fired by the declarations of rights in France and in America. Proudhon and the utopian socialists, who had founded their systems on justice and morality more than on a sober class analysis, were for a long time the most popular authors in radical circles. The Marxists had to wage a very long and hard ideological battle against the various illusions inherent in utopian socialism, including the idea that a "constituent assembly" could solve all problems. In bourgeois circles the concept of natural law was attacked and discarded by the positivists, who began to dominate legal science in the 1870's.[41] During the next decades only a few academic outsiders, Chicherin and Solovyev, expressed open hostility toward positivism, and instead endorsed an idealistic approach to the philosophy of law.[42] Chicherin was plainly an individualist, while Solovyev, in Gurvitch's words, conceptualized law as a *"synthesis of freedom and equality."*[43] In the mid-1890's, however, the tradition of idealism on a neo-Kantian basis revived in Russia. This revival also affected the philosophy of law. Gurvitch placed himself without reservations in the idealist tradition when he wrote an overview of Russian legal science in the early 1920's.[44] A very important element in neo-Kantian idealism which now became popular was the emphasis on natural law, often accompanied by a pluralist methodology. Several philosophers of law, such as W. M. Hessen, Paul Nowgorodzeff and F. W. Taranowsky (one of Gurvitch's teachers in Dorpat), strongly supported the concept of natural law.[45] The contradictory position of the bourgeoisie was clearly expressed in the natural law concept that now emerged, and is evident, for example, in *The Crisis of the Legal Consciousness* (1909), a work by Paul Nowgorodzeff.[46] Nowgorodzeff was the most important figure in the revival of idealism in the Russian philosophy of law, and *Crisis* was one of his major works. In this work he argued that the legal principles of the French Revolution were irreconcilable. Equality and liberty, he wrote, were contradictory demands that could only be realized in the ideal. To think otherwise, as Marx did, was pure utopianism, Nowgorodzeff asserted. According to Nowgorodzeff, man always displayed a "natural egotism."[47]

 The central figure in Russian legal science before the Revolution was Lev Petrazhitsky, another teacher of Gurvitch.[48] Petrazhitsky's work is usually considered to belong to the positivist tradition, but this is a superficial classification.[49] The most interesting aspect of Petrazhitsky's work is his serious attempt to give idealism a firm scientific-positivistic basis. This fusion of science and idealism is exactly what characterizes Gurvitch's notion of social law as well.[50] Petrazhitsky, in his attempt to elaborate on a positivistic theory of law based on the principle of "active love," turned away from the state as a law-giving organ and looked instead to man's legal consciousness. Law, according to Petrazhitsky, emerges spontaneously and can be grasped intuitively. "Justice," he wrote, "is nothing but intuitive law in our sense."[51] In short, Petrazhitsky's ideas reveal the difficulty a bourgeois thinker had, at this historical conjuncture, uniting a serious scientific work with a genuine desire for change. Petrazhitsky's dissatisfaction with the existing social structure pushed him, methodologically, into a realm of the intuitive and the irrational, i.e., into actually negating the importance of positive science and reason.

The Russian philosophy of law expressed the main class strategy of the bourgeoisie. Chicherin, Petrazhitsky and Solovyev were all liberals, as were the majority of the Russian jurists.[52] Gurvitch, however, was much more progressive. In his work he expressed the class strategy of the radical wing of the bourgeoisie. Sergius Hessen, in *The Legal Problem of Socialism,* expressed a similar viewpoint.[53] Gurvitch's radicalism in *L'Idée du Droit Social* is evinced by, for instance, his interest in workers' councils. There had to be workers' control, Gurvitch argued, if social law was to be instituted in the factory. This opinion is undoubtedly a reflection of Gurvitch's active experience in the Russian Revolution for three years.[54] His interest in Proudhon's legal philosophy is another element which separated Gurvitch from the liberal philosophers of law.

Indeed, the most progressive part of Gurvitch's philosophy of law is an outgrowth of his appreciation of Proudhon. The main section of *L'Idée du Droit Social* is devoted to Proudhon who, according to Gurvitch, was the first person to unite socialism with respect for the law.[55] However, Proudhon was essentially a utopian socialist. In a time when the ideology of *laissez-faire* capitalism was expressed in the notion of the Rights of Man, Proudhon mistook cause for effect and built his idea of socialism on the notion of justice.[56] Gurvitch wrote, "The right to credit, the right to assistance, the moralization of property, the right of groups to their autonomy—that was Proudhon's political program."[57] Proudhon's work—as well as Gurvitch's—was clearly a form of juristic socialism.[58]

The Russian intelligentsia's long-lasting sympathy for utopian socialism has been mentioned before and explained by the late development of capitalism in Russia. Capitalism, however, changed drastically after the days of Proudhon, and so did the function of law in bourgeois society.[59] The legal systems in the most advanced capitalist countries at the turn of the century needed to adjust to the emerging monopoly capitalism. Consequently, a decisive change in the legal ideology occurred.[60] Vague appeals were made to "social justice," and the individualistic notion of law began to be replaced in advanced bourgeois legal circles by the notion of "institution."[61] As a corollary, juristic socialism started to flourish in reformistic circles in France, Germany and Italy.[62] Gurvitch, with his idealistic methodology, had no real way of distinguishing between the new bourgeois ideology and the old utopian cry for social justice. This problem is evident in Gurvitch's depiction of the development of social law in *L'Idée du Droit Social.* Up to Proudhon, Gurvitch very much followed the radical bourgeois tradition: Rousseau, Kant, Fichte. But after Proudhon, there was a clear decline in radicalism and Gurvitch turned to Otto von Gierke, the Solidarists and the School of Legal Objectivism. Gurvitch's total rejection of the Marxist tradition in law — only Renner is briefly mentioned — and his preference instead for the Proudhonist tradition had severe consequences: it pushed Gurvitch straight into the arms of bourgeois legal scholars who, though innovative, were intensely hostile to socialism. But, as Engels wrote in *Juristen-Sozialismus,* "that's the way it goes when one reduces a world historical movement to legal slogans."[63]

L'Idée du Droit Social is, however, not exclusively related to Gurvitch's Russian experience. In 1925, Gurvitch emigrated to France — he wanted to get to know Proudhon better — and some years later he became a French citizen.[64] From 1928 on, he was active in the French labor movement (C.G.T.).[65] The class struggle was more advanced in France than in Russia.[66] The bourgeoisie had violently oppressed the proletariat in the latter half of the nineteenth century; however, the bourgeoisie's need to integrate the working class into society was strong. The concept of "Solidarity" more or less became the official slogan of the Third Republic.[67] World War I disclosed the depth to which the notion of "Solidarity," or class collaboration, had sunk into the French labor movement; the class strategy of the bourgeoisie was effectively incorporated into large parts of the working class. Indeed, Gurvitch's *L'Idée du Droit Social* describes the fate of the radical bourgeoisie; it changed from being the ideological leader of the "people" to becoming a part of the reformist wing of the working class movement.

Le Temps Présent et L'Idée du Droit Social (1932), Gurvitch's second and minor thesis at the Sorbonne, was more explicit about the political implications of Gurvitch's philosophy of law than *L'Idée du Droit Social* had been. In this work, Gurvitch tried to prove that the most important issues in legal science could only be solved with the notion of social law. As Gurvitch phrased it, just as all roads had once led to Rome, so all contemporary legal research would inevitably lead to the notion of social law.[68] He also claimed that society itself was moving toward social law, i.e., toward socialism,[69] which was an obvious misjudgment, as evidenced by world events in the 1920's and 1930's.

In *Le Temps Présent et L'Idée du Droit Social,* Gurvitch analyzed three main areas of legal thought—labor law, international law, and sources of law—in order to prove that they were all unconsciously moving in the direction of social law. Gurvitch's argument was essentially quite simplistic. Each group, he claimed, has a "superstructure," i.e., an organization, and an "infrastructure," i.e., an underlying spontaneous community. Every community produces its own law—social law—which is often "perverted" by the individual law imposed by the organization. Thus, the argument that only the state can make laws, Gurvitch repeated, was wrong. This idea that the source of law encompassed more than the state was generally acknowledged in contemporary debate on international law, according to Gurvitch. Many theoreticians of labor law, such as Hugo Sinzheimer, Walter Kaskell, and Maxime Leroy, had come to this conclusion as well. The labor law theoreticians thought that the economic community, rather than the state, produces its own law. Gurvitch considered that a strong tendency in contemporary discussion about the true sources of the law was toward conceptualization of the problem in terms of social law.

Since in Gurvitch's judgment, reality was moving toward social law, one had to open up the organizational superstructures to the progressive underlying communities. This had not been done sufficiently, and as a result there was a "revolt of the facts against the law" (Morin), a demand for a freer interpretation of the law (*Freirecht*). Hence, the superstructure and the infrastructure had to be brought into harmony with each other in each group. In the factories, for instance, the workers' councils that had been introduced after World War I had to become more receptive to the demands of the workers. The workers' councils also needed to be effectively integrated into the economic community via the national economic councils that existed in, for example, Germany and France. The economic community, in its turn, had to become an organic part of the national community, which was increasingly taking its place in the international community, i.e., in the League of Nations. This method, Gurvitch thought, would move society slowly toward socialism.[70]

It is clear that Gurvitch's analysis was far too idealistic to be able to come to terms with the class struggle in the 1920's. The pluralist idea that small groups harmoniously fit into larger ones and that larger groups, in their turn, fit into the national and the international community was unsophisticated and led to serious misjudgments of the political situation. To view the capitalist factory as an isolated unit, as Gurvitch did, was fallacious in the sense that it abstracted from the larger whole. To Gurvitch, the advent of any workers' council meant progress. Gurvitch, for instance, did not understand that the system of workers' councils guaranteed by the Weimar constitution was not socialistic, but rather a clever and strategic compromise by the German capitalists at a time of crisis. Gurvitch, from his formalistic standpoint, considered as progressive even the workers' councils that Rockefeller instituted after World War I in order to outmaneuver the unions.

Gurvitch's analysis of the League of Nations also illustrates the weakness of his methodological approach. To Gurvitch, the League of Nations was an expression of international solidarity. In reality, the League of Nations had not been formed to create "solidarity," despite the proclamations to that effect by Bourgeois and other capitalist statesmen, but mainly to redistribute the colonies of a defeated Germany among the winning capitalist countries — a fact which on the ideological level was expressed as the need to take care of nations that were still unable to govern themselves. Gurvitch, taken in by this ideology, was impressed by the benevolence of the "organ of the international community" toward "insufficiently civilized people."[71] Significantly, Gurvitch never mentioned the Third International in his analysis of the "international community." One of the functions of the League was to reunite the capitalist powers after the war, the consequences of which the Bolsheviks, unlike Gurvitch, were well aware.[72] Throughout the 1920's, according to Harold Laski, the League of Nations could easily have been mobilized to attack the Soviet Union.[73] To proclaim, as Gurvitch did, that the International Labor Organization was the universal representative of labor, was an equally ideological move. I.L.O., as the Russian Communist Party early pointed out, was based on the idea of class collaboration, and was therefore directed against the international working class movement.[74] In short, Gurvitch's analyses in *Le Temps Présent et L'Idée du Droit Social* were ideological and, more important, were incorrect, as history has shown. The co-opted workers' councils failed, and the League of Nations was a fiasco. Gurvitch's optimism, which was organically tied to his scientific methodology, led him to a severe misjudgment of the tendencies of his time.

In the 1920's, it was still possible for those with a reformist view of reality to gloss over the objective development of the class struggle without experiencing too many inconsistencies. Hence, Gurvitch was able to maintain his illusions about a slow and peaceful development toward socialism.[75] The events in the 1930's, however, collapsed this rose-colored view of the future. It was only a question of time before Gurvitch realized that his analysis of social law had totally failed, and that he somehow had to refashion his ideas to bring them closer to reality.

Gurvitch's attempt to adjust his ideas to the restoration of capitalism can be understood in terms of the shift of emphasis in his metaphysics and, consequently, his methodology. The major work that illustrates this is his long essay, "The Juridical Experience," which was published in 1935 in a collection of articles entitled *L'Expérience Juridique et la Philosophie Pluraliste du Droit*.[76] Gurvitch's definition of "justice" in the essay reflects the decline of revolutionary utopianism in the second half of the 1920's. The focus was no longer on revolutionary *Geist* as in the Fichte book; Gurvitch now conceived of justice as positioned somewhere between the "revolutionary" *Geist* and the more "traditional" Logos.[77] Justice lacked the *élan* and creativity of morality, but it substituted security and realism for them. This attempt to adjust to the tendencies of the time made Gurvitch confront reality more squarely but it also pushed him into a historical moralism, as Lukács had predicted. In *L'Idée du Droit Social* Gurvitch characterized all "laws of subordination" as "perverted"—but practically every law fell into that category.

A question not answered by *L'Expérience Juridique et la Philosophie Pluraliste du Droit* is the method Gurvitch intended to use to explain the new developments in the 1930's. On the one hand, Gurvitch openly admitted that the political perspective had "totally changed" from that of the 1920's.[78] Gurvitch acknowledged that the rise of Fascism and the economic crisis of the 1930's rendered a slow and peaceful development toward socialism impossible. On the other hand, there are signs in *L'Expérience Juridique* that Gurvitch was changing his basic methodology. There was, however, only one way that Gurvitch could proceed and that was to force apart the "facts" and "values" that he had tried to unite in the notion of "normative facts." This action was a logical outcome of his methodology. In Gurvitch's scheme, there was a realm of objective values which were partly realized in empirical reality. The content of these values, as has been established, was an expression of the distinct experience of the radical wing of the Russian bourgeoisie which was becoming increasingly irrelevant in the 1930's. To Gurvitch, however, those values represented an objective ideal toward the fulfillment of which society must move. His analysis of social law was fundamentally built on the idea that, under the deceptive surface of oppressive facts, society was silently progressing toward instituting transpersonal values. History, however, proved Gurvitch to be mistaken. With his orientation, Gurvitch had only two alternatives—he could retreat into the metaphysics of Fichteanism and thus retain his moralistic utopianism intact, or he could move toward a more realistic point of view by separating the sphere of transpersonal values from his scientific analysis. Gurvitch chose the latter alternative. Sociology was to prove congenial to this approach.

4 Sociology and the Impasse of the Liberal Bourgeoisie

From the middle of the 1930's, sociology became Gurvitch's main concern, and it was to remain so until his death in 1965.[1] The titles of his works in law indicate the change in his thought. *L'Idée du Droit Social* in 1932 was succeeded by *Eléments de Sociologie Juridique* in 1940.[2] In the former work, the focus was on the necessity to implement "social law" via workers' councils, and in the latter, on the need for a neutral, sociological description of law in society.

Gurvitch chose to work in sociology from then on and to express a strong need for separating value judgments from judgments of reality not because he had given up his socialist ideals and reconciled himself to the present.[3] It was rather the contrary: Gurvitch's values, in the late 1930's, came into an increasingly sharp conflict with reality. When in his intellectual autobiography he looked back at *L'Idée du Droit Social,* Gurvitch stressed, ". . . I should have distinguished here more clearly between value judgments and judgments of reality."[4] In other words, Gurvitch tried to solve the general dilemma he faced in the 1930's with the help of sociology. Sociology promised to let him keep his personal values intact by keeping them apart from his scientific analysis. It also promised a better contact with reality. The catch, of course, was that in the new science Gurvitch now embarked on, his personal values were seen as totally irrelevant to his scientific analysis and therefore had to be eliminated from it. In the long run sociology did not solve Gurvitch's problems; it made them worse. Indeed, Gurvitch's difficulties with the utopian methodology he used in *L'Idée du Droit Social* were minor in comparison with the ones he was now to encounter in relation to sociology's artificial separation between value judgments and judgments of reality. In *L'Idée du Droit Social,* Gurvitch's analysis had been organically tied to the notion of progress — society was moving in the direction of social law and social democracy. Gurvitch had also stressed the necessity to organize the workers into workers' councils. Now he gave up both these ideas. Gurvitch's sociological methodology looked more

rational on the surface than his earlier utopian analysis, but his scientific
methodology actually lost the few progressive traits it originally had.

Gurvitch's sociology, like his theory of law and his philosophy, was quite
eclectic in nature and showed the author's familiarity with works in French,
German, and Russian. In many ways, it is true that Gurvitch's sociology in its
totality is the product of his own thought. But it is also helpful to take a closer
look at sociology in France, Germany and Russia around the turn of the century, because there is a distinct relationship between the sociology that Gurvitch tried to develop in the 1930's and the development of sociology in
general. This relationship can be thought of in terms of "influences" but more
accurately perhaps in terms of parallel class strategies. A thinker, it will be suggested here, is influenced by another thinker if the two somehow articulate the
same class strategy while struggling with similar problems. The point in examining the different origins of Gurvitch's sociology is to show that the basic problem that Gurvitch faced in the 1930's — namely, how to keep value judgments
and judgments of reality apart — was also central to classical sociology and expressed a similar class strategy.

Indeed, one of the basic tenets in sociology as a science is its sharp separation between value judgments and judgments of reality. This distinction was
elaborated especially around the turn of the twentieth century. The meaning it
had then is somewhat different from today for various reasons. In brief, the
social science of the bourgeoisie has gone through three main stages of
development. The first was the utopian stage in which "values" and "facts" fully
coincided. The notion of progress was strong, the mood was optimistic, and
bourgeois values were fairly intact. The works of Saint-Simon, for instance,
belong to this stage, the period of emerging capitalism. The next stage cor-
responds to the beginning of monopoly capitalism at the turn of the century
and is characterized by the ideologically contradictory position of the liberal
bourgeoisie. On the one hand, belief in the basic bourgeois values was still
strong enough at this time to inspire some hope. On the other hand, the
bourgeoisie needed to orient itself practically to the new reality of monopoly
capitalism that was emerging. Hence, there was a clash between "values" and
"facts". The mood was ultimately pessimistic; hope had to become irrational
in order to survive and the notion of progress was absent. In the third stage,
the age of fully developed monopoly capitalism, the original bourgeois values
have lost their grip. The articulation of reality is no longer considered as conflicting with deep-seated personal values. Value judgments and judgments of
reality are kept apart in a spirit of indifference. At this stage, sociology
unreservedly expresses the class strategy of advanced capitalism.

These outlined stages, however, are only general tendencies. Sociology
has evolved in different ways in different countries due to the uneven development of capitalism. In Germany, for instance, the absence of a revolutionary

bourgeois tradition greatly influenced the sociology that developed there. Russian and French sociology have their own distinct traits, too.

The direct influence of Russian sociology on Gurvitch is minor. In his sociological works from the 1930's, Gurvitch never refers to Russian sociology, while references to German and French sociology abound. Gurvitch, of course, acknowledged the general influence of his Russian background on all his work. [5] In his intellectual autobiography he also mentions the experience of the Russian Revolution as a very important factor in the sociology he tried to develop in the 1930's.[6] During the turbulent years of 1917-1920, he writes, two ideas dawned upon him which he explored after he completed his works in the philosophy of law: the idea that social reality can be conceptualized as having different strata which interpenetrate and clash, and the idea that society is a macrocosm of groups, just as the group is a microcosm of forms of sociality.[7]

In a deeper sense, however, Gurvitch's sociology is very much the outgrowth of Russian sociology. His early rejection of Marxism, his enthusiastic espousal of Proudhon, and his study of sociologically oriented jurists — especially Petrazhitsky — all clearly indicate his contacts with the three major strands of Russian sociology: subjectivistic-utopian sociology, Marxist sociology, and liberal-positivistic sociology.[8] The salient links are Gurvitch's adoption of Proudhon's utopian methodology and his rejection of historical materialism. These developments in his ideas facilitated his switch from the idealistic methodology of *L'Idée du Droit Social* to the positivistic methodology in *Essais de Sociologie* and *Eléments de Sociologie Juridique.*

The conflict between utopianism and positivism played an important role in the Russian class struggle in the nineteenth century. The Subjectivistic School, of which Mikhailovsky was the acknowledged leader, corresponded to the utopian phase in Central Europe. The Subjectivistic School was the work of the radical intelligentsia, more precisely of the populists.[9] In it value judgments and judgments of reality were firmly united.[10] Mikhailovsky, for instance, opposed the increasing division of labor on the grounds that it fragmented man, and he claimed that true progress was "the fullest possible and most diversified division of labor among man's organs and the least possible division of labor among men...."[11] However, the strong connection between ethics and positivism that characterized the Subjectivistic School increasingly led it into methodological and practical difficulties. Timasheff, himself a sociologist of Russian origin, later noted:

> Perhaps the main reason for the collapse of [the Subjectivistic] school was that it made sociology dependent upon a social ideal and emphasized value judgments as an intrinsic part of sociology. Subjectivism could not prevail against the forceful demonstration

of Durkheim and Weber that value judgments must not intrude in the development of theoretical sociology.[12]

Why value judgments should not "intrude," however, Timasheff does not say and for this information one must turn to Lenin's *What the "Friends of the People" Are* (1894).[13] In this pamphlet, which is still the most solid critique of bourgeois sociology that exists, Lenin points out that the utopian methodology which had served the populists well at an early stage of the Russian class struggle was becoming increasingly insufficient in the 1890's. The development of the class struggle in Russia was such, Lenin argued, that unless the "friends of the people" shifted over to the politics of the Social Democrats and to the methodology of historical materialism they would be driven into the arms of the bourgeois. In order to understand the objective development of society, Lenin said, one had to use a *"scientific* sociology" (that is, Marxism) as opposed to the metaphysical sociology of the populists.[14] To focus on people's thoughts and intentions, as Mikhailovsky did, was methodologically incorrect since this procedure could not lead to a distinction between what is "important" and what is "unimportant" in society.[15] One needed an objective criterion, and this could only be found in the relations of production, i.e., in the social formation. There were, according to Lenin, natural-historical laws that governed the development of capitalism, and Mikhailovsky's emphasis on people's capacity to create a "just" society was as unscientific as it was idealistic.

After the turn of the century both Marxism and Utopianism lost their appeal to large segments of the intelligentsia and a new type of sociology appeared.[16] This sociology was not developed in the circles of the bohemian intellectuals, but by liberal professors in the universities, often from the law faculties.[17] The main concern of these university sociologists was to separate ethics from sociology and to make concrete, non-philosophical analyses of specific topics. The most extreme example of this tendency was the behavioristic or "objectivistic" sociology that some followers of Pavlov developed. According to this school, it was possible to exclude all subjective judgments from sociology and make it totally objective.

Many sociologists were attracted to the new positivistic sociology that was propagated quite openly in the universities, and they adopted its fundamental tenets. It was especially easy for the populists to do this, since their own analysis of society had proven increasingly insufficient. Sorokin, for instance, who had been an active Socialist-Revolutionary until 1918, became one of Pavlov's sociological followers.[18] But adopting a crudely positivisitic approach could not help Sorokin to reconcile general humanism with a stringent scientific approach.[19] To a certain extent, the difficulties that Sorokin was to encounter later were the same as Gurvitch's: how could one replace the original unity of value judgments and judgments of reality which had existed in the thought of the early Russian intelligentsia with a new and similar synthesis of new elements?

Though the tendencies of Russian sociology made their mark on Gurvitch, German sociology had a much more direct impact on his thinking. In Gurvitch's sociological works from the 1930's one can find traces of the influence of Weber and Scheler especially and also, to some extent, of von Wiese. From Weber, Gurvitch took the notion of *Verstehen* and the "ideal type."[20] Moreover, he was very interested in Weber's attempt to make sociology value-free.[21] In Scheler, Gurvitch found a solution to the problematic relationship between sociology and philosophy.[22] Scheler's attempt to construct a sociology of knowledge and a sociology of morality was also an inspiration to Gurvitch.[23] Finally, in von Wiese's *Allgemeine Soziologie* Gurvitch found a system of social relations that in some aspects appealed to him.[24]

All of these elements from German sociology, which Gurvitch with varying degrees of success integrated into his own sociological system, had one thing in common—they were the outgrowth of the crisis of the liberal bourgeoisie in Germany between 1890 and 1930.[25] The history of Germany during these years allowed the disjunction between value judgments and judgments of reality to be clearly expressed among its social scientists.

The crisis of the liberal bourgeoisie was most dramatically articulated in Max Weber. Politically, Weber was a liberal.[26] As such, he was extremely concerned with the transformation from *laissez-faire* capitalism to monopoly capitalism.[27] He was convinced that nothing could stop this development; however, he was ready to resort to imperialist wars, charismatic leaders (*Führersdemokratie*) and similar measures to keep capitalism dynamic, to prevent it from turning into a closed system. His strong aversion to socialism was based on the belief that socialism would destroy the little room left for human dignity in society by placing all the power in the hands of the state.[28] He was, to quote Mommsen, "a liberal in despair."[29]

Weber's sociology was a forceful attempt to deal with the impasse facing the liberal bourgeoisie. It is from this point of view that his intense struggle for a value-free sociology must be seen. Weber realized well that reality was moving out of harmony with his liberal beliefs, and his honesty impelled him to report this. Being a strongly moral man, however, he felt urged to fight against this development. The only way he could fight was to draw a sharp line between political behavior and scientific work.

His line, however, was illusory. "This seemingly scientific character, this rigorous 'valuefreedom' in sociology," Lukács has noted, "represents...in reality the highest stage of irrationalism. . . ."[30] Indeed, Weber gave the irrational tendencies of the bourgeoisie and its social science a new and superior expression. The subjectivistic tendency in sociology and its methodological separation from political economy were accentuated and refined in his notion of *Verstehen*.[31] Moreover, the notion of "ideal type" was extremely irrational in nature.[32] With the help of these types one could mix together phenomena with virtually nothing in common, such as socialism and old Egyptian bureaucracy or a Shaman and Kurt Eisner.[33] Society was reduced to a series of "ideal types" without any inherent connection to each other. In effect, Weber helped sociology make the transition from *laissez-faire* capitalism to monopoly capitalism by violating his most personal beliefs. However, he never succeeded in going beyond the reality of bourgeois society itself. In the end Weber only captured what Colletti has called the "false objectivity" of capitalist society, that is, the objective ideas and notions which grow out of monopoly capitalism and which are necessary to reproduce it.[34]

Neither in Scheler's nor in von Wiese's work can one find the same intense struggle as Weber waged to keep value judgments and judgments of reality separate. For both thinkers the question was easily settled. Scheler freely acknowledged that sociology had several biases which were impossible to transcend.[35] But he considered this problem to be of little consequence because the eternal values could be directly apprehended through intuition in philosophy. Scheler shifted the problem of value judgments to philosophy, in which it was dissolved into the irrationality of "pure essences." Sociology was secondary to philosophy in Scheler's thinking. The general task of the sociology of knowledge and the sociology of morality was to provide empirical material for philosophy, since each epoch, culture, or nation could only see one side of the infinitely rich ideal.

To von Wiese, sociology was as objective as the natural sciences.[36] "Sociology," he said, " . . . must deal with interhuman relations without immediate references to ends, norms or purposes; it involves a wholly different kind of abstraction."[37] Von Wiese was influenced by Simmel and carried the distinction between form and content to its extreme. As Gurvitch was to do later, von Wiese developed an enormously complicated and formalistic scheme showing how people interact. From a sociological point of view, von Wiese's *Beziehungslehre,* like Gurvitch's system of sociality, was a failure. From a historical point of view, his system demonstrated the liberal bourgeoisie's increasing willingness to reproduce a reality to which it was becoming reconciled. The step from Weber to von Wiese expresses the movement of the liberal bourgeoisie from a position of struggle against monopoly capitalism in the name of individualistic values and ideals to a position of full reconciliation with it in the name of science.

Despite the considerable influence of German sociology on Gurvitch, French sociology had the strongest impact on his sociological thought. When Gurvitch had read Durkheim in the 1910's, he felt fairly indifferent.[38] Now, however, Gurvitch was ready for sociology and he lived in France. The

Durkheimians, like Gurvitch, were socialists with reformist tendencies.[39] Celéstin Bouglé, for instance, was a Proudhonist like Gurvitch.[40] Lucien Lévy-Bruhl, Marcel Mauss, and Maurice Halbwachs were socialists in the tradition of Jaurés, and they all advocated a moralistic-humanistic socialism which was closer to Utopian Socialism than to Marxism.[41] Gurvitch became friendly with all these thinkers and was greatly influenced by their ideas.[42]

Gurvitch's work in the 1930's was affected very directly by Durkheimian sociology. From Durkheim himself, for instance, Gurvitch took the idea of *conscience collective* and from Mauss, he got the notion of "total social phenomenon."[43] However, Gurvitch was also influenced by Durkheimian sociology in a more general way.[44] He often explored problems that the Durkheimians had raised, although he came to different conclusions about them. For instance, Gurvitch's ideas on the role of religion in the development of society and on the relationship between moral philosophy and the sociology of morality differed from those offered by the Durkheimians.[45]

The question of value judgments versus judgments of reality was worked out somewhat differently in French and in German sociology. The liberal bourgeoisie in France came from a more progressive tradition and consequently found it very difficult to accept its new and subordinate role in monopoly capitalism.[46] Nonetheless, on the whole, the problems of the French liberal bourgeoisie at the turn of the twentieth century were similar to those of the liberal bourgeoisie in other capitalist countries. In France, there was the same need to replace the ideology of individualism and the same need to fend off the threat from the working class. What was distinctly different about the French liberal bourgeoisie was its belief that it could play a key role in the transition to advanced capitalism and even renew itself in the process. This was partly an illusion, but it had some reality in the unstable political situation of the Third Republic.[47] In order to defend itself against the attacks from the right wing, the republican bourgeoisie needed the support of the working class. However, the working class, which had been severely repressed in 1871, was suspicious of the bourgeoisie and preferred to keep out of politics. In the *Charte d'Amiens* (1906), for instance, C.G.T. maintained its independence of any political party. Nevertheless, the liberal bourgeoisie continued to seek the support of the working class. The doctrine of Solidarity that swept bourgeois circles in the last decades before World War I was an ideological expression of this need.[48]

Solidarity was a doctrine seeking both to reconcile and replace "individualism" and "collectivism."[49] It proclaimed class struggles as destructive and considered that decent social legislation could remedy the ills of private property.[50] If the French people only united in the spirit of Solidarity, most social problems would be solved. The amorphousness of the doctrine no doubt contributed to its success, as Bouglé has pointed out.[51]

The ideology of Solidarity was quite popular with the scientists in the Third Republic. Some biologists and zoologists, for instance, proclaimed Solidarity to be not only an ideal but also a scientific fact.[52] Several sociologists also rallied to the cause. The classic example is Durkheim's *Division of Labor in Society* (1893), in which he posits that society moves from "mechanical solidarity" to "organic solidarity."[53] Moreover, Durkheim originally intended to call his thesis "The Relationship of Individualism and Socialism;" he saw his work as an attempt to find some common ground between the working class and those who were against *laissez-faire* capitalism.[54] Alfred Fouillée, one of the most important ideologists of the Solidarity movement, expressed the same concern in *Le Socialisme et la Sociologie Réformiste* (1909), in which he advocated "a synthesis of individualism and socialism."[55]

In all of Durkheim's work one can trace his attempt to balance carefully the interests of "the collective" against those of "the individual." Too much power to the collective was just as destructive to Durkheim as too little ("altruistic suicide" versus "egoistic suicide").[56] If the individual was not very developed, solidarity would be "mechanical" and the laws "repressive;" if the individual and the divisions of labor progressed, solidarity would become "organic" and the laws "restitutive." A society in which the state was the supreme ruler would constitute a "sociological monstrosity," while no authority at all would lead to "anomie."[57] The human group, for Durkheim, constituted a delicate balance between the interests of the individual and of the collective.

Durkheim's sociology answered very well to the needs of the liberal bourgeoisie in its "belle époque," since the limitations and illusions of both were quite similar.[58] As a result, Durkheim's sociology never became as sharp nor as realistic as Weber's. Compare, for instance, Weber's demand for value neutrality with Durkheim's article on "Value Judgments and Judgments of Reality" (1911), in which he says: "Sociology moves from the beginning in the field of ideals — that is its starting point and not the gradually attained end of its researches."[59]

The basic tendencies in Weber's and Durkheim's sociology, however, were very much the same. Like Weber, Durkheim separated political economy from sociology.[60] He also constructed sociology on an idealistic and subjectivistic basis with his notion of *conscience collective*.[61] The idea of progress in Durkheim's work was ultimately incompatible with his moralistic analysis of "anomie." The only hope for mankind was in a new stage of "collective effervescence," which, in its irrationality, resembled Weber's notion of "charisma."[62]

Both the strength and the weaknesses of Durkheim's sociology emerged very clearly in the works of his disciples. Durkheim's emphasis on a strict positivistic approach, which was most clearly articulated in *The Rules of*

Sociological Method (1895), pushed sociology toward concrete empirical studies.[63] However, Durkheim's idealism made it difficult for his disciples to deal with contemporary society, especially post-war France which had nothing in common with the France Durkheim envisioned. Bouglé, for instance, saw society as "a great flame that stretches toward the sky," which hardly describes the capitalist France of his day.[64] Fauconnet and Davy saw society in an equally idealistic way.[65] Mauss, with his notion of the "total social phenomenon," was very concerned with demonstrating that every aspect of society involves the whole soul and being of that society (as illustrated in Mauss' famous *The Gift*).[66] This idealistic streak in the Durkheimians can explain their strong focus on primitive societies which are strong and cohesive.[67] The distorting influence of Durkheim's idealism, however, is as clear in the works of Halbwachs and Simiand, the only Durkheimians who studied contemporary France. Halbwachs, for instance, tried to capture the "ideals" of the various classes and this strained his otherwise clever analysis.[68] Simiand made vain attempts to analyze prices as expressions of collective opinion.[69]

Despite the expressed idealism of the Durkheimians, they still maintained a sharp distinction between value judgments and judgments of reality. This is particularly apparent in the works of Lucien Lévy-Bruhl, who scorned moral theory as totally "unscientific" in *La Morale et la Science des Moeurs* (1902).[70] Moreover, on political questions, the Durkheimians separated themselves into "scientists" and "politicians." On the whole, however, they were uncomfortable with this distinction, and their methodology was often closer to the utopian thinkers, such as Saint-Simon and Proudhon, than to the one-sided empirical methodology that would become the norm a few decades later. The Durkheimians' great concern was justice and morality, not scientific methodology *per se* or professionalism. The impasse of the liberal bourgeoisie, however, eventually spelled the end of Durkheimian sociology.

The general problem that Gurvitch was struggling with in the 1930's had already been worked through by these other thinkers in France and Germany. This is attributable to the fact that capitalism and the class struggle were more advanced in France and Germany than in Russia. Gurvitch thus picked up problems which, for instance, Durkheim and Weber had confronted earlier, and this is one of the reasons why Gurvitch's sociology did not become epoch-making — his solutions to the problems that faced the liberal bourgeoisie were neither novel nor original.

A question which should be settled in this context is the extent to which Gurvitch's sociology was already present in his earlier works, especially in *L'Idée du Droit Social*.[71] Interestingly enough, the answer to this question is another reason why Gurvitch's sociology was not definitive, why it failed. In short, when Gurvitch decided in the 1930's to become solely a sociologist ("I was becoming more and more a sociologist and only a sociologist..."), his basic method of analysis was already set.[72] Hence, the actual extent to which one can find sociological passages in Gurvitch's earlier works is not decisive; the important consideration is the general structure of his thought.[73] Gurvitch's sociology, it must be stressed, was a giant effort to move his whole earlier analysis in a new direction. The changes Gurvitch made, however, never really altered the basic structure of his thought; it was merely on the surface that he became "only a sociologist."[74] Though this fact is what ultimately made Gurvitch's sociology incapable of dealing with the new reality of the 1930's, the strong structural affinity between Gurvitch's early legal-philosophical work and his sociology accounts for the non-conformistic nature of his work.[75]

The tendency to reshape only the "tip of the iceberg" of his analysis is clear in all of Gurvitch's sociological works from the late 1930's: *Morale Théorique et Science des Moeurs* (1937), *Essais de Sociologie* (1938) and *Eléments de Sociologie Juridique* (1940). The result is somewhat complicated. On the one hand, Gurvitch tried to construct a sociology which was different from his earlier value-oriented analysis, one that was closer to reality. On the other hand, he failed to make sufficiently radical changes in the basic structure of his thought.

Gurvitch's sociology in this period easily falls into three categories: a confrontation with Durkheimian sociology, an attempt to construct a general sociology, and an application of this general sociology to law. Gurvitch's wrestling with Durkheimian sociology is mainly found in *Morale Théorique et Science des Moeurs* and in three of the articles in *Essais de Sociologie:* "Le Problème de la Conscience Collective dans la Sociologie de Durkheim," "La Science des Faits Moraux et la Morale Théorique chez E. Durkheim," and "La Magie et le Droit."[76] Gurvitch's attempt to construct a general sociology begins in the fourth article in *Essais de Sociologie,* "Les Formes de la Sociabilité," and is continued in *Eléments de Sociologie Juridique.*[77] In the latter work, Gurvitch also applied his general sociology to law.

There were two elements in Durkheim's sociology that especially attracted Gurvitch: the notion of *conscience collective* and his sociology of morality.[78] The *conscience collective,* Gurvitch argued, constituted the most fundamental aspect of Durkheim's sociology and was the key to all his work.[79] Gurvitch accepted the notion of *conscience collective* as the basis of his own sociology, too, but with important modifications. Durkheim had erred, Gurvitch claimed, by making the *conscience collective* transcendent, by identifying it with the Spirit, and by conceiving of only one instead of several *consciences collectives.*

Durkheim's difficulties with the notion of *conscience collective,* according to Gurvitch, were basically due to his incapacity to consider the individual consciousness as "open." For Durkheim individual consciousness was always "closed;" consequently, it was impossible for Durkheim to deal with the idea of collective consciousness except as a "thing" outside of people's minds. Modifying Durkheim and following Husserl, Gurvitch defined individual consciousness as a tension within a psychic totality. The collective consciousness, according to Gurvitch, could then be seen as another tension in this psychic field. Indeed, there was a "reciprocity of perspectives" between the individual and the group in which both penetrated each other. The individual's consciousness and the collective consciousness were just different sides of the same coin to Gurvitch.

Gurvitch also attacked the idea that there was only one *conscience collective* in Durkheim's society. Each group, he argued, has its own collective consciousness. The idea of "reciprocity of perspectives" also supported this argument in Gurvitch's mind.

Gurvitch, in taking up the question of *conscience collective,* accepted as the basis for his sociology the more idealistic and subjective aspect of Durkheim's sociology. This did not exclude an empirically oriented sociology *per se.* However, a closer look at Gurvitch's sociology reveals that it was firmly connected with his earlier legal-philosophical ideology. Though Gurvitch's criticism of the notion of the closed consciousness was no doubt justified, his solution – the reciprocity of perspectives – was a pseudo-solution. It did not originate in concrete research but in Gurvitch's old attempt to synthesize the interests of the group and the individual.[80]

Gurvitch's critique of the "monism" in Durkheim expressed the same dilemma. Durkheim's idea that society had to be united and permeated with solidarity – which was, of course, the reason for his "monism" – Gurvitch criticized from the point of view of his own equally ideological notion of "pluralism." Instead of trying, like Durkheim, to determine which groups were the most important in society, Gurvitch just made general references to the richness of groups and conflicts in society. His main concern, in works like "Magie et Droit," was an old one – the notion of the all-powerful state, be it in contemporary or primitive society.

The second element in Durkheim's work that attracted Gurvitch's interest was his attempt to develop a sociology of morality or a *science des moeurs* as it was then called.[81] On the whole, Gurvitch was very critical of Durkheim on this point. Durkheim, he claimed, had tried to deduce morality from science. Gurvitch considered this to be impossible because he thought value judgments could not be deduced from judgments of reality. Lévy-Bruhl, Gurvitch said, had made this perfectly clear in his admirable look *La Morale et la Science des Moeurs* (1902). In it, Lévy-Bruhl had convincingly argued that the sociology of morality could only become a real science when it was as totally cleansed from all value judgments as the natural sciences were.

On one point, however, Gurvitch disagreed with Lévy-Bruhl and supported Durkheim's position. This was on the question of whether moral theory is possible. Lévy-Bruhl, with his crude positivism, had declared all moral theories to be a hindrance to the emergence of the true *science des moeurs*. Durkheim, on the other hand, had said in some of his last works that the sociology of morality needed the support of moral theory, and Gurvitch fully concurred.

Nevertheless, Durkheim's attempt to "reconcile science and morality" (*Division of Labor in Society*) was rejected by Gurvitch on the grounds that it would lead to an impoverishment of morality.[82] Morality, if already in society, as Durkheim claimed, would have to be conformist. Integration into existing society would be considered "good," and the lack of integration would be considered "evil." This, Gurvitch argued, was contrary to the whole nature of moral experience.

> The moral experience is thus nothing but a perpetual rebellion of the spirit: a rebellion against the present in the name of the future, a rebellion against what already exists in the name of that which shall exist, a rebellion against goals in the name of ends, a rebellion against the laws of causality in the name of imperatives, a rebellion against the ends and the imperatives in the name of values, and a rebellion against the values in the name of creative freedom. The moral experience is revolutionary *par excellence*; it is a spiritual revolution, always going deeper and becoming more and more moral as it is revolutionized.[83]

Why Gurvitch separated value judgments from judgments of reality is clear — the separation enabled him to maintain his Fichtean utopianism intact.

In two direct ways, however, Gurvitch did not succeed in making his sociology value-free. First, it is impossible to have a value-free sociology — that is a technocratic dream. Consequently, Gurvitch's utopian-pluralistic vision is present, in modified form, in his sociology. That this is the case becomes very clear when one takes a closer look at Gurvitch's general sociology. Second, Gurvitch's analysis of the relationship between philosophy and sociology was also not value-free. Moral philosophy, Gurvitch argued, had several tasks to fulfill, such as verifying moral experience, distinguishing it from other kinds of experience, and establishing its main variations. However, Gurvitch constructed moral experience — as can be seen in the quotation cited above from *Morale Théorique et la Science des Moeurs* — in full harmony with his earlier political beliefs. The way Gurvitch worked out the relationship between sociology and philosophy thus prevented him from getting closer to a sociology that could capture either the objective dialectics of capitalist society or its "false objectivity" (Colletti).[84]

The ambition to create a totally scientific and hence value-free sociology came to its clearest expression in Gurvitch's general sociology.[85] According to Gurvitch, social reality could be conceptualized as having two dimensions, one horizontal and one vertical. The vertical dimension was developed in Gurvitch's analysis of the "depth levels" of society.[86] In order to reach the essence of social reality, Gurvitch argued, one had to use Husserl's method of inversion and reduction. Dialectic, like other empty intellectual constructions, would be of no use. If one proceeded according to the general principles of the phenomenological method, one would first reach the most easily perceptible reality: the demographic and geographical level of society (level I). A further effort would take the sociologist to the level of symbols (level II). Below these symbols, there was a layer of organizations (level III). Gurvitch considered organizations to be always hierarchical, centralized and predetermined. Organizations, combined with the next level — that of unorganized collective behavior — constituted social institutions. However, organizations were separated by an "abyss" from the spontaneous aspects of reality which first began to appear at the level of unorganized collective behavior (level IV). The next level constituted the deepest level of collective behavior. Unpredictability and collective effervescence characterized this stratum (level V). Beneath the three levels of collective behavior could be found the values and ideals that inspired them (level VI). Here, the spiritual world intervened for the first time. Finally, the deepest layer consisted of the collective mind (*conscience collective*). Only the collective mind could seize and experience the values and ideals which were incarnated in social reality (level VII). Between the collective mind and the spiritual realm of ideals and values there was an inseparable abyss.

Compared to *L'Idée du Droit Social,* Gurvitch's "depth sociology" was undoubtedly more realistic. It represents a serious attempt to deal with different types of collective behavior. Moreover, by drawing a firm line between the collective mind and the spiritual realm of ideals and values, Gurvitch opened up his analysis to a more realistic approach.[87] On the whole, however, Gurvitch's old concerns still held a tremendous grip on his mind. As in his earlier thought, there was a clear conflict in Gurvitch's depth sociology between voluntarism and determinism. The most solid and materialistic aspect of social reality — the demographic and geographical surface (level I) — was also the most superficial. The deeper one probed into social reality, the closer one got to its essence — namely, to collective effervescence, values and ideals. This design brought accusations that he favored the deeper levels of social reality and that his depth sociology was not objective. Gurvitch protested vigorously against this, but the charge has much validity.[88] Gurvitch's lack of awareness prevented him from getting closer to a social reality that had little in common — especially in the 1930's — with his problem of determinism versus voluntarism. In addition, by removing only the most superficial aspects of his political beliefs from his analysis, Gurvitch broke the last remaining link in his thinking between rationalism and irrationalism. From now on, Gurvitch—like Weber and Durkheim—could only appeal to effervescence in general.

The other component in Gurvitch's scientific description of social reality, the horizontal dimension, he divided into forms of sociality, groups, and societies. These divisions were types, as opposed to the individual phenomena dealt with in history or the very general phenomena studied in the natural sciences. Forms of sociality, Gurvitch claimed, constituted the object of "microsociology." In the 1930's, Gurvitch devoted most of his energy to analyzing the various forms of sociality or, as he defined them, ways of being bound to a whole and by a whole. These forms, Gurvitch thought, were the most elementary aspects of social life. Hence, the first question which sociology must address was the meaning of sociality.

According to Gurvitch, microsociology or "social microphysics" could handle the most indeterminate elements of social life. Earlier sociologists had only cataloged a few of these forms, such as mechanical solidarity-organic solidarity, or *Gemeinschaft-Gesellschaft.* But there was an infinite richness of forms of sociality. In addition, Gurvitch considered that Durkheim and Tönnies had made the fundamental mistake of identifying forms of sociality with historical epochs. Durkheim's analysis in *Division of Labor,* for instance, was no longer a reality. Gurvitch wrote:

> The development of big industry and the growth of unemployment in certain epochs and especially in ours—not to mention the recent affirmation of political dictatorships—shows very strongly how rash it would be today to speak like Durkheim about the progressive march of "organic solidarity" . . . .[89]

Scheler, who had realized the impossibility of identifying forms of sociality with historical epochs, had, however, committed the equally serious mistake of identifying certain forms of sociality with certain values. This was impossible, Gurvitch argued, since sociology could not issue any value judgments. Finally, Gurvitch claimed that forms of sociality should not be confused with groups. A group constituted a mobile equilibrium of many different forms of sociality. Which of these predominated at a certain time depended on concrete circumstances.

Gurvitch constructed a very complicated scheme of sociality using eight different criteria which could be partially crisscrossed (see illustration on page 66). Sociality could first of all be active or passive—(I). If it was active it could be uni-, multi-, or super-functional depending on whether it had one, several, or an infinite number of tasks to fulfill—(II). If the sociality was active and multi-functional, it could serve either a general or a particular interest—(III). Active sociality, as opposed to passive sociality, could also be organized as well as spontaneous — (IV). Organized sociality could be open or closed to the underlying structure in various ways — (V). The forms of sociality could originate from either a partial fusion into a "we" or from a simple interdependence — (VI). Depending on the intensity of the fusion, the "we" consititued a mass, a community, or a communion — (VII). Sociality by simple interdependence, in its turn, could also be differentiated according to the degree of approachability, separation, or a combination of both — (VIII).

The analysis of the "we" and of the "relations with the other" was inspired by von Wiese and constituted Gurvitch's most original contribution to his scheme of sociality. Most important was Gurvitch's distinction between the different forms of "we". The intensity of the fusion into a "we" was weak in the mass, strong in the community, and strongest in the communion. The pressure of the group, however, was felt to be the strongest in the mass. In a communion, the individual felt no group pressure; in a community, the pressure was of medium strength. Gurvitch insisted that one could not attach any value judgments *per se* to these three forms of sociality. Not surprisingly, however, he added that community was the most favorable for the development of *"decentralized, federalist and pluralistic democracies."*[90] It is clear that Gurvitch in his analysis of the different forms of sociality was trying to draw closer to social reality. As in his depth sociology, however, this process was prevented from realization by the residues of his earlier thinking. Gurvitch's voluntarism made him stress the infinite richness of forms of sociality, which resulted in an extremely formalistic and abstract scheme. Indeed, Gurvitch's classification was only a slight modification of the analysis in *L'Idée du Droit Social.* This similarity is probably the most fundamental reason why Gurvitch's classification failed to take root among contemporary bourgeois sociologists. Originally, the "we" versus the "I", active versus passive sociality, and so on had been organically integrated into a heavily value-oriented analysis. Now, instead, Gurvitch was trying to switch to an approach which demanded from him a very different type of analysis. Gurvitch's answer was to refurbish his old categories by making them supposedly value-neutral. The "we," which had been the embodiment of hope in *L'Idée du Droit Social,* was now elevated into scientific neutrality as "mass," "community," and "communion" with different degrees of "pressure" and "intensity." The "I", which had been the basis for the despised individual law, now became a neutral scientific category denoting relations with others and nothing else.

Gurvitch's attempt to construct a "macrosociology" was more successful. Groups and global societies are by nature less abstract than forms of sociality; thereby Gurvitch was forced into a more direct confrontation with reality. His classification of groups, however, was very much influenced by his earlier legal-philosophical analysis and was consequently not that useful. Gurvitch distinguished between groups with and without unconditional constraint, be-

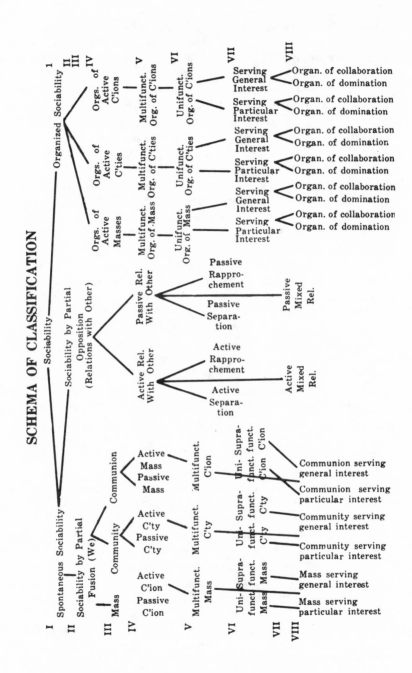

Illustration. From Phillip Bosserman, *Dialectical Sociology,* p. 150. The scheme is, with some minor terminological exceptions, the same as in *Essais de Sociologie,* pp. 30-31.

tween groups that had a unitary, federalist, or a confederalist structure, and so on.

The construction of a typology of global societies was a new task for Gurvitch, and therefore the imprint of his earlier analysis was not as strong here. On the other hand, the limits of bourgeois sociology immediately manifested themselves in his typology. Primarily following Weber, Gurvitch developed a typology of seven global societies. Because each society constituted an ideal type, there was no attempt to make an organic connection between them. What Gurvitch called "feudal society" was, for instance, not organically linked with "contemporary society". This failure to link societies was not inherent in the notion of the ideal type *per se* — Weber's own work testifies somewhat to the contrary — nevertheless, Gurvitch's design expressed the same tendency as Weber's, namely, the rejection of historical determinism and causality in a time when the liberal bourgeoisie had no future.[91]

The same tendency is evident in Gurvitch's conception of global society as a "total social phenomenon" (Mauss). Looking at the whole of society meant, to Gurvitch, rejecting the theory that one aspect could predominate and accepting the relativisitic position that religion, economy, etc., could all play a central role in the development of society. Like Weber and Durkheim, Gurvitch, in the last hand, favored ideal factors over material ones.

In *Eléments de Sociologie Juridique* Gurvitch applied his general sociology to law; consequently, this work has the same drawbacks as his general sociology. Gurvitch's formalism, which was connected to his pluralism, reached new heights in this work. In each group, for instance, one could detect at least 162 different types of law. Gurvitch argued that to each form of active sociality and to each depth level a different "kind" of law answered. The 162 kinds were just a preliminary result. Gurvitch also tried to relate law to his classification of groups. To each group there was a corresponding "framework" of law. Since the number of groups was less than that of forms of sociality, there were fewer frameworks. Finally, in his classification, there were seven so-called "systems of law," each corresponding to a different type of global society. Here again, the basic contradiction in Gurvitch's sociology is very clear — the further he distanced himself from social reality, the more room he created for his vision of a pluralist society and *vice versa*.

Eléments de Sociologie Juridique shows the road Gurvitch had travelled since *L'Idée du Droit Social*. The emphasis in his analysis of law in the early 1930's had been on a synthesis of law and socialism; now it was on an "objective" description of law in society. Earlier, in the tradition of progressive bourgeois social science, Gurvitch had tried to unite value judgments and judgments of reality. Now they were firmly separated.

Eléments de Sociologie Juridique, like *Essais de Sociologie* and *Morale Théorique et Science des Moeurs*, represents the trivial nature of Gurvitch's sociology in the 1930's. None of these works struggled with the concrete problems of the time. Trotsky asked *Whither France?,* but to Gurvitch this was not a question of urgent scientific concern.[92] On the whole, French sociology — like bourgeois sociology in other countries — was totally thrown by the depression and the rise of fascism.

In France, Durkheimian sociology had reached its demise. Since it had long ago separated politics from science, it saw no reason to concentrate scientific effort on the immediate problems of the time.[93] *Annales Sociologiques* (1934-1942), the journal of the Durkheimians, does not contain one serious analysis of either the class structure in France, the rise of fascism, or the great depression.[94] In contrast, the scholarly Marxist journals of the time, such as, *Die Gesellschaft* (1924-1933) or *Zeitschrift für Sozialforschung* (1932-1941), were entirely devoted to these and similar issues.

The sociology of the French liberal bourgeoisie indeed reached its final impasse in the thirties; it lost contact with concrete, living reality. In total disgust at the irrelevance he found in the works of Durkheim, Fauconnet, Brunschvicg, and the whole liberal intelligentsia, a young author wrote:

> These soap bubbles, which aged thinkers blow, burst on contact with the wind that sweeps through the factory yards and the desolate boulevards of the working-class suburbs.[95]

The author was Paul Nizan and the book, *The Watchdogs* (1932). Nizan spoke from the perspective of historical materialism, which after World War II would increasingly challenge both the liberal sociology of the Durkheimians and the technocratic sociology of monopoly capitalism. In the meantime, however, the war was coming, and Gurvitch, who was known for his pro-labor sympathies, in addition to being a Russian Jew, had to flee to the United States to avoid persecution. There he encountered the technocratic sociology of monopoly capitalism in full bloom.

5 North American Sociology and the Triumph of Bourgeois Hegemony

Gurvitch arrived in New York in October 1940. He was one of the many scholars that Alvin Johnson of the New School for Social Research succeeded in saving from German fascism at the last minute.[1] Gurvitch stayed in the United States for five years, returning to France when the war was over. His intellectual production during these years was naturally quite fragmented. In a series of articles, for instance, he introduced his earlier works to his new American audience.[2] He also translated into English, with some minor additions, *Eléments de Sociologie Juridique*.[3] These works are all of minor importance and shed little light on the development of Gurvitch's thought during the war years. Much more significant works are the symposium that Gurvitch edited with Wilbert E. Moore entitled *Twentieth Century Sociology* (1945), and his plan for the post-war reconstruction of France, *La Déclaration des Droits Sociaux* (1944).[4] These two works, along with a couple of articles in political sociology,[5] constitute Gurvitch's major work between 1940-1945 and are the only ones of interest here.

There are two tendencies in Gurvitch's work of these years that appear contradictory at first sight. On the one hand, Gurvitch made a swing to the right in his sociology in the very conventional *Twentieth Century Sociology*. On the other hand, he moved to the left in *The Bill of Social Rights,* in which he developed his plan for a socialist France run by workers organized into workers' councils. Gurvitch did not see these contradictions in his own work. He claimed that his sociology was simply becoming more "realistic" and that in the *The Bill of Social Rights,* as opposed to *L'Idée du Droit Social,* he had succeeded in distinguishing more clearly between "value judgments" and "judgments of reality."[6] However, his explanation is unsatisfactory. In order to understand the fundamental unity of Gurvitch's thought, one has to broaden the perspective and consider Gurvitch's work as part of the general class struggle of the 1940's.

The unifying link between the two tendencies in Gurvitch's thought can be found in the triumph of bourgeois hegemony over the movement to the left that occurred in the 1930's and during World War II. During the 1930's, the economy in the United States and in Europe partially collapsed. The result was a resurgence of radicalism. During World War II, this radical activity continued strongly. The Soviet Union cooperated with the anti-fascist, capitalist states in a popular front against fascism, and it gained tremendous prestige throughout the capitalist world. The extreme sacrifices that the common people in England, Greece, and elsewhere made in order to defeat fascism gave birth to an intense desire for a new, better world after the war. Except for the years following World War I, the Left was never in such an advantageous position as just after World War II.

Within the non-fascist countries, the tremendous strength of bourgeois culture and ideology, however, prevented the cooperation of the working class and anti-fascist elements from turning to the advantage of the former. Undoubtedly, the leadership of the various communist parties — especially CPSU — played a negative role in this development. Stalin had little understanding of how to forge a successful popular front. A popular front, as Gramsci had made clear, must break the alliance between the ruling class and its supporting classes and link these latter classes to the working class mainly through non-political means, i.e. through culture.[7] The crucial question in any political alliance is which class is to exert hegemony, the ruling class or the working class.

In the alliance that took place in the 1930's and 1940's between the working class and the anti-fascist elements, the proletariat definitely lost out. The tremendous strength of bourgeois hegemony showed itself, and the drift to the left of the masses as well as of many intellectuals was effectively stopped and slowly turned around.

This general development was reflected in Gurvitch's work with its simultaneous emphasis on the need for a positivistic sociology and for socialism. Gurvitch was a very strong anti-fascist, involved in Paris with the Italian underground *Giustizia e Libertà*.[8] He was also an ardent supporter of the popular front as well as a participant in the French undergound.[9] His sociology from the 1930's, however, reveals no trace of these radical activities and Marxism is not seriously discussed in, for instance, *Essais de Sociologie* (1938). Despite the work of such creative Marxists as Paul Nizan, Georges Politzer, and Henri Lefebvre, bourgeois hegemony remained intact in France in the 1930's.

In the United States, bourgeois hegemony was far stronger than in France and Gurvitch's work suffered as a consequence during 1940-1945. Marx, Engels, and Lenin had all agreed that the United States had the most "purely bourgeois institutions" in the world and that there were tremendous obstacles to the development of a revolutionary Marxism in the United States.[10] Lenin especially had noted that the rule of the bourgeoisie and the notion of political freedom had become practically identical in the United States.[11]

After the crash in 1929, the North American working class, as well as many intellectuals, slowly began to move to the left.[12] The majority of the intellectuals adopted Roosevelt's mild brand of reformism, but a sizable number also became members of CPUSA.[13] In the social sciences, Marxism became a serious consideration for the first time. Such a conventional American sociological magazine as *Sociology and Social Research,* for instance, stated in 1937 that an "unprejudiced social science must seek to answer the validity of historical materialism."[14]

The American Left, however, was in a difficult position and was never able to develop a solid theoretical basis in the 1930's. By following the Soviet Union instead of developing its own political strategy adapted to American conditions, the American Communist Party soon began to lose its attraction for many intellectuals who had pursued it.[16] When the first radical enthusiasm wore off and the implications of Stalinism became clear, the American left-wing intellectuals had little to fall back on for theoretical guidance.

Marxism, in retrospect, made very little impact on bourgeois social science. The opposite, in fact, occurred. Bourgeois social science eventually succeeded in disarming the Marxists in the United States. Indeed, a very important function of U.S. sociology in the 1930's and 1940's was to present a scientific alternative to Marxism. The successful fulfillment of this task is directly related to the weakness of the working class movement in the United States. People like Philip Selznick, Nathan Glazer, Seymour Martin Lipset, and Daniel Bell, to mention only a few, all started out as Marxists of various shades who later became prominent bourgeois sociologists.[17] A variety of anti-Marxist social scientists like Weber, Michels, and Pareto became very popular during these years and were used to counteract the Left.[18] The so-called Pareto Circle at Harvard was especially active in formulating alternatives to Marxism.[19] Georg C. Homans, for instance, a member of this group, claimed that communism was "unrealistic" in that it didn't view "society as an organism."[20] This was due, he said, to the fact that "revolutionists are not sociologists."[21] This kind of thinking – that Marxism is unfeasible because unscientific – was the main strategy used by the bourgeoisie to counteract the possible influence of Marxism on social science. It was no accident, therefore, that Gurvitch during his sojourn in the United States further developed the idea that "values" and "facts" should be split and that scientific analysis and political analysis should be separated; it was very clearly related to the triumph of bourgeois hegemony in the United States during the 1930's and 1940's.

The difference between Gurvitch's sociology and American sociology is often stressed.[22] The phenomenological side of Gurvitch's thought and his tendency to philosophize rather than to do empirical research are usually cited as the main reasons why Gurvitch's sociology failed to become popular among American sociologists. This explanation, however, is mystifying in the sense that it conceals the basic similarities between North American sociology and Gurvitch's sociology, especially in the early 1940's. It is part of the tendency of conventional sociology to view European sociology as philosophical in nature and North American sociology as empirical whereas they are actually very similar. In order to understand why Gurvitch so easily assimilated North American sociology in *Twentieth Century Sociology,* it is imperative to grasp these structural similarities between U.S. and European sociology.

North American sociology can be easily divided into three periods: the stage of reform (the founding fathers), the "quest to make sociology scientific" (the Chicago School), and the stage of technocratic sociology (from the 1940's onward).[23] These three stages relate to different periods in the integration of the liberal bourgeoisie into monopoly capitalism. During the first stage, there was — as in French sociology at the turn of the century — a great hope among the liberal bourgeoisie that *laissez-faire* capitalism would give way to a harmonious society based on class collaboration.[24] This hope was shattered by World War I.[25] To orient itself effectively to the reality that emerged after the world war, the demoralized liberal bourgeoisie had to abandon its earlier hopes and become "objective." This quest for "objectivity" slowly eroded the old value system of the liberal bourgeoisie and diminished its autonomy. It also helped to produce the kind of social scientists needed by monopoly capitalism for its "social bookkeeping."[26] Finally, and most importantly, sociology's embrace of "objectivity" surrounded monopoly capitalism with an air of neutrality which facilitated its legitimation.[27]

The general parallels between the development of North American and European sociology (including that of Gurvitch) are consequently striking. To establish the exact links between Gurvitch's analyses in *Twentieth Century Sociology* and North American sociology, however, it is necessary to take a closer look at each of the three stages that North American sociology has passed through. Only then is it possible to "decode" Gurvitch's sociology during the war and to understand it properly.

In nineteenth century American sociology no sharp distinction was made between values and facts.[28] On the contrary, the two were intimately connected, and the faith in progress was very strong. Ward, for instance, saw himself as an "apostle of human progress", and Ross and Small had great confidence in the future.[29] Sociology, by combining science and ethics, was to construct a new and better society. This society was to be based on class collaboration.[30] Socialism, all the founding fathers agreed, was destructive of society.[31] As a doctrine, it was totally unscientific and utopian.[32] However, they thought *laissez-faire* capitalism and unrestricted individualism should also be avoided. Small expressed this very clearly when he stated: "the social problem of the twentieth century is whether the civilized nations can restore themselves to society after the nineteenth century aberrations of individualism and capitalism."[33] The good society was to be found somewhere between the extremes of socialism and individualism.

The belief in class collaboration, as Dusky Lee Smith has pointed out in "Sociology and the Rise of Corporate Capitalism" (1965), made sociology the ideological *"avant-garde* of . . . corporate reality."[34] Schwendinger and Schwendinger have elaborated upon this theme in *Sociologists of the Chair* (1974) and have drawn attention to the ideological similarities between the German *Kathedersozialisten* and early American sociologists.[35] In a general sense, sociology did indeed articulate the need of the ruling class to appease the working class with reforms. However, given the strength of the ruling class and the difficulty of organizing the working class into a reformistic political party, the early sociologists badly overestimated this need. As a result, their sociology was soon viewed as utopian, and it was mostly discarded after World War I. In retrospect, Small found it "pathetic."[36]

Though in many ways Ward, Small and Ross failed, they did succeed in laying the ideological foundation for modern American sociology – namely, the mediation of individualism and collectivism. Without going too deeply into this question, one can easily see how favorable the new stage of capitalism was to the development of sociology. Under monopoly capitalism, it was important to relate the individual to the group, not just to another individual, as in *laissez-faire* capitalism. The same development took place in European sociology, but because North American capitalism was so strong, the ideological struggle between the individual and the group came to a much clearer expression in American sociology.

An illustration of early American sociology's solution to the problem of individualism versus collectivism can be seen in the notion of social control as developed especially by Ross.[37] This concept – which Gurvitch chose to elaborate upon in *Twentieth Century Sociology* – tried to strike a balance between the interests of the individual and those of the group. If there were no control over the individual, chaos would result and society would cease to exist. However, the group should not suppress the individual; both could coexist harmoniously through self-regulation by the group.[38]

The reform movement from the 1880's to World War I, of which early North American sociology was a part, became a failed attempt to stabilize capitalism.[39] It was too optimistic and naive to survive the test of World War I. However, the bourgeoisie continued its attempt to bring the capitalist system under control. President Hoover's restless efforts in this direction testify to the magnitude of the problems involved.[40] Sociologists also continued to grapple with the problem of how to stabilize and contain the anarchic forces of monopoly capitalism. Like their predecessors, they tried to find a workable midpoint between individualism and collectivism. According to Park and Burgess' *Introduction to the Science of Sociology* (1921), which marked the transition from pre-war to post-war sociology in the United States, social control was still "the central problem of sociology."[41] ". . . Unlimited liberty, without social control," Park and Burgess wrote, "ends in the negation of freedom and the slavery of the individual."[42] A "society" would become possible only if "competition" was held in check by "social control." Social control could assume three different forms—"conflict," "accommodation," and "assimilation"—each of which represented a more advanced stage of stabilization.[43]

The continuity between early sociology and the Chicago School is easy to perceive. However, there are crucial differences between the two, especially in relation to the notion of progress and the place of values in sociology. Progress had been conceived in an optimistic and bourgeois-reformistic spirit by Ward, Ross, and Small. The attitude of the Chicago people, however, was defeatist. "Progress," Park said, "was a terrible thing."[44] In the section on progress in *Introduction to the Science of Sociology,* it is clear that the belief in man's ability to create a harmonious society has greatly eroded.[45] "Herbert Spencer," Park and Burgess wrote, "asserts the perfectibility of man with an assurance that makes us gasp."[46] Park and Burgess also characterized the radical as having "a boundless confidence in even the most impossible future."[47] The two men were not ready to reject completely the notion of progress—there was still a reformistic element in them—but they totally undermined it: progress was what anyone considered to be progress.[48] This conclusion was in line with the general tendency of bourgeois sociology to avoid objective reality—the historical-dialectical unfolding of class society—and to conceive of society instead in irrational and subjective terms. Combined with this tendency was Park and Burgess' rejection of sociology as a "philosophy of history" and their espousal of multicausal explanations.[49]

Though progress was not yet eliminated from the thought of bourgeois sociology, it was not long before it was totally rejected as "unscientific." Park and Burgess quoted Ellsworth Faris who argued that since "there is no insurance that progress will take place," the concept might as well be dispensed with.[50] Faris added: "The conception which seems to be superseding the idea of progress is that of control."[51]

The attitude Faris articulated is very clear—in order to re-orient itself to the class struggle, the liberal bourgeoisie had to give up its earlier values and get closer to reality. As in Europe, this need led to a strong emphasis on sociology as a science dealing with facts, as opposed to a philosophy dealing with values. In short, sociology became "a philosophy of non-philosophers" as Gramsci has called it.[52] Thus, in *Introduction to the Science of Sociology,* Park and Burgess wrote that to decide what is the "ultimate good" is not a question for sociology but for philosophy. "[Sociology] does not even need to discuss it," they argued.[53] This kind of thinking set the scene for the demoralization of sociologists. Park, the ideological leader of the Chicago School, was well known for the firmness with which he rejected any attempts to introduce value judgments into sociological discussions:

> Park was probably the only one [of the leading sociologists at Chicago] who directly attacked the humanitarian attitude when it appeared among sociologists. More than once he drove students to anger or tears by growling such reproofs as "You're another one of those damn do-gooders."[54]

Most of the graduate students, however, did not need to be pushed into line. Philip M. Hauser, reminiscing about the days when he was a student at the University of Chicago, says: "That sociology was a science, not a vehicle for social action, was a tenet of faith on the part of the faculty and the predominant portion of the graduate students at Chicago [in the 1920's and 1930's] ..."[55] The rest of the students ("those damn do-gooders") soon left, Robert E. L. Faris tells us.[56]

The Chicago School's importance, however, does not reside in the fact that it expressed the impasse of the liberal bourgeoisie, but in that it succeeded in re-orienting itself to the new post-war reality by carrying out huge researches. Those researches were considered to be scientific, and what is known as the Chicago School's "empirical breakthrough" was seen as the "transition [of sociology] from a pre-scientific to a scientific stage."[57] The ultimate importance of the Chicago School thus resides in the fact that it re-oriented the liberal bourgeoisie to the new concrete tasks of monopoly capitalism and labeled these concerns "scientific." In short, it helped to supply monopoly capitalism both with fresh information and with a new sophisticated scientific legitimation.

There was, no doubt, a certain uneasiness at Chicago over the new role of the sociologist as a "neutral" scientist. The resistance to quantification and statistics at Chicago can be seen as part of this discomfort.[58] Some students, such as Louis Wirth, Everett C. Hughes, and Herbert Blumer, expressed misgivings stronger than others. Even in Park himself there was a certain tension between science and reform, as Hughes has pointed out.[59] Perhaps a suitable symbol for Chicago sociology is the notion of "marginal man." Like the marginal man, the Chicago sociologist was part of two cultures, to neither of which he fully belonged: the old reformistic and optimistic sociology of the pre-war days, and the new technocratic sociology of the 1930's and 1940's.

The final transformation of American sociologists from progressive reformers to technocratic scientists, from constituting a "learned society"

(Hughes) to becoming a "profession" (Parsons and others), was completed in the 1930's and 1940's.[60] Whatever was left of the old reformistic ideology was then totally wiped out. Gunnar Myrdal noted in the 1940's: "The reaction against reformism and philosophical system-building has been particularly violent in American sociology. . . ."[61] The new professional ideology, as Oberschall has pointed out, came to a particularly clear expression in Ogburn's work.[62] In his presidential address to the American Sociological Society in 1929, Ogburn stated, "sociology as a science is not interested in making the world a better place in which to live. . . ."[63] "It will be necessary," Ogburn continued, "to crush out emotion and to discipline the mind so strongly that the fanciful pleasures of intellectuality will have to be eschewed in the verification process; it will be desirable to taboo ethics and values [except in choosing problems]."[64] "Science," Ogburn concluded, "is interested in one thing only, to wit, discovering new knowledge. . . ."[65]

Ogburn is relevant in this context not only because his articulation of the need for "objectivity" in sociology is fittingly brutal but also because he was personally involved in bourgeois politics. The same year that he gave his address to the American Sociological Society about the need for objectivity, he was chosen by Hoover to head a study on "recent social trends" in American society.[66] This virtual acceptance of monopoly capitalism, combined with an attack of every other position as "unscientific," exemplifies the general erosion of humanist values which had taken place in the liberal bourgeoisie as well as in society in general.[67] The "destruction of values" in American sociology, to paraphrase Lukács, was now more or less complete.

American sociologists now began to work directly for business and government and to supply them with social information. Loren Baritz has documented part of this development in *The Servants of Power: A History of the Use of Social Science in American Industry* (1960).[68] Market research, studies of public opinion, and similar types of research became popular in the 1930's and were furnished with scientific legitimation by prominent sociologists such as Robert K. Merton, Paul F. Lazarsfeld, Hadley Cantril and others.[69] In 1937 Lazarsfeld became director of the Office of Radio Research at Princeton University which two years later was transformed into the Bureau of Applied Social Research at Columbia University.[70] Thus "administrative research," as Lazarsfeld called this new type of sociology, was launched several years before Gurvitch's arrival in the United States.[71]

American sociology has continued to express the class strategy of monopoly capitalism to the present day. It tries to present solutions to whatever problems emerge in the day-to-day struggle in capitalist society without questioning that society's basic structure. This close connection between North American sociology and the everyday problems of monopoly capitalism accounts for its pragmatic character and also for its micro·

perspective. Monopoly capitalism, however, has to solve more important problems than how to sell hair shampoo and war bonds; it must contain the giant anarchic forces of capitalism and try to keep society together. The first time this was directly understood by North American sociologists was in the 1930's. "The depression of the early 1930's was like the explosion of a bomb dropped in the midst of society," Ogburn noted in the preface to a study sponsored by the Social Science Research Council. Ogburn's feeling seems to have been quite general among sociologists.[72] Serious attempts were made to understand the causes of the depression and to get the economy going, all of which miserably failed, as Kolko has pointed out.[73] However, the need to understand monopoly capitalism as a giant social system with a very precarious equilibrium began to emerge among some bourgeois theoreticians, such as Talcott Parsons and other members of the Pareto Circle at Harvard.[74] There was a growing realization that the most basic task of social thought was to develop strategies for keeping society together. This accounts for the popularity in the 1930's of, for instance, Durkheim's notion of cohesiveness, or Pareto's idea of society as a social system.[75]

Ideologically, an emphasis on the social system meant a de-emphasis on the individual. Social control, for example, was increasingly understood as the need to keep the individual in check.[76] Nevertheless, the general tendency of American sociology to mediate between individualism and collectivism remained very powerful and was reflected in the popularity in the 1930's and 1940's of such concepts as role and occupation.

The symposium on sociology that Gurvitch and Moore edited in 1945, *Twentieth Century Sociology,* was an uncritical appraisal of contemporary sociology. The first part of the work was supposed to present the existing state of the various fields in sociology. Merton, for instance, contributed an article on "The Sociology of Knowledge," Parsons discussed "The Present Position and Prospects of Systematic Theory in Sociology," and Znaniecki wrote on "Social Organizations and Institutions."[77] As a non-American reviewer has pointed out, however, the first part of the symposium might as well have been called "American sociology" because it only covers North American contributions to sociology.[78] In the second part of the work, the state of sociology in various countries was surveyed. Among the contributions in this section, Albert Salomon's article on "German Sociology" and Claude Lévi-Strauss' on "French Sociology" are worthy of mention.[79]

What the two parts of *Twentieth Century Sociology* have in common is that they both express some of the most fundamental tenets of the technocratic sociology which was then in vogue in the United States. The contributors confirmed that sociology must have nothing to do with human values if it was to remain scientific.[80] All "humanistic interferences" in sociology, as one author phrased it, had to be eliminated.[81] Sociology, in Ernest W. Burgess' words, was "a natural science distinct from ethics or history."[82] Being a natural science, Robert E. L. Faris added, sociology must slowly accumulate knowledge and insight and "disregard for the time being the urgencies of a suffering mankind."[83] A sociologist was both a citizen and a scientist, Faris concluded, and one must not confuse these two roles.[84]

The writers in *Twentieth Century Sociology* also attacked viewing sociology as a philosophy of history. Parsons and Sorokin were most emphatic on this point.[85] Connected with the tendency to confuse sociology with philosophy of history, they claimed, was the idea that there was one predominant factor governing social life.[86] Consequently, they dismissed Marx as "unscientific" on two accounts—that he had been more or less obsessed with the idea of "linear progress" and that he had overemphasized the importance of economics.[87] As an alternative to the idea that one factor dominated social life, an eclectic multi-causal perspective was offered by MacIver in the collection.[88] Moreover, Parsons asserted that sociological theory had left behind the less mature stage of "competing schools" and now constituted one coherent theory.[89]

Another characteristic of *Twentieth Century Sociology* is that it attempted to go beyond narrow-minded empiricism and to grasp the problem of society on a macro-level. The result is a fairly vague groping toward a more comprehensive view of society which manifests itself both in the idea of a "social system" (Parsons, Znaniecki) and in the attempt to replace the notion of conscious social values with unconscious functions (Merton, Lévi-Strauss).[90] Merton, for instance, tried to describe how the sociology of knowledge had emerged at the time in western civilization when "the intrinsic content of the avowed belief or point of view [of a person]" was no longer taken at face value.[91] "Thought becomes functionalized," Merton wrote, "[and] it is interpreted in terms of its psychological or economic or social or racial sources and functions."[92] Lévi-Strauss articulated the same idea in a very sophisticated analysis of Durkheim's methodology. Durkheim's basic problem, he claimed, had been to determine how society could continue as a "meaningful whole" without "finalism."[93] For the human mind, Lévi-Strauss argued, the answer to the "blindness of history" and the "finalism of consciousness" had been found in the "unconscious teleology of mind."[94] A similar model, Lévi-Strauss hinted, could be worked out to analyze society as a whole.

Twentieth Century Sociology is nonetheless a monument to the incapacity of bourgeois sociology in the 1940's to understand the major problems of capitalism. Nowhere in its more than seven hundred pages is a serious attempt made to analyze the great problems of the time: the Russian Revolution, colonialism, the depression, the rise of fascism, etc. The refusal to conceive of sociology as a "philosophy of history" and as a "value-filled social science" indeed took its toll; it reduced sociology to a trival empirical science incapable of dealing with anything but the most minor problems of capitalist society.

Gurvitch's own contribution to *Twentieth Century Sociology* consisted of a brief introductory note, written in collaboration with Wilbert E. Moore, and an article on social control. Of the two, the preface is the more important because it shows the extent to which Gurvitch had assimilated the basic tenets of contemporary American sociology.[95] Twentieth century sociology, Gurvitch approvingly noted, had broken the link between sociology and philosophy of history. It had passed beyond the futile debates over progress and order and had also rejected the concept of one predominant factor. These ideas, Gurvitch claimed, had "threatened to compromise the scientific character of early sociological research."[96] Gurvitch considered that the eternal discussions in nineteenth century sociology over progress versus order, the individual versus society, and so on, had just been poorly stated problems, i.e. false problems. Twentieth century sociology, he said, had left these problems far behind in its "new trend toward maturity."[97] "Positive-empirical research" combined with a more constructive way of posing the important problems was what characterized contemporary sociology, Gurvitch concluded.[98]

It is quite clear that Gurvitch was totally overtaken by North American sociology. The ease with which this process took place was no doubt connected with his acceptance in the 1930's of the basic tenets of Durkheim and Weber. Moreover, there is an organic link between Gurvitch's early utopian analysis and his sociological positivism — both tendencies are ahistorical, both are deeply idealistic and both disregard political economy. The difference between the two is primarily one of time; utopianism represents a very early and radical stage of bourgeois social thought while sociological positivism represents a later and semi-conservative one.

In the article on social control, the more progressive elements in Gurvitch's thought are apparent.[99] Here he firmly rejected attempts to consider social control as an oppressive mechanism through which the individual could be kept in line by society.[100] Instead he instinctively sought out Ross and Cooley's notion of social control as the harmonious and democratic reconciliation of the individual and the group.[101] Gurvitch also approved of Ross' notion that law represents the most advanced form of social control.[102] This idea, of course, struck a chord with Gurvitch's old ideal of the perfect society as a social *Rechtsstaat*. However, there are definite drawbacks to Gurvitch's analysis of social control. In his usual ideological manner Gurvitch analyzed social control without looking at its political implications. Thus, his article contains a very sharp analysis of the history of the notion of social control from Ross onward but says nothing about its ideological role. The general transformation of social control from a key concept in the reformistic vocabulary of Ross, to a technocratic concept in the manipulative terminology of sociology in the 1940's, was hidden from Gurvitch's eyes.[103] Though he reacted instinctively against the technocratic notion of social control, which went against his voluntarism and his penchant for spontaneity, he was incapable of analyzing what had caused this transformation.

During his stay in the United States, Gurvitch only published one article in a conventional sociological magazine, "The Social Structure of Pre-War France" in *The American Journal of Sociology* (1943).[104] This article is important because it is the only work of Gurvitch's that can properly be called empirical.[105] Its significance, therefore, resides in the fact that in it, for the first time, Gurvitch's sociology was put to a concrete test.

In comparison to the abstract and formalistic *Essais de Sociologie* and *Eléments de Sociologie Juridique,* "The Social Structure of Pre-War France" reads like a breath of fresh air. Finally, Gurvitch confronted a concrete and significant social problem. The main focus of his analysis is the "strange defeat" of France in 1940, and his general thesis is that French society had become extremely unstable and demoralized by the end of the 1930's.

Gurvitch first analyzed the "social structure" of France which he found to be quite stable in the 1930's. To prove this stability he analyzed the situation of the various classes and professions. Some factors, he acknowledged, had caused a certain disintegration of society. In the 1930's, for instance, it had become increasingly difficult to accommodate the millions of immigrant workers because the economy had declined. World War I, by decimating so many people, had also created a huge generation gap, and the political structure of the Third Republic was conducive to fragmentation. The social structure, nonetheless, had remained quite stable until the late 1930's, Gurvitch argued.

Gurvitch then turned his attention to the "culture" of French society. He emphasized the strength of the revolutionary tradition in France and stressed its strongly democratic character.[106] French culture, he said, was basically rationalistic in nature and hostile to mysticism. However, in the nineteenth century, a conservative and counter-revolutionary movement had developed which appealed to irrationalism. This second trend in the French cultural tradition, in Gurvitch's opinion, had never attracted more than a minority of people. The syndicalists, he argued, had seen irrationalism merely as an inspiration to freedom and had not been influenced by its mystic quality. French culture, Gurvitch concluded, was basically democratic and hostile to all kinds of totalitarianism. But during the last years of the 1930's the situation drastically changed. Faced with a series of new problems, the very stability of French society now became a factor of instability. Such events as the mass strikes in 1936, the difficulty of dealing with the Nazis politically, and the several mobilizations of the army put a heavy strain on the French nation which in turn failed to deal constructively with them. The French democratic tradition had not been sufficiently renewed in the twentieth century, Gurvitch argued, and as a result, apathy and resignation easily spread in the difficult years of the late 1930's. The combination of apathy with the treason of some politicians and with the general ineptitude of the French army made it inevitable that France fell when the Germans attacked. Only a small minority of Frenchmen supported the Vichy regime, Gurvitch claimed. The immense majority of the people supported the resistance, and when France was liberated, its strong democratic tradition would re-emerge in a Fourth Republic.

Gurvitch's analysis of the fall of France is not without merit. It contains a fairly good appraisal of the various political groups and the various classes in France. The reader is introduced to the *Comité de Forges,* the *Croix de Feu,* the difficulties of the Popular Front, and so on. Nevertheless, the analysis — and this is its basic weakness — could have been written equally well by any person with newspaper knowledge of the French situation. But then nothing in Gurvitch's carefully developed sociology was of any help to him in this analysis. What could have been the point of looking at the seven or eight "depth-layers" of French society? Would it have helped to know which form of "sociality" predominated in, for instance, the *Comité de Forges?* Could one get to the "essence" of fascism by "bracketing" it? Evidently not. When faced with the concrete situation of France in the 1930's, Gurvitch's sociology collapsed like a house of cards.

It is not difficult to be ironic about the utter incapacity of Gurvitch's sociology to deal with the events that led to the establishment of the Vichy regime. Moreover, if one scrutinizes his scattered remarks on German and Italian fascism, it becomes clear that he had little understanding of fascism in general. Gurvitch viewed fascism as "totalitarian" and characterized by "mystico-ecstatic" elements in combination with a "charismatic" leader.[107]

However, Gurvitch shared his incapacity to understand fascism scientifically with the rest of the bourgeois sociologists, especially the North American ones. If one takes a closer look at the way American sociologists dealt with fascism in the 1930's and 1940's, it becomes clear that they failed to deal with it at all.[108] No American (or European) sociologist produced a major work on fascism.[109] This was no doubt due to the general triviality that characterized American sociology in the 1940's; sociologists did not consider fascism to be of scientific interest.[110] There are, for instance, many articles of the early 1940's devoted to "sociometry" but there are no articles on the extermination of European Jews and socialists. However, even if North American sociologists had tried to understand fascism, it is difficult to imagine what they could have accomplished. Their theoretical tools were mainly those of Weber, Durkheim and the Chicago School: "charisma," "rationalization," "anomie," "cultural lag," and "social movement."[111] All of these concepts were indeed used by American sociologists; none of them, however, was specifically fit to deal with such a difficult phenomenon as fascism. Thus, the few analyses that were produced by American sociologists were unable to go beyond the most superficial aspects of fascism.[112] Just as North American sociologists had failed to understand the depression because of their incapacity to deal meaningfully with the larger socio-economic structures of society, so they failed to understand fascism. Reviewing the literature on fascism from the 1930's to the 1960's, H. Stuart Hughes has noted:

> On balance, a broadly Marxist canon of interpretation had worked better in the critique of fascism than any alternative schema. It had adhered more closely to the concrete details of existence under the rule of Mussolini and Hitler than had the method subsequently proposed — the loose ideal type procedure epitomized in the work of Hannah Arendt and Ernst Nolte.[113]

Consequently, Gurvitch's failure to meaningfully analyze the fall of France and fascism in general was not a unique phenomenon — it was a sign of the general incapacity of bourgeois sociology to understand the most essential aspects of contemporary society.[114]

The Bill of Social Rights (1944) is Gurvitch's most important work written in the United States and it represents his move to the left during these years. As cited earlier, Gurvitch had attributed the failure of L'Idée du Droit Social to his incapacity to keep value judgments and judgments of reality apart.[115] In L'Idée du Droit Social, as Gurvitch saw it, he had tried too hard to "tie together [his] sociological analysis and [his] politico-social convictions which favored decentralized economic planning."[116] This "mistake" was not repeated when, in the 1940's, Gurvitch returned to the question of workers' councils. Following the cult of objectivity in bourgeois sociology, he systematically separated values and facts. Thus, he did not attempt to make a scientific sociological study of the workers' councils but produced instead what he called "a program of politico-social action."[117]

Gurvitch's reluctance to try to unite his scientific and political views was directly related to what has here been called the triumph of bourgeois hegemony. Because Gurvitch, as a result of this hegemony, refrained from treating the question of workers' councils and workers' self-management in a scientific and sociological manner, his work, The Bill of Social Rights, has not been seriously considered as part of Gurvitch's "scientific" contribution.[118] The write-up that The Bill of Social Rights received in American Sociological Review illustrates this:

> A professor from the University of Strasbourg and editor of the Journal of Legal and Political Sociology while in this country during the war addressed himself to the problem of drafting a bill of rights to cover the needs of free men in the modern world. He

states his conceptions under such headings as Right to Labor,
Right of Labor, Right to Rest and Retirement, Right to Freedom
and Labor Unions and Right to Strike; Social Rights of Consumers and Users; Social Duties and Social Rights Concerning
Property; Social Rights of the Common Man. To verbalize liberal
ideals abstractly may be one function of intellectual leadership, but
most sociologists will probably be inclined to ask "So what?"[119]

In short, by removing his analysis of workers' councils from the field of
sociology, Gurvitch made himself vulnerable to an easy attack in the name of
science ("So what?").

The Bill of Social Rights is in many aspects a remarkable work and con-
tinues the progressive tradition begun in *L'Idée du Droit Social* but abandoned
in *Essais de Sociologie* and *Eléments de Sociologie Juridique*. Jean Duvignaud
has said that in *The Bill of Social Rights* "one can see, for the first time, a
sociologically and legally defined *system of workers' self-management* within
the framework of a socialist plan."[120] In addition, Georges Balandier has
noted that *The Bill of Social Rights* contains "a program of social and political
action for the [post-war] reconstruction — viewed as a socialist society *centered
on workers' self-management.*"[121]

As an attempt to deal with the post-war world, *The Bill of Social Rights*
was part of a series of works by social scientists which appeared during World
War II and which tried to outline the correct class strategy to adopt after the
war.[122] Gurvitch's work was much more progressive than most of these. This
can be illustrated, for instance, by a comparison of his work with that of
Mannheim, the last of the great liberal sociologists. Mannheim, who readily
admitted the "wreckage of liberalism" in the twentieth century, dealt with the
problem of reconstruction in a series of works, the most important of which is
Man and Society in an Age of Reconstruction (1935, 1940). The whole thrust
of Mannheim's analysis was that *laissez-faire* capitalism had to be replaced
with "planning." "As if everything [does] not depend on who regulates whom,"
Adorno wryly noted in his review of Mannheim's work.[123] A closer look at
Man and Society in an Age of Reconstruction indeed reveals that the liberal
bourgeoisie had reached the end of its progressive period. Mannheim's work is
permeated with a deep distrust of the masses and with a glorification of elites,
an attitude which has certain quasi-fascist overtones.[124]

Gurvitch's work was far more progressive than Mannheim's. He
understood clearly that some form of socialism was necessary in order to
create a truly democratic society. In this sense, Gurvitch's *The Bill of Social
Rights* was closer to another work on the reconstruction of post-war society
written during the 1940's: Anton Pannekoek's *Workers' Councils.*[125] Both of
these works contained a sophisticated discussion of the organizational form

that an anti-authoritarian socialism must create—namely, a system of workers' councils.

The Bill of Social Rights was primarily conceived as a draft for the constitution of the Fourth Republic. But Gurvitch claimed that the principles he expounded in it were applicable to other countries as well. The book consisted of a constitutional draft, written in conventional legal language, with explanatory notes. The thrust of Gurvitch's argument was that western democracy had to renew itself in order to be capable of avoiding new catastrophes like fascism and World War II. The strong tendency of countries toward technocracy and "economic feudalism" (Gurvitch's term for monopoly capitalism) threatened to destroy the peace after the war, unless vigorous action was taken. Democracy, Gurvitch said, had to become an inspiration again, an ideal to which people could strive, and the only way for this to happen was to complement political democracy with a solid industrial democracy. What was needed, Gurvitch said, was a "1789 in the economic sphere" (Proudhon).[128]

During the last decades, Gurvitch said, there had been many attempts to institutionalize man's "social rights." The Weimar Constitution (1919), the Constitution of the Spanish Republic (1931) and the Soviet Constitutions (1918, 1924-25, 1936) were examples of this. Gurvitch also alluded favorably to some of Roosevelt's famous speeches, such as the one on "the four freedoms" (1941), and the draft for a new Bill of Rights which the United States National Resources Planning Board had worked out in 1943. But for Gurvitch none of these bills had gone far enough. Attempts to institutionalize workers' control between the two wars had failed, primarily because there had been no economic planning and nationalization involved. There were other reasons for the failure as well, such as the difficulty of eliminating the antagonism between workers' councils and unions, the tendency to let the workers control only minor details of their lives in the factories, and the failure to link the local councils with councils on the national level.

Gurvitch's draft was supposed to be a correction of the earlier attempts to bring about workers' control. In each factory, Gurvitch said, there had to be a "controlling committee." This organization was to be responsible for the inner regulation of the factory or the office. More important was the organization that Gurvitch called the "management council." This council, elected by the workers in every factory, would run the whole factory, i.e., be responsible for the general direction of the company and its administration. It would decide all the economic and technical problems involved in the running of the company.

Gurvitch's faith in the workers' capacity to run the factories by themselves contrasts strongly with the contempt for the masses shown by liberals like Mannheim. Gurvitch wrote:

> . . . it seems . . . necessary to elaborate upon [the] *management councils,* in order to answer a possible objection: would it not be dangerous to call upon workers to participate in the technical and economic administration of enterprises, in view of their incompetence in this domain? Our answer would be that the difficulty here is imaginary rather than real: the functions of management councils will consist in the general direction and the running of enterprises and industries, and will not take over the functions of the technical personnel. The latter will be appointed by management councils and receive from them general directives only. In general questions the workers on one hand, and the users on the other, being directly interested in the efficient functioning of production, are more competent than the present-day members of directing boards of trusts, corporations, and stockholding companies, and the directors appointed by them and by individual owners. This technical personnel, e.g., engineers, will be chosen by management councils among the persons possessing academic degrees qualifying them for this kind of position. In judging the personal qualities and experience of these candidates, workers are more competent than anyone else. After appointment of the technical personnel for a limited period by management councils, it may be desirable to submit them to periodical re-elections by workers. This would be a very effective means of combatting the technocratic trend without interfering with "technical competency." A qualified engineer, or any technician, would lose none of his qualifications in being submitted to periodical re-elections. Without requisite degrees he could neither be appointed nor elected.[127]

Besides the local councils in the factories, there were to be Regional Economic Councils, National Economic Councils, and an International Economic Council, according to *The Bill of Social Rights.* The workers in one factory would thus be connected with other workers' councils in their own country as well as in foreign countries.

If workers' self-management was the first theme in Gurvitch's scheme for a socialist society, his concern for the individual was the second. As he saw it, each individual had to be able to belong to different groups in order to become really free. Different organizations for people as workers, citizens, consumers (of products), and users (of services) had to be created. A person's interest in a low price as a consumer or a user, for instance, would be counterbalanced by his or her interest in a higher salary as a worker. A person's political power organized into the state, would be counterbalanced by the economic organizations, and so on. The whole society, as Gurvitch saw it, would consist of a pluralist system of checks and balances so that no person or group would be abused. If a deadlock occurred between two different interests, a court would decide the result. The ultimate arbitrator in the nation would be a Supreme Court, and on the international scene, an International Supreme Court would be the highest power (see illustration on next page).[128]

The positive element in Gurvitch's scheme for his *Rechtsstaat* or *Sozialrechtsstaat* is apparent — the workers would run the factories by themselves. There are, however, several weak points in Gurvitch's proposal. These are generally centered around Gurvitch's difficulty to come to terms with his own penchant for juristic socialism, which, along with the tradition of natural law, was revived at the end of World War II. Thus, Gurvitch's approach was still very unrealistic; he overestimated the importance of changes in the superstructure and he underestimated the strength of capitalism. For instance, Gurvitch did not deal with the question of power in a realistic way; he hoped that a parliament would simply vote capitalism out of existence. Moreover, Gurvitch's use, for instance, of both Roosevelt and Proudhon as predecessors of the Bill of Social Rights illustrates the confusion of class strategies in his mind: he united the aims of a Roosevelt, who essentially wished only to reform capitalism, with the aims of a Proudhon who desired to crush capitalism. Gurvitch made a similar mistake on the question of nationalization. In several places in *The Bill of Social Rights,* Gurvitch claimed that the workers would own the means of production, but in other places he said the opposite; on the whole his position on this central issue was one of vacillation.[129]

The separation between "values" and "facts" that was very strongly developed in North American sociology due to the triumph of bourgeois hegemony thus pushed Gurvitch into simultaneously developing a very docile sociology and a quite militant political philosophy. After the war, however, this separation between "values" and "facts" would increasingly be seen as false by many European thinkers. Gurvitch's struggle with this problem constitutes the focus for the following two chapters on Gurvitch's post-war sociology.

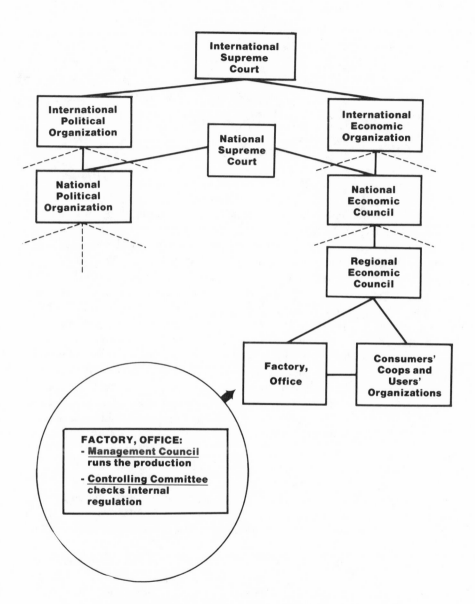

Illustration. Gurvitch's plan for the reconstruction of post-war society according to *The Bill of Social Rights* (1944).

6 The Task of Sociology in Post-War France (1945-1952)

If Gurvitch had remained in the United States after the war his sociology would undoubtedly have become different in emphasis. In the United States, cooperation between the anti-fascist forces had worked to the advantage of the bourgeoisie. The various sections of the new petty bourgeoisie (Gramsci's "organic intellectuals") had rallied to the war effort and had willingly subordinated themselves to the leadership of the bourgeoisie. Whatever was left of an opposition to the ruling class in the United States after World War II was quickly suppressed. In social science, the years after the war were characterized by tremendous conformity. Most of North American sociology was narrowly empirical in character, and it conceived its main task to be the solution of the problems that capitalism had created. This tacit acceptance of the major values of capitalism meant that most of sociology's energy was spent on research techniques and other questions of minor importance.[1] Functionalism now emerged as the major theory. For people like Parsons and Shils, the post-war period constituted a "golden age."[2] The main thrust behind functionalism was the belief that capitalism as a social system worked very well without conscious participation of the masses. The unintended consequences of social behavior were given a privileged status in this doctrine, and the conscious *telos* of "man" in the Enlightenment tradition was now replaced by the unconscious *telos* of the capitalist social system. The moral indifference generated by capitalism was not only ideologically justified in functionalism but constituted its very basis.

In 1945, the United States was the only major capitalist power that had not been destroyed by the war. Indeed, North American capitalism emerged tremendously strengthened by the war and fully intended to assume responsibility for the whole capitalist world.[3] For several years it seemed as if the new super power could not be challenged and that the United States and the U.S.S.R. controlled the fate of the world (the "Cold War"). However, by 1953-1954 it was already apparent that the United States was unable to control the "free world," just as the U.S.S.R. was unable to control the socialist bloc.[4] In the last hand, World War II created a situation which was far too contradictory for the capitalist class in the United States to manage. The United States was unable to replace the European powers as a colonial master, and the "Third World" emerged with irresistible force after World War II. Gabriel Kolko, who has written two excellent books on the failing class strategy of the ruling class in the United States between 1943-1953, summarizes the ultimate significance of World War II:

> World War Two, like the first orgy of bloodletting that had preceded it, was profoundly significant to the following generation not in the manner in which it led to diplomatic settlements or even permanent new power relations, but in the way it unleashed forces in the world that no one — neither Americans nor Russians — anticipated. For the war made permanent revolutions and the momentum from the Left the central irresistible theme in the history of our times, and while it temporarily resolved capitalism's difficulties it ultimately intensified them as it made the problems of world politics and economics yet more indivisible.[5]

The challenge presented to U.S. capitalism eventually registered in North American sociology. Functionalism and theories like "the end of ideology" were increasingly seen as what they had always been — ideologies in the classical Marxist sense of the word. But this awareness was belated — it did not really register among North American sociologists until the 1960's — and this testifies to the tremendous strength of bourgeois hegemony in the United States during the post-war period.

Gurvitch, however, left the United States and went back to France, where he remained for the rest of his life. In France, as in Italy or Germany, the post-war situation was very different from in the United States; in Europe the bourgeoisie underwent a crisis of hegemony. The French bourgeoisie's capacity for "moral and intellectual leadership" (Gramsci) was seriously questioned just after the war for several reasons. Most of the bourgeoisie had collaborated with the Nazis and was therefore discredited in the eyes of many people. Important sections of the petty bourgeoisie had taken part in the Resistance and had been radicalized as a result. Increasing numbers of the working class were turning to the French Communist Party which had emerged from the Resistance with tremendous prestige. There was a general feeling in France that the Third Republic had been responsible for its humiliating defeat in 1940 and that a new, much more democratic society had to be created. The Resistance, with its ideal of liberty, freedom and fraternity, enjoyed enormous popularity just after the war.

The central problem that faced all classes in France was the crisis of bourgeois hegemony. Would the bourgeoisie be able to restore its leadership by reintegrating the rebellious parts of the petty bourgeoisie and of the working class? Would the working class, under the leadership of the Communist Party, be able to break the hegemonic alliance between the petty bourgeoisie and the capitalist class and draw the petty bourgeoisie toward the working class? Would the radicalized petty bourgeoisie be able to renew itself, or would it gravitate back into the field of bourgeois hegemony? These were the major questions that the post-war period posed in France. It is consequently within the dialectics of the crisis of hegemony that the development of post-war French sociology (including that of Gurvitch) must be considered.

The Durkheimian School had vanished along with the Third Republic, symbolically enough, and had left behind a certain ideological and institutional vacuum.[6] The title Gurvitch used for his first sociological article in France, as well as for his major post-war work in sociology, "The Present Task of Sociology" ("La Vocation Actuelle de la Sociologie"), was therefore very pertinent.[7] What role was sociology to play in the hegemonic crisis that France underwent after the war? Would sociology help to reintegrate the petty bourgeoisie into capitalism? Would it support the Communist Party and as a result alienate the vacillating petty bourgeoisie? Or would it try to develop a "third way" which would tie the progressive petty bourgeoisie to the working class? These constituted the three main alternatives; each represented a different class strategy and consequently a different social theory.

Gurvitch's sociology did not articulate any of these three major class strategies very clearly. On the whole, he took a vacillating position, and it is quite complicated to determine the practical significance of his post-war sociology. To delineate it properly, one must draw a clear picture of the main social theories in post-war France and illustrate their relation to the bourgeois crisis of hegemony. Briefly, on the level of social science, the bourgeoisie leaned toward a "value-free" empirical sociology, the French Communist Party tended to advocate dogmatic Marxism, and the radicalized petty bourgeoisie found its most congenial expression in existentialism.

The French bourgeoisie, as just mentioned, was in a very difficult position after the war since it had collaborated with the occupation forces.[9] The resistance movement, with its vague ideal of nationalization and its genuine hope for social democracy, had the upper hand for the moment.[9] In a number of areas during 1944-1947 the bourgeoisie had to yield to its opponents. Laws on workers' councils (*comités d'entreprise*), on welfare and nationalizations of major industries and banks were passed through in fast succession. A new constitution which forbade the formation of trusts and guaranteed a person's social rights was accepted in a referendum in 1946. These concessions, however, were all minor and the bourgeoisie was soon in a position to either turn them to its own advantage or to empty them of any substantive content. The nationalizations, for instance, served essentially to modernize French industry,[10] and the laws on workers' councils, as well as the constitution itself, were soon reduced to empty letters.[11]

During the period between 1945-1947 the bourgeoisie was very careful and did not openly try to seize the momentum but under the surface it steadily gained power. The relative ease with which the bourgeoisie achieved ascendancy had specific causes, the most important of which was undoubtedly the support it got from the North American bourgeoisie. Since 1943 — the year Nazi Germany was stopped — the United States had been concerned with preventing the resistance movements in Europe from growing too strong.[12] The United States was very aware that revolutions might follow upon the defeat of Germany, and eruptions of this kind would destroy its dream of a capitalist Europe integrated into an international bloc led by North American capitalism. Only small-scale weapons, for instance, had been given to the resistance movements during the war. The United States had also been active in trying to make the Underground accept pro-capitalist leaders. In the case of France, the United States first supported Giraud but later switched over to De Gaulle, who had originally been Great Britain's rival candidate. De Gaulle had the advantage of being a firm right-winger with high prestige among opposition circles within France. If De Gaulle turned out to be unable to manage the situation in France, the United States was willing to suppress an uprising with arms.[13] From 1948 onward the United States mobilized a lot of capital through the Marshall Plan and this aid, of course, strengthened the position of the French bourgeoisie in relation to the other classes. Moreover, the United States helped to split the French labor movement by supporting the anti-communist S.F.I.O.[14]

Several other factors worked to the advantage of the bourgeoisie. One of the most important of these was the after-effect of Stalin's war policy which had been aimed at weakening Nazi Germany at all costs.[15] When De Gaulle decided to back Stalin's efforts to get the Allies to open a second front, he got Stalin's full support in return, and also that of the French Communist party.[16] After the war, the French Communist Party let De Gaulle dissolve all the major resistance organizations, and during the next years the Party told the workers that the most important goal was to raise France's production and restore capitalism.

In the area of production, the bourgeoisie also re-established itself quickly. Few capitalist collaborators were punished because, in general, De Gaulle was not interested in punishing the collaborators. The workers' councils met with strong resistance by managers and were soon without any importance. Behind the neutral shield of the state, the capitalists proceeded quickly to re-establish strong capitalism via national planning (the Monnet Plan). The politically inexperienced resistance movement was finally moved into a pro-capitalist stance through a clever regrouping of the political parties (M.R.P. and P.R.F.).

By 1947-48 the bourgeoisie's position was considerably strengthened and its basic crisis was over. Apathy among the masses made it easier for the bourgeoisie to operate more openly now. The collaborators, for instance, emerged in public life in 1947-48 to the outrage of the anti-fascists. Neofascism was rampant, and the need for a "strong man" was felt in wide circles. [17]

On the level of social science, the bourgeoisie's interests were best pro-tected by an empirically oriented, "value-free" sociology which could re-establish the separation between "economy" and "society" (a separation people had tended to forget in the Resistance) and absolve the social scientist from any responsibility for his/her work. In more direct terms, the bourgeois strategy was to "smother socialism with [bourgeois] social science," as Lafargue once put it. [18] Here, as elsewhere, ideological support from the United States was considerable. French sociology was ready for its "opera-tional jump," to use an expression of Lazarsfeld, and the United States had the world's most sophisticated empirical sociology at its disposal. [19] "As soon as the war ended," Lazarsfeld has noted apropos France and other European countries, "the pent-up interest in empirical studies broke through, appealing especially to the younger generation. The only source of literature and methodological experience was the USA. No wonder then that much of the material available to us mentions the period around 1946 . . . as a turning point in their sociological development." [20]

It would, however, be wrong to portray the bourgeois-empirical sociology that, from 1946 on, became so popular in France as merely an im-ported product. France, like any capitalist country, had its own non-academic tradition of "social book-keeping." [21] The strength of France's own technocratic tradition facilitated the development of a positivistically oriented sociology. [22] To summarize, the bourgeoisie gravitated naturally toward the "value-free" sociology of the Weberian-American type in its general strategy of legitimating capitalism, as well as in its more specific task of neutralizing and reintegrating the radicalized petty bourgeoisie into capitalism.

The crucial question just after the war was whether the French working class, led by the Communist Party, would take power. As mentioned earlier, the French Communist Party came out of the war with tremendous prestige. It had lost more than a hundred thousand members in the Resistance and was known as the "Party of the Executed" (*Le Parti des Fusillées*). [23] Most resistance organizations, including those that consisted of intellectuals, were either controlled or dominated by the Communists. In 1945, the Party got more votes than any other political organization. Kolko writes:

The party almost doubled its membership in the six months after December 1944, its Paris newspaper was the largest in the city, the communists won a controlling position in the French trade union movement, but, above all, their role in the resistance permitted them the moral right to build up France. It was, in its role in politics, in the economy, among intellectuals, the only party with sufficient power to consider defining the tenor and character of France.[24]

The French Communist Party, however, did not seize power. Thorez argued, thinking of Greece, that British and North American troops would be used if an attempt was made to start a revolution. This was indeed true; when there was a rumor of a communist upheaval in 1946, the United States prepared to move in.[25] Fernando Claudin, in *The Communist Movement* (1970), argues that the French Communist Party should have seized power over the resistance movement in the early 1940's and then presented the Anglo-American troops with a *fait accompli* in 1944.[26] Tito showed, in Yugoslavia, that this action was possible. This strategy, however, presupposes one quality that was sorely lacking in the leadership of the French Communist Party — namely, independence from the U.S.S.R.

During 1944-1947, the French bourgeoisie underwent a severe crisis of moral and intellectual leadership which afforded the French Communist Party an excellent chance to seize the momentum through a "war of position" in Gramsci's terminology, that is, through a cultural-ideological offensive as opposed to a direct attack on the state ("war of movement").[27] This offensive, however, did not occur because the leaders of the French Communist Party followed U.S.S.R. policy too closely. As early as 1943, Stalin acknowledged that France belonged to the Western "sphere of influence."[28] Hence, during the first years after the war, the general strategy of the Communist Party was to restrain the working class and prepare for a peaceful transition to socialism. This policy had one especial weakness — it was not openly discussed by the Communist Party. Indeed, there were a number of questions that the Party refused to explain and clarify; for instance, its glorification of the Allies during the war, the campaign to raise production during 1945-1947, and so on.[29] Because of its equivocation, the Communist Party became increasingly forced into a contradictory position. In short, the Party had to rely more on obedience, discipline, and faith to win support than on persuasion and reason, the essential elements needed to win over the masses in a successful "war of position." After 1947, when the whole policy of the Soviet Union changed very quickly, the chance of an open communist policy became even smaller. According to Zhdanov in 1947, the first duty of the Communist Parties in Western Europe was to support the "anti-imperialist, democratic camp" and especially its "base" (U.S.S.R. and the Popular Democracies), as opposed to "the imperialist and anti-democratic camp."[30] This strategy was meant to lead to a new balance of power between the United States and the Soviet Union. The French Communist Party now had to attack Tito, defend the Soviet labor camps, support the show trials in the Popular Democracies, and so on, using as its only argument that "the fatherland of socialism" had to be defended at all costs.

A successful "war of position" requires a very careful policy toward the "organic intellectuals" of capitalism, those that ideologically and culturally justify capitalism to the working class. The French Communist Party's failure from 1945-1952 to strengthen its position among the petty bourgeoisie was therefore of great consequence. Important segments of the petty bourgeoisie had become radicalized in the Resistance and were open to socialist ideas. This was especially true of teachers, artists, and authors.[31] The basic intention of the Communist Party was to attract these people to the Party, as can be seen from Roger Garaudy's famous speech at the Tenth Congress of the French Communist Party in June 1945, entitled "The Intellectuals and the French Renaissance."[32] Garaudy argued that the best way for an intellectual to serve communism — be he/she an engineer, artist or historian — was to excel in his/her profession. In other words, Garaudy expressed the belief that the advancement of knowledge and true humanism was in full harmony with the Communist Party's policy.[33] This, however, was not the case. During 1945-1947, the Communist Party took a stern line toward progressive intellectuals. Jean-Paul Sartre, for instance, was treated as a "traitor" during those years.[34] The intellectual atmosphere within the Party was stifling, according to Edgar Morin.[35] After 1947, the attitude of the Communist Party hardened considerably, and many intellectuals left the Party.[36] Casanova, Kanapa, and other leading ideologists constantly stressed that it was the duty of intellectuals to wholeheartedly support the Party's position on all questions.[37] Intellectuals were increasingly viewed as unreliable by the leadership in the Party when they did not understand that Tito was an American spy, that there were no labor camps in the U.S.S.R. and so on.[38]

The development of Marxism within the French Communist Party during 1945-1952 was very meager. This, of course, was due to the fact that the Communist Party had committed itself to follow the line of the U.S.S.R. instead of developing its own class strategy. "The function of Marxist ideas [in the Communist Party]," Merleau-Ponty noted in 1945, "is no longer so much to determine policy as to comment upon it and give it an *aura* of Marxism."[39] As a result, Merleau-Ponty continued, there was little knowledge about U.S. imperialism, the situation in Europe, and other important subjects.[40] Morin, in his *Autocritique* (1958), noted the same absence of knowledge in the Party.[41] In 1948, he wrote that no serious analyses were being made in the Party. The ideologists of the Party were content to predict the coming collapse of U.S. capitalism and to extol the virtues of the Soviet Union.[42] "The works that advance knowledge," Sartre exclaimed in 1956, ". . . are *never* written by people in the Communist Party."[43] The Marxism of the French Communist Party was, as a result, very deterministic and mechanical in character, much closer in spirit to the Marxism of the Second International than to that of Lenin.

The Party was very hostile to sociology, which was considered to be a bourgeois science mainly preoccupied with maintaining the status quo.[44] The Party ideologists impatiently brushed it aside as bourgeois rubbish and were not even interested in critiquing it.[45] The only exception to this negative attitude was Henri Lefebvre. In a series of works, Lefebvre tried to develop a non-dogmatic Marxism.[46] Marxism, Lefebvre argued, following Lenin, was essentially a "scientific sociology."[47] In an article entitled "Marxism and Sociology," published in Gurvitch's magazine *Cahiers Internationaux de Sociologie* in 1948, Lefebvre discussed in detail the relation between sociology and Marxism.[48] He considered that "scientific sociology," as opposed to the "official sociology of the French bourgeoisie," had Marxism as its basic method. However, scientific sociology must be flexible, Lefebvre stressed, and should use all the new research techniques available to it. "Marxists," Lefebvre summarized, "are of the opinion that only by using the *method* of Marxism and sharing its concrete preoccupations can French sociology get over the impasse it is in and become freed and creative in spirit."[49]

The Communist Party, however, had no intention of backing Lefebvre's project of a "scientific sociology," especially after 1947.[50] In the spirit of the Cold War, the Communist Party now asserted that one had to choose either U.S. imperialism and pragmatism or the Soviet Union and historical materialism. The line of the Party was expressed in an article entitled "From Psychological Techniques to Cop-Sociology," in *Nouvelle Critique* in 1951.[51] The article condemned Burnham, Friedmann, Gurvitch, and Merleau-Ponty as "cop-sociologists" and part of a "Marshall Plan of Ideas." That Lefebvre's ideas were also not considered favorably can easily be seen from this quotation.

> Concerning sociology, it is ridiculous to see how idealistic sociologists in bourgeois countries ask themselves whether Marxism-Leninism constitutes a sociology or not. In the U.S.S.R. an abstract sociology which is independent from political economy and history is certainly not being taught. On the contrary, all the social sciences are taught with real social content and *the recent work of Stalin in linguistics proves that the U.S.S.R. is in the forefront of the world in social science as in other cultural areas.*[52]

The hegemonic crisis in 1945-1947 came to its clearest expression in the vacillations of the petty bourgeoisie. During the war important segments of the French petty bourgeoisie had moved to the left.[53] During the Resistance, a vague ideology of freedom and fraternity had developed in these circles, and just after the war they were ready to support a revolution.[54] The Communist Party, as has been established, had no intention of making a revolution, and quite soon the petty bourgeoisie started to move back into the camp of the bourgeoisie.[55] The Communist Party, incapable of a true Popular Front strategy, repulsed many people from the petty bourgeoisie, especially after 1947, and further isolated itself.

Nevertheless, some of the petty bourgeois intellectuals who had been radicalized by the war did not become passified and reintegrated into capitalism. Their struggle to keep from falling into the arms of the bourgeoisie came to its finest ideological expression in French post-war existentialism. The people around *Temps Modernes,* especially Jean-Paul Sartre, Maurice Merleau-Ponty and Simone de Beauvoir, tried to challenge the cultural hegemony of the bourgeoisie and to link the progressive petty bourgeois intellectuals to the working class.[56]

The productivity of *Temps Modernes* during the first years was remarkable. A real attempt was made to "tear humanism from the clutches of the bourgeoisie," as Simone de Beauvoir put it, and to develop a socialist world view.[57] During 1945-1950, one can find in *Temps Modernes* analyses of prejudice (Sartre, *Anti-Semite and Jew*), literature (Sartre, *What is Literature?*), colonialism (Tran-Duc-Thao), ethics (Simone de Beauvoir, *The Ethics of Ambiguity*), women (Simone de Beauvoir), justice (Merleau-Ponty, *Humanism and Terror*), and much more.

Politically, the French existentialists were in a difficult position because they received no support from the Communist Party. On the contrary, they were constantly rebuffed. Sartre later recalled:

> We had to defend Marxist ideology without hiding our reservations and hesitations. We had to go a part of the way with people, who, in turn, treated us like police-intellectuals. We had to thrust and parry without being insulting or sever relations; criticize freely but with moderation these cadavers who didn't tolerate a single disagreement; affirm, in spite of our solitude, that we were marching along at their side, at the side of the working class — (reading us, the bourgeois laughed derisively) — but without forbidding ourselves, when necessary, to take sides hastily with the Communist Party, as we did at the beginning of the war in Indo-China, or to fight for peace and the lessening of tension, within the confines of our confidential review, as though we were publishing a popular daily.[58]

As a result, Sartre, Merleau-Ponty and de Beauvoir had to grope their way toward Marxism without any help. To the Communist Party, the people around *Temps Modernes* gave their qualified support — "without illusions" as Merleau-Ponty put it in 1945 — but were not willing to give up their independence.[59] The political strategy that the existentialists tried to advocate was the formation of a true Popular Front.[60] When in 1947 Sartre and Merleau-Ponty joined R.D.R. (*Rassemblement Démocratique Revolutionnaire*), it was to help establish a link between "the advanced segment of the reformist *petite bourgeoisie* and the revolutionary workers," as Sartre wrote.[61] The existentialists were drawn to the working class but repelled by the French Communist Party and its Stalinism. "Have I fallen into the unacceptable dilemma of betraying the proletariat in order to serve truth or betraying truth in the name of the proletariat?" Sartre asked.[62] "It is impossible to be an anti-Communist and it is not possible to be a Communist," Merleau-Ponty seconded.[63]

The existentialists concentrated on one of the most important hegemonic ideas in bourgeois thought: the liberal notion of responsibility. "Bad faith," "ambiguity," "choice" — these key concepts in the existentialists' vocabulary relate to this issue. It was no doubt their experience in the resistance movement that led the existentialists to break with the liberal-formal notion of responsibility. Each act always entails an objective and historical responsibility, Merleau-Ponty wrote in "The War Has Taken Place."[64] During the war, Merleau-Ponty and his comrades had learned not to "play into the hands of the enemy under any circumstances" and this experience was carried over into the post-war world.[65]

In *Humanism and Terror,* which contains a profound Marxist analysis of justice, Merleau-Ponty discusses the differences between responsibility according to "the judicial dream of liberalism" and according to Marxism.[66] In bourgeois thought, responsibility is directly tied to subjective intention. Guilt is established by reconstructing a direct link between the crime and the criminal. Marxism, on the other hand, admits a historical-objective responsibility as well. An act cannot be judged on intention only; it also has to be judged on its objective results. The Marxist notion of justice is directed primarily toward the future. What will the consequences of someone's actions be? — that is the crucial question. In Marxism, there has to be a balance between the subjective and the objective dimensions of responsibility. To stress either the subjective dimension exclusively (as, for instance, liberalism does) or the objective dimension (as, for instance, Stalinism does) means to avoid the basic ambiguity of history, according to Merleau-Ponty.

The most important section of Merleau-Ponty's work is his discussion of the disharmony between a person's intentions and his acts. What we intend to do, Merleau-Ponty argued, often results in something different, yet we still have to bear the responsibility for our actions. He wrote:

> We suggest that every man who undertakes to *play a role* carries
> around him as Diderot said of the actor on stage, a "great phan-
> tom" in which he is forever hidden, and he is responsible for his
> role even when he cannot find in it what he wanted to be.[67]

To Merleau-Ponty, the disjunction between intentions and results is the
tragedy of modern man. Nevertheless, the only solution — and this applies to
the individual as well as to the Communist Party — is to assume responsibility
for one's acts and try to create a society in which alienation in its Hegelian-
Marxist sense can disappear. Evidently, on the question of moral responsibility, Merleau-Ponty took a position which was opposite to the North American
functionalists, who accepted alienation as a natural condition of human beings by complacently viewing the unintended consequences of social behavior
as the key to the secrets of society. To Merleau-Ponty, this view of behavior
was (like the secretive policy of the French Communist Party) just another way
to "mask" the class struggle at a time when it desperately needed to be clarified
through analysis and discussion.

Intellectuals, the existentialists argued, had a definite historical responsibility for their productions. "There are words," Simone de Beauvoir noted,
"as murderous as gas chambers."[68] An author, Sartre contended, must not
describe and explain what already exists but has a moral responsibility to
depict what can be:

> We no longer have time to *describe* or narrate; neither can we limit
> ourselves to *explaining*. Description, even though it be
> psychological, is pure contemplative enjoyment; explanation is ac-
> ceptance, it excuses everything. Both of them assume that the die is
> cast. But if perception itself is action, if, for us, to show the world
> is to disclose it in the perspective of a possible change, then, in this
> age of fatalism, we must reveal to the reader his power in each con-
> crete case, of doing and undoing, in short of acting.[69]

Responsibility, according to the existentialists, is only possible if there is
freedom. If everything is predetermined, there is no room for freedom and
morality. "Ethics is the triumph of freedom over facticity," as Simone de
Beauvoir put it.[70] Sartre especially elaborated the theme that though every person is socially conditioned, he/she is always free to make choices. The point,
Sartre said, is to create a society in which people can always "choose life."[71]
This argumentation led him to confront Stalinist Marxism, which used the notion of historical necessity to justify whatever policy the U.S.S.R. was advocating. People make history, Sartre argued, and they have to be made aware
of their collective power and not have historical necessity thrown in their faces

at all times. In "Materialism and Revolution" (1946), Sartre attacked the concept of determinism in vulgar Marxism, which he said constituted a "radical denial of man's freedom."[72] Contemporary Marxism, he stressed in another article, "has been degraded to a stupid determinism."[73] The fatalistic type of philosophy of history that the Party subscribed to, Sartre wrote, could only have paralyzing effects.

Unlike bourgeois sociologists, however, the existentialists accepted the idea of a philosophy of history. Merleau-Ponty has elaborated on this point:

> Shouldn't politics abandon the idea of basing itself on a philosophy of history and taking the world as it is no matter what our wishes, dreams, or judgments may be, define its end and its means by what the facts authorize? But one cannot do without a perspective, and, whether we like it or not, we are condemned to wishes, value judgments, and even a philosophy of history. It has not been sufficiently noted that, after demonstrating the irrationality of history, the skeptic will abruptly abandon his methodological scruples when it comes to drawing practical conclusions. If one wishes to regulate action, certain facts must indeed be considered dominant and others secondary. No matter how realistic it wishes to be, no matter how strictly based on facts, skeptical politics is obligated to treat (at least implicitly) certain facts as more important than others and to that extent it harbors an embarrassing philosophy of history—one which is lived rather than thought but which is no less effective. . . . In point of fact, historical skepticism is always conservative, although it cannot, in all strictness, exclude anything from its expectations—not even a revolutionary phase of history. Under the pretext of objectivity it freezes the future and eliminates change and the will of men from history. When it believes it is simply facing facts by admitting the necessity of an "elite" in every society or acknowledging the omnipotence of natural riches and geographical conditions, it is really making a bet, expressing a preference and a wish and assuming a responsibility.[74]

The existentialists did not succeed in carrying out their ambitious project of a true Popular Front themselves; they were far too isolated. However, they attacked bourgeois ideology at its most sensitive point in relation to the petty bourgeoisie—the question of moral responsibility. They ripped apart the cloak of neutrality-objectivity that the petty bourgeoisie liked to shroud itself in and revealed how this behavior objectively "played into the hands" of the oppressor.

The shifts in Gurvitch's thought that are noticeable in his post-war production acquire their full significance only if, to repeat, they are placed within
the struggle for hegemony just described. Only when one has first understood
the organic relationship between the bourgeoisie and "value-free" sociology,
between the Communist Party and dogmatic Marxism, and between the petty
bourgeoisie and existentialism, can one proceed to decipher the development
of Gurvitch's thought after 1945. From this perspective, one can see that Gurvitch's position vacillated during those years. He was primarily committed to a
value-free empiricism and defended this position with great vigor; it was the
main thrust of his sociology. His deep-seated voluntarism, however, pulled
him in the opposite direction. The chance of a revolution occurring just after
the war excited him tremendously, as his political writings from those years
testify.[75] Moreover, the impact of the struggle for hegemony caused Marxist
and existentialist themes to appear in his sociology too.

An awareness of the class struggle in France after the war is also necessary
in order for one to fully understand the central role Gurvitch played in French
social science during the years after the war. In Russia, Gurvitch had been too
young to be a major figure in university circles, and in France in the 1930's he
had remained second to the Durkheimians. In the United States, of course, he
was only a refugee scholar and never got a real footing in the academic hierarchy. But in post-war France, Gurvitch finally got his chance. Durkheimian
sociology had disappeared, leaving behind an ideological and institutional
vacuum, and Gurvitch came back to fill it. In 1945-46 Gurvitch was the main
animator behind the creation of a *Centre d'Etudes Sociologiques* in Paris
which replaced Bouglé's *Centre de Documentation Sociale*.[77] In 1946 Gurvitch
founded his own sociological magazine, *Cahiers Internationaux de Sociologie,*
France's only sociological magazine until the reappearance of *Année
Sociologique* in 1949.[78] The next year *Twentieth Century Sociology* appeared
in a French translation, and this work constituted the first introduction of
many French sociologists to North American sociology. In 1948 Gurvitch was
appointed to the chair in sociology at the Sorbonne,[79] which meant that he had
reached the pinnacle of France's hierarchical university system, and in 1950 he
started his own sociological book series, *Bibliothèque de Sociologie Contemporaine.*[80] In 1950 Gurvitch also published *La Vocation Actuelle de la
Sociologie,* which represented his attempt to give French sociology a new
theoretical direction. When Lucien Goldmann in 1952 and Armand Cuvillier
in 1953 sharply attacked French sociology, they singled out Gurvitch especially.[81] In short, during the post-war period Gurvitch was France's leading
sociologist.[82]

Nineteen forty-five might have been "year one in the Gurvitchean era," as
Georges Davy has put it, but toward the middle of the 1950's Gurvitch's star
was in decline.[83] Somewhere between 1955 and 1960, Goldmann says, a

"qualitative transformation" took place in French philosophy and social science.[84] In 1958, when Gurvitch published his autobiographical sketch which has so often been quoted here, he described himself as "excluded from the horde" and noted with bitterness that he was rejected by both contemporary sociologists and philosophers.[85] Gurvitch had ultimately failed to fill the ideological vacuum left behind by the Durkheimians. He himself attributed this to his attempts to unite theory with empirical research and sociology with philosophy:

> French and American sociologists today consider me a philosopher who entered through the wrong door; and the "philosophers" think of me as a "traitor" who changed sides long ago.
>
> However, this painful, isolated position seems to me quite natural: my position implies the necessity of a close collaboration, not only between theory and empirical research, but between sociology and philosophy as well, both renouncing their dogmatism and imperialism . . . . It is only when this attitude . . . is accepted, that I keep the hope that I will cease to be banished from both clans.[86]

This explanation is not the reason why Gurvitch became unpopular in the 1950's; he came closer to the truth when he noted that "the rhythm of my thought has almost always been out of step with fashion."[87] In short, it was the way the class struggle developed in the mid-50's that made Gurvitch's influence diminish.

After the war Gurvitch continued to maintain a strict separation between values and facts, between his political thought and his sociological work.[88] A comparison between Gurvitch's post-war political writings and his post-war sociology reveals this separation. Besides *The Bill of Social Rights,* which was reissued in France in 1946 and which in many aspects belongs to a discussion of his post-war production, Gurvitch's post-war political writings consist of two articles published in 1946 in the left-wing Catholic magazine *Esprit.*[89] Two quite different kinds of class strategies are outlined in these articles, and this constitutes their most interesting aspect.

The first article, entitled "Representation of Labor and the Problem of Nationalizations," adds little to the ideas Gurvitch put forward in *The Bill of Social Rights.*[90] The article stated that the workers must be allowed to run the factories themselves rather than have control only over insignificant details. In the choice between "technocratic nationalizations" and "nationalizations with direct representation by labor," Gurvitch declared that France must choose the latter.[91]

Gurvitch also emphasized the importance of coordinating nationalizations with economic planning on a national level: "The planned economy, the
nationalized sector and industrial democracy must unite, inter-penetrate and
become one and the same thing."[92] The class strategy advocated by Gurvitch
in this article, as in *The Bill of Social Rights,* is characterized by reformistic illusions. The content — a self-managed economy — is radical enough, but the
means of achieving it, a constitution, is a form of juristic socialism. Gurvitch
hoped to vote in self-management and to vote out capitalism.[93] This was a
naive idea which, however, was not without popularity in the circles of the
radicalized petty bourgeoisie. Especially the group around Emmanuel
Mounier at *Espirit* held similar ideas and had, throughout the war, discussed
what the new Declaration of Rights should look like.[94] *Temps Modernes,* on
the other hand, brushed aside the notion of a "revolution by law" as totally
meaningless.[95] A constitution must come after a revolution, not before, they
argued. The Communist Party realized, of course, that the establishment of
socialism was not going to be decided by the constituent assembly. To expect
socialist institutions without a revolution would be "absurd," Fajon said in his
discussion on the constitution in *Cahiers du Communisme* in 1945.[96]
Bourgeois politicians were in full agreement with the communists on this
point.[97] They happily wrote promises of workers' control, no unemployment,
and expropriation of all monopolies into the constitution of the Fourth
Republic, knowing well that it meant nothing.[98]

Gurvitch's second article on the political situation in 1946, entitled
"Toward the Unity of Labor," articulated a more realistic class strategy for the
working class. In the article, Gurvitch warned that the workers were letting the
revolutionary momentum slip out of their hands. To prevent this, he argued,
the Socialist Party and the Communist Party must unite into one strong working class party. The various ideological and organizational differences between the two parties did not constitute unsurpassable obstacles in his mind.
The new tone that Gurvitch revealed in this article is especially noticeable in his
discussion of the ideological differences between the Socialist Party and the
Communist Party. Communism, Gurvitch wrote, is usually seen as a collectivism which crushes the individual, while socialism is credited with seeking a
synthesis of Marx and Proudhon, of collectivism and individualism, and so
on. This view, Gurvitch argued, exaggerates the differences between the two
doctrines. Lenin, for instance, had stressed the voluntaristic and anti-statist
sides of Marx, and the communists were ultimately against a centralized state.
In short, Gurvitch had begun to reevaluate communism and to take a more
realistic view of the political situation:

The French working class and the political parties that represent it
must realize: *It is now or never.* If the unity of the working class is

not produced very quickly, the Socialist Party as well as the Communist Party will inevitably face a defeat, leaving France empty
and without hope.[99]

When one compares Gurvitch's post-war sociology with his political
writings, one is struck by the disparity between the two. Politically, Gurvitch
was convinced that workers' self-management must be instituted and that the
fate of France would stand or fall with the unity of the working class.
However, in Gurvitch's giant sociological work of the period, *La Vocation
Actuelle de la Sociologie* (1950), the working class and workers' self-
management play no role whatsoever. In his political writings, Gurvitch felt
free to express his own value judgments, but in his sociology he felt restricted
to "judgments of facts." Indeed, one could characterize Gurvitch as radical in
his politics and "value-free" in his sociology. But this characterization would
be too simplistic. The class struggle was as present in Gurvitch's sociology as in
his political writings, but it was more "masked," as Merleau-Ponty put it. Gurvitch's sociology was the outcome of two opposing forces. The first — the
dominant one — was classical bourgeois sociology which Gurvitch had adopted
in the 1930's from Weber and Durkheim and which was reinforced during his
stay in the United States. The second was connected with Gurvitch's voluntarism and with his faith in socialism which made him take up some of the
problems that the Marxists and the existentialists were wrestling with just after
the war. The combined result of the two forces in Gurvitch represents his position in the struggle for hegemony in post-war France.

As we know, the basic tendency in Gurvitch's sociology was to maintain a
strict separation between values and facts and to adhere to the bourgeois concept of objectivity. "No one would contest today," Gurvitch wrote in *Vocation,* "that every normative tendency must be extirpated from sociological
work, as Lévy-Bruhl demonstrated [in *La Morale et la Science des Moeurs* in
1902], and that one must definitely renounce all hope of being able to know
and prescribe at the same time."[100] The sociologist must under no circumstances interfere with the facts which could be approached only from the
outside in a "hyper-empirical" and "super-relativistic" way, that is, without
any dogmatism whatsoever.[101] Gurvitch considered that sociology was on its
way to becoming a "positive and empirical science," and no preconceived
philosophical notions must stand in the way of its development. [102] This,
however, did not mean that sociology could dispense with philosophy. On the
contrary , Gurvitch advocated a close collaboration between philosophy and
sociology. The division of labor between the two was to be the following:
sociology would furnish the material and philosophy would validate it. Once
"positive knowledge" was acquired, it could be applied in a way similar to that
outlined by Lévy-Bruhl in 1902.

The impact of North American Sociology on Gurvitch's own post-war sociology was very strong. The three-page preface to *Twentieth Century Sociology* was, for instance, expanded into a thirty-page chapter in *Vocation* called "The False Problems of Nineteenth Century Sociology."[103] In this chapter, Gurvitch elaborated on already familiar themes, that sociology must have nothing to do with philosophy of history, that there are no predominant factors in social life, and so on. At the end of this onslaught on "nineteenth century sociology," Gurvitch raised the following important questions:

> Twentieth century sociology consequently no longer proposes to solve: 1. the problem of the fate of mankind; 2. the problem of order and progress; 3. the problem of the conflict between the individual and society; 4. the problem of the opposition between the psychic and the social; 5. the problem of predominant factors; 6. the problem, finally, of sociological laws. Under these circumstances, what remains for sociology to do? Should it yield to a more fruitful human science which could preside more effectively over the cooperation between the social sciences and their integration into a coherent ensemble?
>
> It would be a mistake to draw that conclusion. Twentieth century sociology is giving up all these problems, which have been fruitless, dogmatic and poorly posed. Instead it is gathering considerable strength and is renewing itself just by passing through this crisis. It is polishing and revising its conceptual model, its method and its techniques. Thus, it will reach its final maturity. The first phase of this process consists of the development of depth-sociology.[104]

Having established that sociology must take no partisan stand, Gurvitch drew the logical conclusion that a sociological system must be developed which tries to capture all social reality, past and present. The result was that Gurvitch proposed an enormously complicated system, by necessity very abstract. Gurvitch had earlier, in *Essais de Sociologie* (1938) and in *Sociology of Law* (1942), presented the first outlines of this system, but *Vocation* represented the first effort to put the whole system together.

The main principle in Gurvitch's complete system remained the same as in the earlier models — social reality was conceptualized as having a vertical and a horizontal dimension. The former consisted of depth layers, the latter, of the three main sociological types: forms of sociality, groups, and global societies. Whereas Gurvitch, in *Sociology of Law,* had distinguished eight different depth layers, he now found ten:[105]

The Morphological and Ecological Surface (I)
Social Organizations or Organized Superstructures (II)
Social Patterns (III)
Collective Behavior of a Certain Regularity
Outside of Organizations (IV)
Webs of Social Roles (V)
Collective Attitudes (VI)
Social Symbols (VII)
Effervescent, Innovating and Creative Collective Behavior (VIII)
Collective Values and Ideas (IX)
Collective Psychic Acts and Mental States (X)

The number of levels, Gurvitch argued, was heuristic, and the levels were arranged in order of accessibility to the researcher. Level I was the easiest to study, while Level X demanded the most sophisticated techniques. The two new levels, "Webs of Social Roles (V)" and "Collective Attitudes (VI)," were inspired by Gurvitch's exposure to North American sociology.[106] Neither of these two new levels changed Gurvitch's system; they simply incorporated some of the new developments of sociology into it. Together, all the levels constituted what Gurvitch, following Mauss, called "the total social phenomenon." Some of the specialized social sciences might concentrate on just one level as their object of study, Gurvitch said, but sociology had to study them all.

The horizontal dimension of Gurvitch's system consisted of forms of sociality, groups, and global societies. Each of these had its own depth-layers and each constituted a "total social phenomenon." "Ontologically," Gurvitch argued, global societies had precedence.[107] This meant that forms of sociality and groups must always be incorporated and understood within the context of a global society. From a methodological point of view, however, it was suitable to start with the forms of sociality because they represented the most elementary parts of social reality. This aspect was a repetition of his analysis in *Essais de Sociologie,* which outlined the complicated scheme of criss-crossing forms of sociality. Some new parts to his microsociology, however, were also added in *Vocation.*

The main novelty in the section on forms of sociality was Gurvitch's use of sociometric methods to verify his microsociology and to give it an experimental basis.[108] Gurvitch was especially eager to prove that the "we" really existed, and sociometry seemed to be able to help him do this. In *Vocation,* he outlined a couple of experimental methods designed to bring out the latent "we's" in a group and to measure the intensity and pressure of the "we's."

Vocation also contained an elaborate taxonomy of groups. In *Sociology of Law,* Gurvitch had defined groups according to seven criteria (scope, duration, function, attitude, ruling organizational principle, form of constraint, and degree of unity).[109] Gurvitch now added eight more: size, time rhythm, degree of dispersion, basis of foundation, mode of admission, degree of externalization, degree of penetration by the global society, and degree of compatability between groups.[110] Gurvitch also included a short section on social classes, a topic to which he had paid little attention earlier.[111] Classes, he argued, first appeared with capitalism. They were groups of "great importance" and were defined in accordance with Gurvitch's typology as:

> *a group that is (1) supra-functional; (2) extended in nature; (3) permanent; (4) dispersed; (5) de facto; (6) open; (7) unorganized but structured (except when it is in formation); (8) divisive; (9) normally resistant to the penetration by the global society; (10) radically incompatible with other classes; (11) without unconditional constraint.*[112]

After the section on groups, the reader would expect to find a discussion of global societies, especially since they were "ontologically prior" to forms of sociality and groups. However, such a discussion does not appear. Gurvitch's manuscript broke off at this point, containing only some vague allusions to the effect that different criteria might be used to construct a typology of global societies. This omission, as Gurvitch himself admitted, is a serious defect of *Vocation.*[113]

How formalistic and technocratic Gurvitch's sociology was at this stage of its development is also clearly revealed in an article entitled "A Sociological Analysis of International Tensions," which Gurvitch presented to a group of UNESCO scholars in 1948.[114] Sticking to the dictum that "It is . . . not the task of scientists to console but to describe reality as we see it," Gurvitch outlined all the major types of tensions in existence: tensions between different strata of reality, between different forms of sociality, within groups, between groups, and between nations. International tensions, Gurvitch claimed, were mainly due to misunderstandings; they were artificial and often exploited by warmongers. However, Gurvitch conceded that there were "certain factors" which could create colonial, economic, and other types of conflicts. He also outlined how one might reduce international tensions. Since they were basically artificial, he argued, it was a fairly easy task to reduce them, but the means would vary according to the type of society, the historical period, and so on. Gurvitch's proposal to improve international relations centered around cultural exchange, information to counteract chauvinistic propaganda, and the establishment of an "International Economic Planning Board." The last proposal, Gurvitch said, perhaps belonged to the future.

Gurvitch's analysis of international tensions, like the main thrust of *Vocation*, was formalistic and ahistorical. The other social scientists who participated in the UNESCO meeting had no difficulty pointing out its weaknesses. Alexander Szalai, a Hungarian sociologist, noted:

> Very few wars, if any, have been "founded" on misunderstandings, or false information. It is a dangerous and misleading illusion to think that imperialistic wars are caused by such psychological factors. What about oil fields, markets, colonies?[115]

On the question of an International Economic Planning Board, Szalai said:

> No International Economic Planning Board is conceivable for capitalistic and socialist countries. There is an inherent anarchy in capitalist production which cannot be changed by international planning, nor even by an "international managerial revolution." Gurvitch is therefore right: an International Economic Planning Board belongs to the future — to the future of Socialism.[116]

Max Horkheimer made a more subtle critique of Gurvitch's analysis, focusing on "the methodological problem."[117] Gurvitch, Horkheimer said, seems to think that "it is the exclusive task of sociology to describe and classify." Gurvitch, he continued, "tried to survey all the possible sources of social tensions in general" instead of dealing with "the tasks which society faces at a given time." Horkheimer summed up his critique of Gurvitch's methodology in the following words:

> In seeking to avoid every possible dogmatism, psychological and political, [Gurvitch] seems to renounce all general or specific explanations of contemporary chauvinism and to content himself with providing conceptual elements which might function in a possible theoretical or practical attempt. The aggressor and the victim can equally make use of them.[118]

The main tendency in Gurvitch's post-war work was indeed technocratic; it was a sociology which the "aggressor and the victim could equally use," as Horkheimer put it. But there was also another side to Gurvitch's sociology. This second tendency, suppressed but nonetheless present, can be seen in Gurvitch's attempt to break the hegemony of bourgeois thought on the level of social science. It is behind the emphasis on conflict and spontaneity in *Vocation* and in the existentialist and Marxist themes that began to appear in Gurvitch's work during 1945-1952, and it is most clearly expressed in Gurvitch's analysis of technocracy in 1948.

Gurvitch's opposition to technocratic sociology is most visible in the emphasis he placed on spontaneity and creativity in *Vocation*. He impatiently attacked North American sociologists for their excessive concern with social order. "Actually," Gurvitch argued, "one can say that in each society and in each particular group, in every moment of their existence, a pointed drama is taking place between the forces of conservation and the forces of innovation or more directly between a permanent revolution and a no less permanent counter-revolution."[119] Gurvitch stressed that social life was filled with conflicts, surprises, and unpredictable events. There was a "quasi-infinitude" of forms of sociality and groups, and no one could predict exactly what was going to happen in society.[120] In a manner reminiscent of Durkheim, Gurvitch stressed the importance of "collective effervescence" in social life:

> The important and decisive role that this type of behavior plays in specific social conjunctures and in precise historical moments is beyond discussion. Examples are social and political revolutions, the great epochs of reforms, the great religious upheavals, civil wars and international wars, migrations, the discovery of new continents and their colonialization. In all these great social movements, collective behavior takes place in unknown milieus and in unknown conjunctures; they orient themselves in totally new directions and adjust to *unknown situations* which are completely unforeseen and in which old patterns and symbols are no longer of any guiding help since they are in a state of total confusion. Then suddenly there emerges the depth level of innovation and collective spontaneous creation which takes precedence over the other levels of social reality . . . .[121]

The limits of this glorification of spontaneity are evident. First, oppression is as spontaneous as liberty; that all spontaneity is positive is a libertarian myth. Second, granted that the concept of spontaneity always signals a certain opposition to the *status quo,* it is nonetheless of little help in making a concrete analysis of oppression.

The influence of existentialism on Gurvitch was helpful in that it inspired him to analyze the obstacles to freedom more clearly and to therefore go beyond a mere hymn to spontaneity. Indeed, one of the existentialists' main concerns was to decide under what conditions people can become free, and this led them to articulate very clearly the problem of freedom versus determinism. Gurvitch had been fascinated by this problem for a long time, and he now began to work seriously with it.[122] In 1951 he published an article called "The Degrees of Freedom" in which he outlined different degrees of freedom: the freedom to choose between alternatives, the freedom to create a totally new situation, and so on.[123] How close Gurvitch was in spirit to the existentialists can be seen from his definition of freedom as *"the victory of man . . . over his own determinism."*[124] Existentialism, on the whole, had a sobering effect on Gurvitch by leading him to analyze more closely the conditions under which human freedom becomes possible. However, it could not provide him with the conceptual apparatus needed for this difficult task.

Marxism, on the other hand, did have the potential to furnish the conceptual tools for an analysis of freedom. Gurvitch, as indicated by the section on social classes in *Vocation,* also showed a renewed interest in Marx after the war. In 1948, to celebrate the centennial of the *Manifesto,* Gurvitch devoted a number of *Cahiers Internationaux de Sociologie* to Marx and contributed an article on "The Sociology of Young Marx."[125] What especially attracted Gurvitch to young Marx was the latter's implacable critique of Hegel's determinism. Gurvitch sharply rejected the later works by Marx, which he found to be too deterministic and economic in nature. He also accused Marx of confusing value judgments with judgments of reality and of not being sufficiently relativistic. Economy, Gurvitch argued, might be important but did not constitute the key to everything, especially not to all types of society. Gurvitch's reading of Marx was consequently quite limited. He counter-posed the young humanistic Marx with the economically oriented Marx of *Capital* and *The Critique of Political Economy* in a manner which cut him off from some of the most important parts of Marxism. Like the existentialists, Gurvitch reacted violently against the type of Marxism that the French Communist Party stood for (Lefebvre excepted), and he extended his dislike to Marx's later works.

Gurvitch's most successful attempt to merge his political analysis with his scientific analysis — "values" and "facts" — can be found in his contribution to a seminar on "Industrialization and Technocracy" which he organized at *Centre d'Etudes Sociologiques* in 1948.[126] The occasion was prompted by the appearance of a French edition of *The Managerial Revolution* by Burnham. Burnham's basic thesis was that a new class, "the managers," was in the process of taking over the world.[127] Gurvitch reacted strongly against Burnham's theory for two distinct reasons. First, Gurvitch was becoming increasingly convinced that the triumph of fascism would have been impossible without the support of the technocratic intelligentsia.[128] Since the technocrats had successfully survived the war, the danger of fascism was still very grave, Gurvitch argued. He wrote:

The advent of fascism, its partial success, its persistence after its military defeat are facts which have not been sufficiently studied in sociology. I think it is precisely the study of the techno-bureaucratic group that constitutes the beginning of a sociological understanding of what fascism was and what it still can become because the

danger of fascism is not at all eliminated, neither in the defeated
countries, nor in the victorious ones.[129]

The second reason for Gurvitch's passionate reaction against Burnham's book
was that technocracy was the very antithesis of everything Gurvitch believed
in—namely, freedom and workers' self-management. The technocrat is, by
definition, someone who knows better than the worker how to run things; the
technocrat is the expert who uses "competence" as a legitimation for despotism
in the factories.

Part of Gurvitch's presentation at the meeting in June 1948 was devoted
to a description of what exactly composed the "techno-bureaucratic class." According to Gurvitch, managers, officers, and engineers, were among the oc-
cupational categories that belonged to the technocracy. The main thrust of
Gurvitch's lecture, however, was on how the technocratic groups could be
prevented from forming a class and taking power. "I am willing," he exclaimed
in a discussion, ". . . to be the first to give my life so that this class will be
prevented from coming to power."[130] But—and this is an important question—who was speaking here, Gurvitch the scientist, or Gurvitch the politi-
cian? Weber, of course, would have said the latter.[131] Gurvitch himself would
have agreed with Weber, and in an embarrassed gesture, he later explained
that the question of how one could stop the technocrats belonged to the field
of "applied sociology."[132] Nevertheless, at one point Gurvitch's militance
made him forget his own distinction:

> To defeat machine guns you need machine guns, not sticks and
> stones. That is why the question of "structural reform" as they used
> to say in France before this war, the question of introducing new
> legal, political and social guarantees to fight the technocratic
> tendency, is so important. It is certainly not a problem that can be
> solved by abstract and unconvincing predictions such as the hope
> that the technicians will one by one join the proletariat or, earlier
> or later, life in the factories will become a dance on roses.[133]

In this section of his argument (which was later omitted when the article was
reprinted in *Vocation*), Gurvitch came very close to articulating the central
problem—the impossibility of sharply distinguishing between thought and
life, between fact and value.[134] Did he not raise here the idea of the "total
man" that Marx spoke of in his early works and to which Gurvitch himself felt
so attracted?[135]

In another passage, Gurvitch denounced the scientific neutrality that
Burnham used to legitimize his anti-democratic ideas:

Burnham says that the "democratic and constitutional factory," which Marx had already anticipated, has become absolutely unrealizable and impossible today due to the very development of technology. In Marx and Proudhon's days the workers would have been able to manage the factories themselves because then the machines and techniques were so easy that every worker could more or less learn to handle them. This is supposedly totally impossible in our day since the machines and the techniques have become enormously complex and efficient and present dangers to those who do not understand them. That is the reason why there must be an authoritarian regime in the factories today. These arguments are really striking in their childishness as well as in their dishonesty. It is clear that the workers can manage the factories themselves through a representative system, by electing those who have been prepared for their tasks and have the necessary credentials, for instance, administrators, technicians, engineers. . . .[136]

But Gurvitch did not take his analysis to its logical conclusion and confront the whole bourgeois ideology of scientific neutrality. Thus, Gurvitch did not succeed in raising the question of moral responsibility to the extent that the existentialists had done. Nevertheless, he clearly understood the crucial role that "organic intellectuals" play in monopoly capitalism with their moral indifference and technocratic ideals. By pointing a warning finger at these groups, he indeed succeeded in articulating an opposition to them.

When *Vocation* was published in 1950 it was met with strong criticism. Some people close to Gurvitch found only good qualities in it, but the majority of critics were negative.[137] The various reactions of the critics reflected their respective positions in the class struggle. The Communist Party, for instance, was extremely hostile to Gurvitch (cf. Fougeyrollas in *Nouvelle Critique*).[138] The radicalized segments of the petty bourgeoisie saw major flaws in Gurvitch's ideas, mainly relating to Gurvitch's notion of social science and values (cf. Sartre in *Temps Modernes,* Lapierre in *Esprit,* and Goldmann in *The Human Sciences & Philosophy).*[139] The liberal-academic intelligentsia felt that Gurvitch had failed to rejuvenate the French academic tradition (cf. Cuvillier in *Oú va la Sociologie Francaise?* and Braudel in *Annales).*[140] Gurvitch, in short, did not satisfy the exponents of any of the major strands in French social thought. The liberal thinkers approved of his academic endeavors but disapproved of his political ideas, while the radicals did just the opposite. It is therefore not surprising that by the late 1950's Gurvitch's reputation among French intellectuals was declining; the "rhythm of his thought" was indeed "out of step with fashion."

Fougeyrollas' criticism in *Nouvelle Critique* followed the Communist

Party line closely and was very dogmatic.[141] Fougeyrollas did not analyze
Gurvitch's sociology on its own terms but pressed it into the theoretical
perspective of the current leadership of the French Communist Party. Thus,
Vocation was conceived in terms of the Cold War between the U.S.S.R. and
the United States, and Gurvitch, like Burnham, Friedmann, and Moreno, was
placed in the imperialist camp. He was accused by Fougeyrollas of being passionately anti-Russian, of mentioning the works of the "traitor and spy"
Bukharin more favorably than those of Lenin and Stalin in his compilation
Twentieth Century Sociology, and so on. Fougeyrollas, however, did make
some pertinent remarks about Gurvitch's sociology. *Vocation,* he said, was
basically an idealistic work. Gurvitch's notion of society was more
psychological than materialistic, and he had replaced the mode of production
as the basis of society with depth-layers. Gurvitch's class concept, he continued, was poor, and he had assigned more importance to tensions between
different strata than to the class struggle in *Vocation.* That no classes existed
before capitalism was totally wrong in Fougeyrollas' opinion.

Cuvillier and Braudel approached *Vocation* mainly from an academic
perspective. To what extent, they asked, had Gurvitch contributed to the
French academic tradition?[142] Cuvillier was extremely critical of *Vocation* and
insisted that Gurvitch had not succeeded in replacing Durkheimian sociology
with a new creative approach. Cuvillier's critique centered on Gurvitch's formalism — the failure, as he put it, of *Vocation* to unite "facts" and "ideas." To
some extent Cuvillier was correct; *Vocation* is indeed a formalistic work.
There is, however, as distinct a link between "ideas" and "facts" in Gurvitch's
theory as in any sociological theory, and what Cuvillier most objected to was
the type of "facts" *Vocation* focused on. Gurvitch, Cuvillier claimed, inor-
dinately stressed conflicts in society and ignored the role of institutions, structures, and history.[143] In sum, what Cuvillier disliked in *Vocation* was Gurvitch's attempt to criticize the *status quo.* Cuvillier wanted all sociology to
elaborate on the stabilized sides of social reality in the detached and amoral
manner which had become so popular in "twentieth century sociology."

Braudel's critique of *Vocation,* though more sophisticated than
Cuvillier's, was essentially the same.[144] In Braudel's opinion, Gurvitch was
ahistorical because he gave priority to the spontaneous, unpredictable
elements in social reality. This went against the very grain of Braudel's own
theory which assigns dominance to "la longue durée" over "l'événementiel,"
that is, to the slow and unconscious development of society as opposed to the
conscious efforts of a minority to make history (be they kings, diplomats, or
revolutionaries).[145] In philosophical terms, Braudel and Cuvillier in effect accused Gurvitch of improperly reproducing the prevailing alienation in the
world (Hegel, Marx), and they both criticized Gurvitch's attempts, however
weak, to oppose this alienation.

Sartre and Goldmann took a very different approach to *Vocation*.[146] What they basically disliked about Gurvitch's work was its failure to contribute to a revolutionary science of society. Sartre's critique of Gurvitch was very brief — it covered only his class concept — but was very well aimed. Gurvitch, like several other scholars, had defined the working class in terms of its present state rather than its future state, Sartre said. The result, in Sartre's estimation, was a mechanistic class concept in which the present atomization of the working class was incorporated into the concept itself. Addressing Gurvitch and other thinkers, Sartre said:

> . . . your sociology is applicable to the worker only if misery has reduced him to despair. It is his resignation that your sociology reflects back to him, his passivity, his surrender. [147]

Goldmann's critique of Gurvitch was somewhat different from Sartre's.[148] Gurvitch's sociology, Goldmann claimed, illustrated the fact that "bourgeois thought in decline is incompatible with sociological theories which are able to capture human reality to some extent."[149] In Goldmann's opinion only a creative Marxism could approach reality with some success; the days of Weber and Durkheim, when bourgeois sociology still had something to say, were over. Goldmann tried to show how Gurvitch's incapacity to deal with history was caused by his attitude toward Marxism. That Gurvitch could describe Marx's thought as "one-sided," "eschatological," and so on, illustrated that he was unable to discuss Marx seriously, Goldmann felt. Goldmann also criticized Gurvitch's attempt to sharply separate the writings of young Marx from those of the more mature Marx as simplistic and detrimental to a correct understanding of Marxism. Like Sartre, Goldmann found Gurvitch's class concept to be very mechanistic. Gurvitch's eleven criteria of class, Goldmann said, were all "peripheral," and his exclusion of class consciousness and place in production from his definition of class led him to minimize the importance of classes in society. In short, Goldmann considered that *Vocation* in general, and Gurvitch's interpretation of Marx in particular, had little to offer.

In conclusion, Gurvitch's sociology between 1945-1952 was a failure in that it did not succeed in articulating the class strategy of any class or class fraction in a coherent and straightforward manner. To do this, Gurvitch would have had to locate the main problems of a particular class and then apply his sociological skill to articulate these problems. Instead, torn between his political ideal of a society run by the workers themselves and his desire to create an objective and "value-free" science, Gurvitch ended up in limbo; he created a sociology which simultaneously refused and accepted the *status quo*. During the rest of his life — Gurvitch died in 1965 — the contradiction between socialism and social science continued to be the main theme of his thought. The momentous turns that the class struggle took after 1952 intensified this contradiction and propelled Gurvitch's thought into new directions.

7 Sociology and Socialism (1953-1965)

During the last years of his life, Gurvitch's production was considerable.[1] He published a series of important works, such as *Déterminismes Sociaux et Liberté Humaine* (1955, 1963), *Traité de Sociologie* (1958-1960, 1963), *Dialectique et Sociologie* (1962), and *Les Cadres Sociaux de la Connaissance* (posthumously published in 1966).[2] These works, as well as the new and enlarged editions of *Vocation* (1957, 1963), were intended to complete Gurvitch's general system of sociology.[3] By 1957, the year in which the second edition of *Vocation* appeared, he had given his sociological system its final form. Gurvitch's work during 1953-1965, however, was not as homogenous as a cursory look might lead one to believe. It was actually characterized by an intensive struggle between two opposite tendencies in Gurvitch's mind: the desire to complete his sociological system from the 1930's and the discovery of the scientific possibilities of socialist thought. The latter tendency, though present in Gurvitch's major and more official publications from this period, came to its clearest expression in a series of courses Gurvitch taught at the Sorbonne and which appeared in mimeographed form: *Le Concept de Classes Sociales de Marx à Nos Jours* (1954), *Les Fondateurs Francais de la Sociologie Contemporaine: Saint-Simon et P. J. Proudhon* (1955), and *La Sociologie de Karl Marx* (1959).[4] In short, during the last period of Gurvitch's life, sociology and socialism directly confronted each other for the first time. This confrontation is the major theme of Gurvitch's last works, and it is also what makes them of special interest.

To what extent is one justified in using 1953 as the year which divides Gurvitch's post-war production into two periods? *Déterminismes Sociaux et Liberté Humaine* was published in 1955, but did Gurvitch not teach a course with the same title in 1949-1950?[5] And did he not devote a course to "Dialectics and Sociology" in 1951-1952 — that is ten years before the book of the same title appeared?[6] Indeed, a couple of Gurvitch's works which appeared in book form after 1953 had been first outlined several years before.

One can nevertheless talk of a distinct shift in Gurvitch's production during the last thirteen years of his life. Gurvitch's interest in Proudhon, for instance, was renewed during this time. He also devoted much time and thought to the question of dialectic and became increasingly interested in Marxism. In his autobiographical sketch of 1958 he emphasized his "new meeting with Marx" in the 1950's, and when he spoke about updating this article shortly before his death in 1965, he stressed his increased interest in Marx.[7] It would consequently be difficult to challenge the idea that Gurvitch's sociology shifted in emphasis during his last years.

The question as to the year of transition nevertheless remains. From what has already been said, it is obvious that there was no dramatic overnight change in Gurvitch's thought. However, there are some very good reasons for singling out Gurvitch's activities during 1953 in this context. During that year Gurvitch taught his very important course in social class at the Sorbonne, *Le Concept de Classes Sociales de Marx à Nos Jours.* He also published his famous article on the use of dialectics in sociology, "Hyper-Empirisme Dialectique." Finally, 1953 was also the year that Gurvitch rejected reformism.[8]

Gurvitch's interest in the 1950's and 1960's in the scientific possibilities of socialism, however, cannot be explained by just referring to a change in his intellectual tastes. One must look also at the class struggle in the 1950's in order to fully understand Gurvitch's works of this period. Nineteen fifty-three, in the Western world as well as in the socialist camp and the Third World, signalled a new epoch, and it is ultimately this turn of events that explains the new direction of Gurvitch's thought.

During the 1950's, capitalism seemed stronger than ever before. Perry Anderson has described the 1950's and 1960's as "the epoch of an unparalleled objective consolidation of capital throughout the world."[9] Henri Lefebvre has called the years from 1950 to 1970 the "idyllic period of world capitalism."[10] The working classes of the western world, especially the United States, seemed thoroughly integrated into capitalism, as did the growing petty bourgeoisie. The contradictions in western capitalism, however, were far from resolved, and the events in 1953 eloquently testify to this.

In the early 1950's, the United States' post-war effort to build up a successful international system of capitalism with itself as the leader collapsed. The United States lost the Korean war, failed to turn Europe into a giant market for U.S. products, and was unable to replace the European powers as an effective colonial master.[11] By 1953-1954, as the Kolkos argue in their excellent study, *The Limits of Power* (1972), the United States began to lose hegemony over the non-socialist countries. "The world," they write, "was too large, the number of local crises too numerous, for the United States to be able to regulate the affairs and fate of every nation."[12] Until then, however, the setbacks for U.S. capitalism were limited to areas outside the United States. It was not until the 1960's, with the escalation of the war in Vietnam, that the class struggle blaringly opened within North America itself.

Nineteen fifty-three also spelled the end of Soviet hegemony over the socialist camp. In March 1953, Stalin died, and within months there was a workers' uprising in Eastern Germany. In 1956, the new Soviet leadership criticized Stalinism ("the cult of the Individual") and the same year severe rebellions broke out in the People's Republics of Poland and Hungary. New types of socialism emerged in the Third World. Yugoslavia started to experiment with workers' self-management, and a growing tension developed between the People's Republic of China and the Soviet Union. All these developments contributed to discrediting the U.S.S.R. as the international leader of communism. By 1960, even those communist parties which supported the Soviet Union, such as the French Communist Party, did it by their own choice. In little more than a decade the communist movement had lost its center and developed in several different directions.

In France, the 1950's was a very prosperous decade, and it was during this decade that mass consumption really developed.[13] While the First Plan (1947-1952) had focused on building up the basic industries, the Second Plan (1954-1957) aimed more at raising the standard of living.[14] The tremendous role played by the state in economic planning spurred on the development of various technocratic groups in French society. Especially after 1958, with the accession of De Gaulle to power and the decline of parliamentary power, the technocrats got a free hand.[15]

The capitalist class in France, however, faced very serious problems in the 1950's. In 1954 France lost Vietnam, and the same year the Algerian revolution started. The Algerian civil war, which nearly caused a civil war to break out in France, did not end until 1962 and brought the fascist right into prominence. The French Communist Party closely followed the course of U.S.S.R. activities during 1954-1962, making Europe rather than the Third World its first priority.[16] As a result, it played a minor and passive role in the struggle against French colonial rule in Algeria. Moreover, the French Communist Party, as opposed to its Italian counterpart, chose to remain Stalinist even after the Twentieth Congress of CPSU (1956), and consequently saw many of its actual as well as potential allies withdraw to other parties or try to develop a new form of socialist party.[17] Thus, in France, as in the United States, capitalism was faced with serious problems during this period, although these were overshadowed by the general capitalist boom. There was, to conclude, a certain calm in Western society, but it was more apparent than real.

The ambiguous character of capitalism in the 1950's — its apparent success combined with its loss of mastery over the world — was expressed with varying degrees of consciousness in the different capitalist countries. In the United States, whose influence on post-war France was tremendous, the hegemony of bourgeois thought remained more or less intact until the 1960's. North American sociology, with a few notable exceptions, continued to be mainly empirical and conformist in nature. In sociology, the conformist tendencies continued to find their most sophisticated expression in structural-functionalism. The main thrust of this ideology, to repeat, was the depiction of society as a unit which regulates itself without conscious intervention by the masses. Attempts to radically change society were seen as disturbances to the system and quite illusory ("the end of ideology"). How strong the position of structural-functionalism was in the United States is evident in Kingsley Davis' presidential address in 1959 to the American Sociological Association.[18] Davis proclaimed all sociological theories to be aspects of functionalism, whether cognizant of it or not.

Lacking a strong socialist tradition, the opposition within U.S. sociology had great difficulties elaborating a powerful critique of society. The liberal-radical tradition was most coherently expressed in conflict theory, which emerged in the early 1960's.[19] Marxist social science first started to become a real force in North America in the late 1960's.[20]

In France, as has been stressed, the general situation was quite similar to that in the United States: capitalism was strong, but its strength was overrated. Social thought also developed in parallel directions. There was a conformist tendency, a liberal-radical opposition, and Marxism. In French sociology, however, the respective influence and development of these three types of thought were very different from that in the United States.

The intensity of the major currents of social thought in France and their internal relationship to each other was fundamentally tied to the position of the petty bourgeoisie. During the 1950's the petty bourgeoisie, especially its technocratic strata, became increasingly integrated into the capitalist system.[21] Positivism — including its most sophisticated expression, structuralism — and empirical sociology consequently predominated. The counter-movement within the petty bourgeoisie was situated mainly around the existentialists and the increasing number of intellectuals who left the Communist Party in the late 1950's. This small group of disparate thinkers tried during the late 1950's and early 1960's to develop a critical and non-dogmatic analysis of contemporary society. Its interest in and knowledge of Marxism was much deeper than that of its liberal-radical counterpart in the United States, and it is within this group that the first tentative meeting between sociology and Marxism took place.

Another group was the intellectuals who remained faithful to dogmatic Marxism. The Communist Party continued to be the main focus of interest for these intellectuals, and their hostility to empirical sociology remained very strong during this period. The class strategies of the three strands of social thought in France were as follows: conventional sociologists advocated a close collaboration between the petty bourgeoisie and the capitalist class; the critical sociologists tried to articulate an opposition within the petty bourgeoisie and establish contact with the working class; and the Communist Party ideologists continued to isolate the working class and progressive elements from each other in accordance with the dogmatic politics of the Thorez clique.

The grip that positivistic thought kept on Gurvitch's mind during his last years was directly related to its great success in France during the 1950's and 1960's. U.S. sociology continued to exercise a strong influence on the development of French sociology.[22] The old-fashioned, semi-philosophical studies of the Durkheimian School were disappearing totally. In their stead came a technocratic, positivistic sociology.[23] The institutionalization of French sociology continued, even if quite slowly.[24] Nevertheless, a new network of social science departments and research centers eventually came into existence.[25] The general need of capitalism for sociologists — by the bourgeois state as well as by private industry — also increased.[26] A new series of sociological magazines appeared, such as *Sociologie du Travail* (1959), *Revue Francaise de Sociologie* (1960), and *Archives Européenes de Sociologie* (1960), which began to rival *Cahiers Internationaux de Sociologie* and *l'Année Sociologique*.

Occasionally, the influence of U.S. sociology had a positive effect on the French intellectuals. The work of Georges Friedmann and his disciples especially reflects this.[27] More often than not, however, what was picked up by the French sociologists was a smattering of methods and the ideological tenets of U.S. sociology. Raymond Aron's work illustrates the impact of North American ideology on French social science. During the late 1950's Aron became one of the most influential figures in French sociology.[28] Aron worked mostly on a non-empirical level and attacked the existentialists and the Marxists in a continuous stream of books, the most famous of which remains *The Opium of the Intellectuals* (1955). He introduced several important phrases into French sociology, such as "the end of ideology" and "industrial society."[29] He questioned the usefulness of the class concept and presented a liberal version of the history of sociology in a famous lecture series at the Sorbonne in 1959-1960.[30] Aron characterized himself as an old-fashioned "incorrigible liberal" and worked for the conservative *Figaro*.[31]

The second major figure that emerged in French social science during the 1955-1960 period was Claude Lévi-Strauss.[32] Lévi-Strauss impatiently brushed existentialism aside ("shop-girl metaphysics") and elaborated a scientific theory centered on the concept of structure.[33] Undoubtedly, as many critics of structuralism have admitted, it is progressive to emphasize the notion of structure in social science.[34] Nevertheless, the structuralists (Lévi-Strauss, Foucault, Althusser, etc.) soon fashioned a scientific meta-theory out of their concept of structure which, in its own sophisticated way, was little more than "an ideology of the *status quo*" (Lefebvre).[35] The main thrust of structuralism was the depiction of society as an unconsciously evolving formation in which human beings cannot interfere.[36] Man's conscious activities were brushed aside as scientifically insignificant and superficial — mere "events" which could only be of interest to the defunct theory of historicism.[37] The anti-humanism of the structuralists was very strong: Althusser advocated that "the philosophical (theoretical) myth of man be reduced to ashes;"[38] Lévi-Strauss stressed that in social science the point is "not to construct, but to dissolve man;"[39] and Foucault prophesied the day when "man [will] be erased, like a face drawn in sand at the edge of the sea."[40] There were few novelties in structuralism as an ideology. Its counter-posing of "science" and "humanism," of "fact" and "value" was in full harmony with the main trend of bourgeois social science in the twentieth century. If one endorses Goldmann's useful definition of positivism ("positivism is not merely a small school, but underlies any claim of radical rupture between judgments of facts and value judgments"),[41] it becomes clear that structuralism was simply a form of neo-positivism. Structuralism indeed follows the old subject-object track and reduces the scientist to the role of detached observer. The social scientist stands on the side lines and watches human reality unfold before his/her eyes. Societies, in Lévi-Strauss' telling metaphor, become "machines for possible combinations."[42]

The most theoretically forceful opposition to positivism in French social science did not, as in the United States, come from within the ranks of sociology itself but from a rather heterogeneous group of neo-Marxists. Gurvitch had good contact with several of these thinkers — he was, for instance, a very close friend of both Henri Lefebvre and Jean Duvignaud — and many of his most important ideas during 1953-1965 were inspired by the revival of Marxism within this group.[43] These thinkers were either closely associated with the increasingly Marxist *Temps Modernes* (Jean-Paul Sartre, André Gorz, Lucien Goldmann, Serge Mallet) or had just left the French Communist Party (Henri Lefebvre, Jean Duvignaud, Edgar Morin, Annie Kriegel).[44] In addition to *Temps Modernes*, their articles could be found in the magazine *Arguments*.[45] The interest these thinkers showed in sociology was directly occasioned by the fact that official Marxism had become increasingly divorced from reality. As a result, Marxism had grown into an ideology which distorted rather than revealed reality. "When will it be understood," Sartre exploded in *Le Fantôme de Staline* (1956-1957), "that it is necessary to gather the facts before explaining them, that Marxist method allows figuring out experience but not suppressing it."[46] Referring to the ideologists of the French Communist Party, Sartre wrote that "Marx would have laughed at these pompous asses who take the class struggle for a Platonic idea or bring it in like a *Deus ex machina*."[47]

Official Marxism with its dogmatic conception of the laws of history and its insistence on the predominance of the infra-structure over the super-structure had, in its own way, deteriorated into positivism. Like functionalism or structuralism, it depicted society as an immense self-regulating system in which individuals could not intervene (unless the highest echelons in the party ordered it). Given this fact, it is not surprising that many of the major unorthodox Marxist works from this period centered on the question of dialectic: Merleau-Ponty, *Les Aventures de la Dialectique* (1955), Goldmann, *Le Dieu Caché* (1955) and *Recherches Dialectiques* (1959), Sartre, *Critique de la Raison Dialectique* (1960).[48] The main question in all these works is the relationship between the individual actors of history and the laws of history, i.e. the subject-object relation. Sartre, for instance, tried to analyze the connection between the individual and history in *Critique de la Raison Dialectique*. Goldmann and Merleau-Ponty revived in their respective works Lukács' profound discussion of the subject-object relation in *History and Class Consciousness*. They reaffirmed that people are part of the motions of history and not merely subjected to the external laws of history. Refuting the "dialectical mechanics" of official Marxism, Merleau-Ponty stressed that ". . . the passage of the subject into the object and the object into the subject is the driving force of dialectic."[49] Like Goldmann and Sartre, he also questioned the applicability of dialectic to the realm of nature. All of this criticism, of course, was against the line of the French Communist Party whose notion of dialectic was closer to that of Engels and Stalin than to that of Marx.

In view of their hostility to Marxist positivism, it was natural that many of the unorthodox Marxists would be very critical of structuralism. Lefebvre and Goldmann especially attacked structuralism.[50] Both men saw it as the ideology of an emerging "technocratic society" in which people assume no responsibilities whatsoever and where no human values exist. Against this type of society they posed the idea of a society with workers' self-management, a society run by workers' councils.[51] This rediscovery of workers' self-management within the circles of unorthodox Marxists in the early 1960's constitutes one of the most important achievements of post-war Marxist thought.[52] Gurvitch's influence in this area was not without significance.

Many of the most important Marxist works in the 1950's and the early 1960's were undoubtedly philosophical in nature.[53] However, several concrete studies of contemporary social reality were attempted. Among these works are Lefebvre's studies of the countryside, Mallet's analysis of the new working class, and Gorz' attempt to outline a new strategy for the working class under neo-capitalism.[54] In general, the unorthodox Marxists rejected the old Communist Party line that sociology constituted a "reformistic bourgeois science."[55] However, their attempt to outline "a sociology of Marx" did not mean that they considered Marx to be solely a sociologist. Lefebvre argued in *Sociologie de Marx* (1966) that "Marx is not a sociologist, but there is a sociology in Marx."[56] Goldmann, in his fine article, "Y a-t-il une Sociologie Marxiste?" (1957), claimed that in Marxism value judgments and judgments of reality are inseparable, and he rejected any attempts to revive Adler's old distinction between Marxist "sociology" and Marxist "ethics."[57]

During these years the French Communist Party made a few concessions to the anti-Stalinist trend, but on the whole it was firmly against any meeting between Marxism and sociology.[58] Not being a party member, Gurvitch was automatically rejected and called a bourgeois reformist.[59] Sartre, Goldmann and the other thinkers mentioned above, were, of course, unacceptable to a party which understood the political implications, for instance, of denying the dialectic of nature. Roger Garaudy, the foremost philosopher in the party after Lefebvre's suspension in 1958, was dogmatic and authoritarian. The revival of French Marxism, as Vranicki has stressed in his *Geschichte des Marxismus,* was achieved by thinkers who were critical of the French Communist Party, not by members of it.[60]

On political questions Gurvitch was very close to the neo-Marxists. Like them, he supported the Third World countries without reservations. He was very outspoken on the Algerian question, and when he signed an appeal against police brutality in *Temps Modernes* in 1961, his apartment was bombed by the right-wing OAS.[61] Shortly before his death on December 12, 1965, he took a revolutionary stand on the question of decolonialization. At the sixth meeting of *l'Association Internationale des Sociologues de Langue Francaise* which was devoted to the Third World, Gurvitch argued that "if one really wants to liquidate colonialism, there is only one way: social revolution."[62] Evoking Fanon, he stated that former colonies as well as the countries that had exploited them needed first and foremost a social revolution.[63]

Like the neo-Marxists, Gurvitch also welcomed the de-Stalinization of the U.S.S.R. His emotional reaction to the 22nd Congress of CPSU was very strong. In a letter to Jean Duvignaud, Gurvitch wrote that he wept for joy when he listened to Khrushchev's speech about the democratization of the U.S.S.R.[64] In general, Gurvitch reevaluated his attitude to the Soviet Union during his last years and took a more radical stance toward it.[65] Before the war Gurvitch had a tendency to equate fascism with authoritarian socialism but no more.[66] He maintained nevertheless that a "new humanism" was necessary in the Soviet Union and that the only way for this humanism to come about was through workers' self-management.[67]

Of Gurvitch's political writings from 1953-1965, the most important ones are those that deal with workers' self-management.[68] The reason for this is that during his last years, Gurvitch, for the first time since the Russian Revolution, unequivocally supported revolution rather than reformism. In 1953, in the Catholic left-wing magazine *Esprit,* Gurvitch wrote an important article entitled, "Les Voies de la Démocratisation Industrielle."[69] Refuting what he now called "the positions that today seem mistaken [in *The Bill of Social Rights*]," Gurvitch attacked reformism and stated that "*Industrial democracy must be revolutionary or it will not exist at all.*"[70] Any form of self-management within capitalism was doomed to fail, Gurvitch argued. The bourgeois state and the general pressure of the capitalist system were too strong for industrial democracy to survive in any other form than as a parody of itself. For workers' control to exist, there had to be a revolution: ". . . industrial democracy cannot come into existence without a social revolution."[71]

In socialist societies, Gurvitch argued, the situation was different. Here Gurvitch envisioned three different ways in which workers' self-management could come into existence. It could spontaneously spring up in a revolution as it did in Russia in 1917. This event, according to Gurvitch, would be the most favorable to the success of self-management. The second alternative could be that a newly established socialist government would create a system of workers' councils. Gurvitch was quite skeptical about this possibility, arguing that few governments would give up power once they had acquired it. The last possibility would be that an old, authoritarian socialist society would introduce self-management in stages. The U.S.S.R., for instance, might do this, Gurvitch argued.

Gurvitch often repeated during his last years that workers' self-management must be revolutionary. "Reformism," he wrote in one article, "has no chance. One has to dare to take radical measures."[72] He showed absolutely no interest in the co-opted versions of industrial democracy that were being experimented with in, for instance, Western Germany. He was more enthusiastic about the development in Yugoslavia, though he was not uncritical of it.[73]

The influence Gurvitch exerted on the neo-Marxists on the question of self-management was considerable. He had dealt with the problem for more than forty years, and they had only recently confronted it.[74] Henri Lefebvre, for instance, was very much influenced by Gurvitch's idea of decentralized socialism,[75] as was Jean Duvignaud.[76] Moreover, the first socialist magazine in Europe to be exclusively devoted to the question of workers' self-management, *Autogestion* (1966-), was originally Gurvitch's project.[77] Yvon Bourdet, the editor of the journal, has written in a letter that ". . . Gurvitch was the principal initiator of the journal *Autogestion* on which he unfortunately, because of his death, was unable to collaborate. Due to this fact Gurvitch does not occupy the place he deserves in the history of workers' self-management."[78]

Aside from self-management, the second major theme in Gurvitch's political writings from 1953-1965 was the technocratic society.[79] As Gurvitch saw it, capitalist society—and to some extent socialist societies like the U.S.S.R. —were moving toward a form of fascist technocracy. Several tendencies within modern capitalist society were working together to produce a tremendous threat to the whole of human civilization: "It is a question of life and death for tomorrow's society and civilization."[80] Only one method could stop this trend, Gurvitch argued, and that was to institutionalize self-management in every society.

Gurvitch's political vision—his forecast of a dangerous fascist-technocratic society which could only be averted by workers' self-management—has been said to "border on hysteria" (Daniel Bell).[81] To socialists, however, Gurvitch's thoughts about self-management and the dangers of technocracy do not seem so farfetched. In his last speech before his death, Gurvitch spoke of the necessity to unite the theories of Marx and Proudhon.[82] Only by omitting dogma from Marxism and synthesizing it with Proudhon's concern for workers' control, he argued, would it be possible to create "a new collectivism."[83] Many socialists would no doubt agree.

After looking at the important problems Gurvitch struggled with in his political writings during 1953-1965, it is disappointing to turn to his main sociological works of these years. Neither the complete version of *Vocation* (1957, 1963), nor *Déterminismes Sociaux et Liberté Humaine* (1955, 1963), nor *Cadres Sociaux de la Connaissance* (published posthumously in 1966) focuses on politically relevant questions. Instead one finds Gurvitch's sociological system in its final and very cumbersome form: fourteen "global societies," ten "depth layers," an infinite number of "manifestations of sociality," and so on. With the concept of "global society," which was first developed in *Déterminismes Sociaux* (1955) and then introduced into the second edition of *Vocation* (1957), Gurvitch now completed his sociological system.

Gurvitch has often been accused of formalism, of expounding "grand theory," and of writing in a style difficult to understand ("Write humanly," Braudel once implored him).[84] Looking at his sociological system in its final form, this criticism is well-founded. He has also been called a "sociological Linnaeus," and he has been reproached for his "love for classifications."[85] All these comments are valid, but they explain very little. Gurvitch was indeed a passionately systematic thinker, but this fact does not account for his development of such a gigantic sociological system. The salient fact is rather that Gurvitch's sociology grew out of the radical separation between value judgments and judgments of reality which came to characterize bourgeois thought beginning at the turn of the century. This separation between subject and object began to be questioned by some Marxist thinkers in France during the 1950's and 1960's. The main trend in the social sciences, however, leaned heavily toward positivism, and Gurvitch's sociology was no exception. A reviewer once described Gurvitch's sociology as "uncommitted sociology," and that is more to the point:[86] the sociologist stands aside, establishes an "objective" distance to reality and turns him/herself into an "absolute spectator" (Merleau-Ponty).[87] This detached position no doubt makes it very tempting for the sociologist to reduce social reality to a few formal elements which, like the pieces in a child's kaleidoscope, can be rearranged to fit different epochs and societies. This is what Gurvitch did and in this he was not alone. Lévi-Strauss and Gurvitch, for instance, are known for their intense dislike of each other's ideas. Gurvitch's antipathy for Parsons is also common knowledge.[88] All three thinkers, however, share one very fundamental trait — they embrace positivism and drive it to its ultimate logical conclusion.[89] Parsons with his attempt to classify every "social action," Lévi-Strauss with his conception of societies as "machines for possible combinations," and Gurvitch with his interminable classifications of "global societies," "classes," "particular groups," and "manifestations of sociality" — all three thinkers, each in his own way, have reached the limit of "uncommitted sociology."

The main theme of Gurvitch's sociological work during his last years was consequently "neo-positivism" (Sartre).[90] Sociology, as Gurvitch saw it, was a neutral tool that anyone could use: "One can apply sociological analyses equally well to plans that benefit trusts and cartels as to plans of the Soviet-type or even to plans for workers' self-management — as is done, for instance, in Yugoslavia and to an extent also in the Nordic countries."[91] Gurvitch's classification of global societies, which completed his sociological system, was indeed conceived in this spirit. According to his design there were fourteen global societies, four of which were called "archaic" and the rest "historical."[92] Historical global societies were said to be "Promethean" since people could consciously intervene in these. Historical global societies were classified as follows: "Theocratic Charismatic Societies," "Patriarchal Societies," "City-States in the Process of Becoming Empires," "Feudal Societies," "Nascent Capitalist Societies," "Democratic-Liberal Societies," "The Managerial Society of Organized Capitalism," "Fascist Techno-Bureaucratic Society," "Centralized State Collectivism," and "Decentralized Pluralist Collectivism."[93] In the four archaic societies, on the other hand, no intervention was possible. These societies were classified as: "Tribes with Mainly a Clan Basis," "Tribes Incorporating Varied and Relatively Unhierarchical Groups," "Tribes Organized on the Basis of Military Division, Domestic and Conjugal Families, and Clans," and "Organized Monarchic Tribes, Which Partly Retain Clan Divisions."[94] A global society was not defined by various forms of human activity as in *Sociology of Law* (1942) but by the precarious equilibrium between the many hierarchies that constituted its "structure": "(1) the hierarchy of groups; (2) the probable combination of forms of sociality; (3) the tendency toward accentuation of certain depth levels; (4) the stratification of modes of division of labor and accumulation of goods; (5) the hierarchy of social regulation or social controls; (6) the system of cultural works, and (7) the scale of social times."[95]

Braudel greeted Gurvitch's concept of "global society" with open arms, but it was also criticized.[96] Why, it was asked, did Gurvitch divide capitalist society into several "global societies"? This and other similar criticisms are quite justified. On the whole, it can be said that the strength of Gurvitch's classification lies mainly in its flexibility; its weakness lies in its lack of a firm basis, like "mode of production," in Marxism.

Gurvitch also gave his sociological system its final touches during these years by establishing the exact relations between sociology and the other social sciences, especially history and philosophy.[97] History, Gurvitch argued, could furnish sociology with indispensable material and with good explanations; sociology, in its turn, could help history through its typologies and its sensitivity to ideological distortions. Philosophy, Gurvitch argued, was needed to verify what constituted law, morality, and so on; sociology was needed to furnish philosophy with concrete material and to make it less dogmatic.

Gurvitch's sociological system was more or less completed by 1955, the year when *Déterminismes Sociaux et Liberté Humaine* was published. The system had the following structure: "vertically," there were the ten depth layers, and "horizontally," there were manifestations of sociality, groups, classes and global societies. After 1955, in a series of works, Gurvitch applied this system to various topics such as knowledge, time, space, determinism, law, and morality.[98] The main idea behind these applications is quite simple. If one considers the concept of time, for instance, one can postulate that there is a different kind of time in each form of sociality, group, class, global society, and depth level. This is exactly how Gurvitch proceeded in his *La Multiplicité des Temps Sociaux,* with one major modification.[99] First, he developed a typology of different times and then assumed a relationship between each type of time and every link in the social system. In the case of time, Gurvitch came up with a typology of eight different categories: "1. Enduring Time (time of slowed-down long duration); 2. Deceptive Time (where under an apparent calm, sharp crises produce a time of surprise); 3. Erratic Time (time of irregular pulsation between the appearance and disappearance of rhythms, the time of uncertainty); 4. Cyclical Time (in which past, present and future turn in a circle); 5. Retarded Time (which is too long awaited); 6. Alternating Time (time alternating between delay and advance); 7. Time Pushing Forward (which makes the future actually present); 8. Explosive Time (explosive time of creation)."[100]

Gurvitch proceeded in a similar manner with many other topics. For instance, he distinguished between eight different "genres" of moral life: "1. Traditional morality; 2. Finalist, specifically Utilitarian, morality; 3. Morality of virtues; 4. Morality of judgments afterwards (blame or encouragement); 5. Imperative morality; 6. Morality of ideal and symbolic images; 7. Morality of aspiration; 8. Morality of action and creation."[101] In his book, *Déterminismes Sociaux,* Gurvitch also outlined determinisms for each part in his system. Different "unidimensional social determinisms" answered to the different depth levels, and "social micro-determinisms" answered to the various forms of sociality.[102] Classes and groups had their "partial sociological determinisms" and global societies had their "global sociological determinisms."[103] To explain something sociologically, according to Gurvitch, meant primarily to integrate the form of sociality into a group, the group into a class, the class into a global society, and the global society into a specific historical conjuncture.[104]

Gurvitch's most elaborate attempt to apply his sociological system is the work that truly constitutes his sociological *summa: Les Cadres Sociaux de la Connaissance.* This work clearly shows the weaknesses and strengths of Gurvitch's system. The book consists of four sections, "Microsociology of Knowledge," "Particular Groups as Social Frameworks of Knowledge," "Social Classes and Their Cognitive Systems," and "Types of Global Societies and Their Cognitive Systems."[105] Within each of these four "frameworks of knowledge," Gurvitch distinguishes seven types of knowledge: "the perceptual knowledge of the external world," "knowledge of the Other, the We, etc.," "common sense knowledge," "technical knowledge," "political knowledge," "scientific knowledge," and "philosophical knowledge."[106] Within each of these seven "types" of knowledge there are five dichotomies of "forms" of knowledge which can be differently accentuated: mystical vs. rational knowledge; empirical vs. conceptual knowledge; positive vs. speculative knowledge; symbolic vs. concrete knowledge; and collective vs. individual knowledge.[107] Gurvitch's sociology of knowledge, in brief, became a kind of "sociology of all knowledge." The areas he tried to cover were, by the very logic of his system, immense, and the result was often meager. To take just one example, what Gurvitch says about the cognitive system of "Tribes with Mainly a Clan Basis" is of little help in understanding this type of society.[108] On the other hand, Gurvitch's method also made him formulate some interesting topics, such as "The Bourgeois Class and Its Cognitive System" and "Factories and Knowledge."[109]

The impact of Gurvitch's system of sociology on French social science has been practically nil. Even the thinkers closest to Gurvitch have rejected his basic system and, at the most, have used only selected parts of it. One of Gurvitch's students has described his sociology as a "gold-mine," and it is indeed true that Gurvitch's work is filled with ideas.[110] On the whole, however, Gurvitch's sociological system is awkward and permeated with the most conventional kind of positivism.

Despite the fact that the main thrust of Gurvitch's sociology was positivistic, he showed little affinity for Western sociology in the 1950's and 1960's. As a matter of fact, during his last years he became increasingly hostile to the prevalent type of sociology in the United States and in France. Though after the war and in the early 1950's he had advocated collaboration between French and North American sociology,[111] he now started attacking the latter.[112] Empiricism, he claimed, did not advance science. It amassed mountains of facts but lacked a theory which could give meaning to them. Part of the reason for this, Gurvitch claimed, was the contempt for philosophy that characterized empiricism.[113] Ignorance of philosophy, as Gurvitch saw it, seemed a prerequisite for acceptance as a good empirical sociologist. The major reason for the failure of contemporary sociology in Gurvitch's mind, however, could be found in the general trend toward technocracy in the capitalist countries. Sociology, Gurvitch argued, was very much a part of this development. In article after article, he denounced "technocratic sociologists" with their "quantophrenia" and "testomania."[114] Capitalism, he argued, was pleased with the "alibis" with which the technocratic type of sociologist could furnish it:

> . . . employers' organizations and the bureaucracies are well aware of the profits they can get from the 'competence' or rather 'incompetence' of their 'sociological experts': these serve as alibi and justification for the camouflaged but still very violent forms of exploitation that the workers, the white collar and the consumers tend to be exposed to by their employers in the ever sharper class struggle and in society in general. Thus, instead of trying to *explain* technocracy sociologically, the sociologists who view themselves as empiricists, turn themselves into *technocrats,* into technocratic clowns if I may say so, into technocrats to parade around and make fun of – if one compares them to technocrats whose competence is based on the natural sciences (as in the case of nuclear arms experts and experts on nuclear physics). In the meantime, no sufficient explanations have been given of the most striking phenomena of our time: fascism, technocracy, and the triumph of social revolution in countries with a very small working class population: first of all in Russia, but also in China and in the whole of Asia and today perhaps also in Africa. . . .[115]

Gurvitch's dislike for conventional sociology was also revealed in his effort to launch an association for French-speaking sociologists. Together with his friend Henri Janne, a Belgian sociologist, Gurvitch founded *l'Association Internationale des Sociologues de Langue Francaise* in 1958 to counteract the predominance of Anglo-Saxon sociology.[116] This association, in which Gurvitch participated actively until just before his death, devoted its meetings to such topics as the Third World, industrial democracy, and social class.[117]

Certain counter-tendencies to positivism also existed within Gurvitch's own sociological system. These came to their fullest expression, as in the immediate post-war years, in Gurvitch's exaltation of spontaneity and in his attempt to construct a "sociology of freedom."[118] During his last years, Gurvitch actually increased his emphasis on spontaneity in social life. According to the second edition of *Vocation* (1957), sociological method is not only characterized by the notions of totality and typology as in the earlier edition (1950), but also by its stress on discontinuity.[119] Sociology, as opposed to history, emphasizes the discontinuous sides of social life.[120] The second edition of *Vocation* also stated that the "total social phenomenon" represented "the vulcanic element in social reality" and was the fullest expression of *"social vitalism."*[121] In most of Gurvitch's works of these years, one can find traces of his elevation of the spontaneous elements in social life. In *Multiplicité des Temps Sociaux,* for example, Gurvitch speaks of "the explosive time of creation," and in his analysis of morality he speaks of "the creative and activistic demiurge type of morality," and so on.[122]

Gurvitch's stress on discontinuity and spontaneity in his sociology made it sometimes come dangerously close to irrationalism.[123] This tendency is especially true of Gurvitch's notion of dialectic which he outlined in a celebrated book entitled *Dialectique et Sociologie* (1962). Dialectic, as Gurvitch saw it, could not really help to explain social reality. What it could do, however, was help eliminate dogma from the sociologist's ideas and in effect sweep the conceptual field free of any preconceived notions. "The first and foremost inspiration of any authentic dialectic is the demolition of all established concepts in order to prevent their 'mummification' which comes from their inability to seize the 'ongoing' totality."[124] Dialectic was for Gurvitch, as one critic has put it, "an appeal to the perpetual overthrow of systems."[125]

Among the group of people close to Gurvitch, *Dialectique et Sociologie* was seen as an exceptionally fine book.[126] Most of them felt uneasy about Gurvitch's gigantic sociological system and preferred his "dialectical sociology" to his complicated schemes of depth layers, forms of sociality, and so on.[127] To these people, most of whom were not Marxists, Gurvitch's sociology was very creative, "subversive" and anti-establishment in a positive sense — a form of radical conflict sociology.[128] However, whether Gurvitch's dialectical sociology was really "subversive" is questionable. Dialectic, as Gurvitch saw it, had to break with all philosophical pre-suppositions:

> . . . the true task for the dialectical method is to demolish *all established and crystallized concepts.* . . . That is why dialectic, in order to be really fruitful, must be essentially *anti-dogmatic,* that is, eliminate every previous philosophical or scientific standpoint.[129]

This separation of philosophy and dialectic, however, weakens his sociology and reduces it to shallowness. Gurvitch's emphasis on spontaneity — his "conflict sociology" — thus ended in the same flat positivism as his sociological system.

Occasionally, however, Gurvitch's emphasis on spontaneity served him

well, even if it did not enable him to go beyond positivism. The concept of
social structure that Gurvitch developed in the 1950's illustrates this.[130] At that
time, there were two prevalent notions of structure: those put forth by French
structuralism and those of North American functionalism. Gurvitch disliked
both notions equally and attacked them severely.[131] What repelled Gurvitch
most in structuralist writings was their attempt to reduce all social reality to
variations of one basis code. Lévi-Strauss, Gurvitch charged, was trying to
develop a *"mathesis universalis."*[132] The French anthropologist's famous notion of structure was labelled a "total failure" by Gurvitch who, as usual, did
not spare his academic invectives.[133] Lévi-Strauss answered in kind, in *Anthropologie Structurale* (1958).[134] The personal aspects of this quarrel,
however, are less interesting than the main question it raises: does the structuralist notion of structure impoverish reality or make it more understandable? Gurvitch was convinced that the former was true and considered Lévi-
Strauss' structuralism to be scientifically unsound.

Gurvitch's feelings for North American functionalism were not any
warmer. What Gurvitch disliked about the structural-functional school in the
United States was its use of the concept of institution. For North American
sociologists, as Gurvitch saw it, structure was more or less synonymous with
institution. The concept of institution, however, was a very unhappy one in
Gurvitch's mind, since it only expressed the most conventional aspects of
social reality. In short, North American sociology was too conformist for Gurvitch. Gurvitch's writings of this period heaped particular abuse on Parsons
("that incarnation of the sclerosis of American sociological theory").[135] Gurvitch claimed that Parsons excluded everything that was unexpected, effervescent and rebellious from his analysis.

> Parsons says nothing about and tries to totally *ignore* all that is not
> expected, sanctioned, regular, as well as the struggle between dif-
> ferent classes, different groups, different value-scales, different
> social times, different determinisms — not to speak of the struggle
> between different depth layers, different forms of sociality, and,
> finally, different kinds of roles: privileged ones, imposed ones,
> regular ones, modified ones, created ones, fluctuating ones, unex-
> pected ones, roles one aspires to, imagined roles, etc.[136]

Gurvitch thus developed his own concept of social structure in direct opposition to the structuralists and functionalists. According to Gurvitch, one
should speak of "structuration" rather than "structure."[137] "Social structure,"
Gurvitch wrote, "is a permanent process: it is engaged in a movement of eternal destructuration and restructuration since it is part of *society in action
(société en acte)* which, as a 'product,' cannot exist one moment without the in-

tervention of an 'action': the ever renewed attempt to unify and orient [the total social phenomenon]."[138] A structure, as Gurvitch succinctly put it, is a *"struggle"* not a "rest."[139] The exact definition Gurvitch gave to social structure is the following:

> *Every social structure is a precarious equilibrium which is constantly being renewed; this equilibrium is composed of a multiplicity of hierarchies at the center of a total social phenomenon of a macrosociological type and the structure is only a weak substitute for this phenomenon. The equilibrium is specifically made up of hierarchies of depth levels, of the manifestations of sociability, of the means of social control, of social times, of mental colorations, of modes of division of labor, of accumulation of groups, and if the situation calls for it, of functional groupings, of classes, and their various organizations. This equilibrium of multiple hierarchies is fortified and cemented by the patterns, signs, symbols, regular and habitual social roles, values, and ideas, in brief, by the cultural works which are proper to these structures, and if they are global, by an entire civilization which invades them and in which they participate as both the creator and benefactor of these cultural works.* [140]

There was no consensus among French social scientists as to the value of Gurvitch's concept of social structure. The structuralists naturally found little of interest in it. Gilles Granger, for instance, said that Gurvitch's concept of structure really belonged to "anti-structuralism."[141] The principal aim of structuralism, Granger argued, was to get to know reality better by translating it into a different language as is customarily done in natural science. Gurvitch, as Granger saw it, achieved exactly the opposite because he refused to "reduce" the richness of the "total social phenomenon." This response, however, does not mean that Gurvitch's notion of structure was unacceptable to all structuralists. Piaget, for instance, prefers, like Gurvitch, to talk of "structuration" rather than "structure."[142] And Goldmann's idea of structure is very close to that of Piaget.[143]

Among the non-structuralists, opinions varied as to the value of Gurvitch's concept of structure. Georges Davy held that a structure was by definition something stable and to make it too fluid, as Gurvitch did, was basically to eliminate it.[144] Jean Cazeneuve, one of Gurvitch's friends, accepted the validity of Davy's argument and acknowledged that the concept of structure constituted the "Achilles heel" of Gurvitch's sociology.[145] Henri Lefebvre, on the other hand, found Gurvitch's notion of social structure perfectly acceptable.[146] However, he pointed out Gurvitch's failure to account for the origin of social structure. For this information, Lefebvre argued, Marxism was necessary.

Gurvitch's most articulate effort to go beyond positivism within the limits of his own sociological system is to be found in the "sociology of freedom" he developed in the 1950's. The main work in this context is *Déterminismes Sociaux et Liberté Humaine* (1955, 1963). What Gurvitch tried to do in this book was establish the strength of determinism in social life and see what opportunity there was for human freedom to intervene. A friend of Gurvitch has called *Déterminismes* his "most characteristic" work and, in a sense, it certainly is.[147] Knowing Gurvitch's background in the Russian intelligentsia, who can fail to see the continuity between the problems Gurvitch raised in this work and the ones he struggled with in the 1910's? Gurvitch himself has acknowledged the close connection between the Russian Revolution and *Déterminismes Sociaux* in an interview with Jean Duvignaud in 1959:

> J.D.-*Has your thinking about the [Russian] Revolution been constitutive for your sociological thinking?*

> G.G.-Yes, but only as a reflection "after the event" which took place after a fairly long interval. What always has preoccupied me and for which I found no explanation before I thought it over in *Déterminismes Sociaux et Liberté Humaine* was how surprised I was that the social revolution succeeded in Russia — a country where industrialization had just begun and where the proletariat was not even ten percent of the population. Lenin tried to explain this extraordinary phenomenon by evoking the "colonial" situation of Russia and by appealing to the revolutionary spirit of colonial workers. These explanations do not seem sufficient to me, since Russia was not exploited as a colony by its allies who were content to invest capital there. Internationally Russia played an independent role during the Tzars as well as after the revolution. The situation was not comparable to that of a colony.

> The problem of the "crack" in determinism is surely posed by the social revolution in Russia. I am not saying the revolution in general because the Tzarist regime was rotten and only needed a small push to fall. But the incontestable success, not only political success but also economical and industrial, of the plans in the Soviet Union ought to give some food for thought to all those sociologists who, like their colleagues the historians, love to *predict the past*. . . .[148]

The basic idea of Gurvitch's "sociology of freedom" was that man is not totally determined by society and that human liberty can always "infiltrate" and "intervene" somewhere in social life.[149] The task of the "sociology of freedom" was to determine under what conditions human freedom could exist. Gurvitch's answer to this question was that there is always room for human freedom within and between the various determinisms in the total social phenomenon. There are, for instance, "discontinuities" and "contingencies" within a "unidimensional determinism," as well as "breaks" and "conflicts" between the different determinisms of this type. The same is true of the other kinds of determinisms ("microdeterminisms," "partial determinisms," "sociological determinisms").[150] There are also, in addition to all these opportunities for freedom to intervene, "breaks" and "discontinuities" between a global society and its structure, as well as between different global societies.

Gurvitch's "conflict sociology" can be said to have reached its peak in *Déterminismes Sociaux*. This work was Gurvitch's most sustained effort to develop a sociological theory of spontaneity. The book was hailed by liberal critics as a very fine work in "the sociology of freedom."[151] T. B. Bottomore, who reviewed *Déterminismes Sociaux* for *The British Journal of Sociology,* found it "libertarian and optimistic [in spirit]" and hailed it as "a welcome change from the fashionable neo-Weberian pessimism which sees in contemporary societies only problems of bureaucratic organization."[152] At his death two of Gurvitch's closest friends, Duvignaud and Balandier, stressed that his sociology was a sociology of freedom.[153] Moreover, Henri Lefebvre characterized Gurvitch's sociology as basically a "philosophy of freedom" similar to Sartre's.[154]

Not only Lefebvre but other critics as well have seen similarities between Sartre's work and Gurvitch's.[155] One person has gone so far as to talk of Gurvitch's "existential sociology."[156] This comparison, however, is misleading. Gurvitch's sociology, even in *Déterminismes Sociaux,* never went beyond positivism as the existentialism of Sartre does. If one takes a closer look at Gurvitch's concept of freedom, one can clearly see the difference between Gurvitch and Sartre. Freedom, Gurvitch explained, could be the freedom to do evil as well as freedom to do good.

> One has, however, to watch out in order not to see in human freedom something good in itself and to identify the infinite richness of its colorations, of its forms and virtualities, with positive values. Like everything that concerns the human condition, liberty is ambiguous and ambivalent. It can decompose as well as construct, push toward perversity as well as generosity, turn to good as well as evil, lead to degeneration as well as to leaps ahead.[157]

This concept of freedom is superficially similar to that of Sartre, but it is really a compromise of the "philosophy of freedom." Gurvitch conceives of freedom in an abstract and idealistic manner, and in doing so opens the door to sophistry: the freedom to oppress is as much a freedom as any other. . . .

The most exciting part of Gurvitch's work during 1953-1965 is undoubtedly his attempt to revive sociology with the help of socialism. This attempt never materialized in a major work such as *Déterminismes Sociaux* or *Cadres Sociaux de la Connaissance*. Instead it was scattered throughout a series of minor works, such as in the courses that Gurvitch taught (e.g., *Le Concept de Classes Sociales, La Sociologie de Karl Marx*)[158] and in some of the minor works that he edited (*Proudhon, Saint-Simon*).[159] These writings did not have one specific focus. Gurvitch tried rather to reorient his sociology in general, and his works, like his thoughts, pointed in different directions. If, however, one theme were to be chosen to represent Gurvitch's main concern in these works, it must be his attempt to write a "History of Sociology." *Traité de Sociologie* (1958-1960, 1963), for instance, contains an article entitled, "Brève Esquisse de l'Histoire de la Sociologie," and several of the courses Gurvitch taught at the Sorbonne were conceived as part of this project.[160] However, some reservations must immediately be made. Gurvitch was not at all interested in Durkheim, Comte, Spencer or any of the sociologists active after World War I.[161] This, no doubt, contributed to making Gurvitch's "History of Sociology" fairly obscure in relation to Raymond Aron's famous courses on the same subject at the Sorbonne in 1959-1960. In contrast to Aron, who celebrated the most conventional sociologists plus two liberal heroes of his own choosing, Montesquieu and Tocqueville, all of Gurvitch's interest was focused on three nineteenth century socialists: Saint-Simon, Proudhon, and Marx.[162] It was on the study of the works of these thinkers that Gurvitch set his hopes for the rejuvenation of sociology. For someone who had edited a work like *Twentieth Century Sociology,* this represented quite a change indeed.

To Gurvitch, as to Durkheim, Saint-Simon was the real founder of sociology. Saint-Simon, as Gurvitch saw it, had anticipated most of nineteenth century social thought and the impact of his ideas had been enormous: "Neither Marx, Proudhon, Durkheim, nor even Comte could have developed their theories without Saint-Simon."[163] Gurvitch especially stressed the influence of Saint-Simon on Marx and Proudhon. Thus it was Saint-Simon rather than Hegel who was Marx's main inspiration, according to Gurvitch. Left-Hegelianism, for instance, was *"only a saint-simonized Hegelianism or a hegelianized Saint-Simonism."*[164] Saint-Simon, as opposed to Hegel, had stressed the central role of liberty in human society and the necessity to construct a "science of liberty." Gurvitch even went so far as to say that most of historical materialism came from Saint-Simon.[165] This assertion is no doubt incorrect. Less polemical was Gurvitch's interpretation of Saint-Simon's impact on Proudhon. As Gurvitch saw it, Proudhon — together with Marx — was Saint-Simon's true successor. Some of Proudhon's most ingenious ideas, Gurvitch claimed, originally came from Saint-Simon.[166]

A question that must be raised in this context is the extent to which Saint-Simon could be of any help to Gurvitch in his search for a critical sociology. The answer must be in the negative. Gurvitch, as we know, had studied Saint-Simon quite extensively in his youth. Then, he had been fascinated by the distinction made between state and society in Saint-Simon's work. Now, however, Gurvitch was interested in Saint-Simon as a sociologist, and his new analysis was intended as a self-criticism of his section on Saint-Simon in *L'Idée du Droit Social*.[167] As Gurvitch now saw it, Saint-Simon's sociological work consisted of three basic propositions: that society creates itself; that social reality contains material as well as spiritual dimensions; and that society is divided into large antagonistic groups.[168] After Saint-Simon, however, all these propositions had been analyzed masterfully by Proudhon and Marx, as Gurvitch himself was the first to acknowledge. Consequently, there was not much that Gurvitch could really extract from Saint-Simon's work for his own use. All in all, Gurvitch's interest in Saint-Simon was symptomatic in the sense that it symbolized his desire to reexamine the roots of sociology and find something different there.

The second socialist Gurvitch turned to for inspiration was Proudhon. Proudhon must not be simply discarded as a "petty bourgeois," Gurvitch argued. Marx's *Misère de la Philosophie*, Gurvitch claimed, was directed more against Hegel than against Proudhon. Proudhon's work, as well as his political behavior, was truly revolutionary in Gurvitch's mind. The project of rehabilitating Proudhon was very important to Gurvitch since he believed that the future of socialism lay in a successful synthesis of the ideas of Marx and Proudhon.[169] Marx, as Gurvitch saw it, was a superior economist and historian to Proudhon, while Proudhon had a deeper insight into the nature of liberty and understood the necessity of decentralizing society much better than Marx.[170]

Thus for the second time in his life Gurvitch tried to launch Proudhon as a scientifically valid figure. This time, however, as opposed to in *L'Idée du Droit Social,* it was not Proudhon's legal thoughts that interested Gurvitch but his "sociology." Following Bouglé, who had been the first to consider Proudhon as a sociologist (1911), Gurvitch now tried to distill a sociology from Proudhon's voluminous writings.[171] He was not very successful in this enterprise. Some of Proudhon's concepts — such as "collective force" and "collective reason" — are indeed useful, but basically there is no scientifically valid core in Proudhon's work.[172] Marx had realized this back in the 1840's.[173] Proudhon's emphasis on workers' self-management, on the other hand, is still relevant today, as are his ideas about pluralism. No doubt his ideas on these points can help to correct an authoritarian socialism — in recognizing this in Proudhon Gurvitch was right, even prophetic. On the whole, however, Proudhon's work could not provide Gurvitch with the conceptual basis of a new social science. To find such a basis Gurvitch had to look to the works of Marx himself.

Gurvitch had studied Marx during the post-war period, but at that time he had restricted his analysis to the works of the young Marx. Following the fashionable trend of the time, Gurvitch had in an artificial way opposed the radical and philosophical young Marx to the deterministic and economically oriented old Marx. Now, however, Gurvitch considerably deepened his analysis of Marx and made an effort to encompass Marx's whole work. The basis of Gurvitch's argument now became that Marx was first and foremost a sociologist and that only by laying bare this side of his work could one revive both Marxism and sociology. Gurvitch wrote, ". . . it is sociology which constitutes the unity of [Marx's] work,"[174] and he added, "Marx was in the first place a theoretician of sociology and a sociological researcher."[175] Dialectical materialism, Gurvitch argued, was more or less the same as Marxist sociology.[176] To deny the possibility of a Marxist sociology, he continued, would lead to a simplified and dogmatic Marxism.[177]

Gurvitch was generally very impressed by Marx's thought and felt increasingly sympathetic to Marxism. He especially praised the works of Marx's "intermediary period" (1848-1852) for their concrete and pragmatic qualities (". . . the most successful works of Karl Marx the sociologist").[178] He also spoke approvingly of Marx's "sociology of economy" in *Capital.* He found many Marxist concepts valuable — especially alienation, ideology, class, and dialectic.

Gurvitch's assimilation of Marx's thought was not total. As a matter of fact, he had so many reservations about the value of Marxism that it is accurate to consider Gurvitch a "non-Marxist" even in his most pro-Marxist works. As Gurvitch saw it, Marx had mixed science and politics too closely. Thus, he thought of Marx's philosophy of history as unscientific. That Marx depicted the proletariat as having a "mission" was equally unscientific. And Marx put too strong an emphasis on determinism and was not relativistic enough.

Gurvitch's analysis of Marx was two-fold. First, Gurvitch did a close textual reading of Marx on ideology and alienation. Second, Gurvitch took up certain Marxist concepts — such as class and dialectic — and independently developed them, confronting their original Marxist meaning with the definitions of a host of other thinkers, as well as with his own thoughts. It is this latter discourse on Marxist thought that is most interesting. Gurvitch's textual analysis of alienation and ideology actually contains very little of substance. Alienation, Gurvitch argued, was an unclear concept which Marxists would do well to clarify. Gurvitch considered ideology to be equally fuzzy in its outlines — he distinguished among no less than thirteen different meanings. This concept would benefit, Gurvitch thought, by being restricted to mean "political knowledge."[179]

Of Gurvitch's discussion of Marxist concepts, his course on class — *Le Concept de Classes Sociales* — was the most successful. This course, taught at the Sorbonne in 1953-1954, perhaps constitutes Gurvitch's best work after World War II. Gurvitch had already discussed the concept of class in the first edition of *Vocation* (1950), but this time he made a much more thorough study, not only of Marx himself but of the Marxist tradition.[180] The result is an exciting and fine work, if not an *opus magnum* such as *L'Idée du Droit Social.*

Marx's concept of class, as Gurvitch saw it, was fruitful but ambiguous: "The Marxist theory of class is at the same time rich in possibilities, rather contradictory in certain aspects, and insufficiently elaborated."[181] The positive side of the notion of class, Gurvitch argued, was that it helped to account for social reality much better than, for instance, the stratification theories of U.S. sociologists. The problem with the class concept was that Marx had not given it a precise definition. The young Marx's concept of class, for instance, was quite philosophical in nature, while it was much more concrete in his later historical works. In Marx's works it was indeed clear that class was not the same as stratum and that it was not based on income. Nowhere, however, did Marx give a positive definition of class. On the whole, Gurvitch argued, Marx saw class as determined by place in production. This conception, however, left several questions unanswered, such as the number of social classes, the distinction between class and group, the role of consciousness in the class concept, and the historical origin of a class society.

In order to find a solution to these problematic points in Marx's concept of class, Gurvitch went through the works of Engels, Bernstein, Kautsky, Lenin, Bukharin and Lukács. None of these thinkers, Gurvitch felt, had clarified the class concept very much. All, except for Lukács, shared a mechanical concept of class. Engels, for instance, identified class with economic groups. Bernstein and Kautsky's ideas resembled the reformistic notions of North American sociologists, and Lenin and Bukharin neglected the role of class consciousness far too much. Lukács, Gurvitch admitted, had emphasized the role of consciousness in *History and Class Consciousness,* but he was too eschatological and mystical for Gurvitch's taste. In brief, Gurvitch felt the Marxist tradition had not advanced far beyond Marx's original position.

Gurvitch then turned to bourgeois sociologists and economists to see if they had solved some of the difficulties that beset the Marxist concept of class. Gurvitch here focused on Schmoller, Pareto, Weber, Schumpeter, Halbwachs and Sorokin. In general, Gurvitch found very little of use in the works of these thinkers. Weber's definition of class, for instance, was flatly rejected, along with the respective definitions of Schmoller, Pareto and Schumpeter. Gurvitch felt that Sorokin and Halbwachs — especially the latter — had advanced some good ideas. Both, for instance, used a variety of criteria to define class and they were not overly political in their analyses. Neither Halbwachs nor Sorokin, however, had succeeded in solving the problems that beset the Marxist class concept.

Gurvitch tried to find a solution to these problems himself. The result of his effort is summarized in the following definition of class:

> *Social classes are specific groups which are very large and which represent macrocosms of minor groups. The unity of these macrocosms is based on their supra-functionality, on their resistance to being penetrated by the global society, on their radical incompatibility among themselves, and on their advanced structuration with a predominant collective consciousness and specific cultural works. These groups, which first appear in industrial global societies where technical models and economic functions are specifically accentuated, have in addition the following traits: they exist de facto, are open, exist at a distance, are permanently divisive, and only have access to conditional constraint.*[182]

What is most important about Gurvitch's definition is his attempt to tie the class concept to, as he put it, "a general theory of particular groups."[183] He also saw class consciousness as an integral part of class. But he felt that the connection between mode of production and class was very weak; classes did not exist, in his opinion, before the advent of industrial society.

Gurvitch's second spin-off from Marxism was the course *Dialectique et Sociologie* which he taught at the Sorbonne in 1961-1962 and which appeared in book form in 1962. The first part of the course was devoted to a "History of the Principal Types of Dialectic," the second part to his own concept of dialectic. As Gurvitch saw it, sociology could not dispense with dialectic: ". . . the object of sociology—the total social phenomena—becomes impossible to understand if one repudiates the dialectic."[184] The existing types of dialectic, however, were quite sterile and needed, in Gurvitch's mind, to be "dialectized" themselves. Dialectic as a method was strong but it was usually "betrayed" in the sense that it was used to justify a pre-established ideal.

Gurvitch's history of dialectic covered the following figures: Plato, Plotinus, Damascius, Pseudo-Dionysius, Kant, Fichte, Hegel, Proudhon, Marx, and Sartre. All of these thinkers, according to Gurvitch, despite their merits, had in some way "domesticated" the dialectic by subordinating it to their own philosophical doctrines. Marx, for instance, had connected the dialectic with the advent of the classless society. Of the ancient thinkers, Gurvitch preferred Pseudo-Dionysius who used dialectic for his "negative theology." Of the German philosophers, Gurvitch's sympathies, as usual, were with Fichte rather than Hegel. Fichte was the first thinker to see society itself as dialectical.[185] Hegel, Gurvitch grudgingly admitted, had introduced dialectic into history, but through his glorification of the concept of synthesis and his sophistic use of contradiction he had also run dialectic into the ground. On the whole, Gurvitch concluded, Hegel's work represented a step backward in the history of dialectic and had, in addition, been an "authentic source [of fascism]."[186] Gurvitch was much more sympathetic to Kant who, though denying dialectic, had actually renewed it in Gurvitch's opinion. Gurvitch was also very positive toward Proudhon. Proudhon's dialectic, he said, was an *"anti-nomic, anti-theological, anti-statist, anti-conformist, revolutionary dialectic."*[187] Along with Marx's dialectic, Proudhon's was the richest and most concrete dialectic in existence. Proudhon's strength was that he recognized contradictions everywhere in social reality without dissolving them — as Hegel did — into arbitrary syntheses. Marx's accusation that Proudhon's dialectic was "petty bourgeois" Gurvitch emphatically rejected. But he found Marx's own dialectic very rich and actually more successful than Proudhon's. Marx had tried to eliminate all philosophical presuppositions from the dialectic in order to make it more sensitive to history, Gurvitch said. On the negative side, he noted, Marx had not properly explored the relations between dialectic as a method and as a movement. Sartre, finally, was too individualistic for Gurvitch's taste. While he fully agreed with Sartre's statement that Engels had "killed the dialectic when he pretended to find it in nature" (*Critique de la Raison Dialectique*), Gurvitch basically rejected the existentialist dialectic as too focused on individual consciousness.[188]

Gurvitch's own version of dialectic was meant to set it free from all bonds that had held it back for centuries. The main inspiration of Gurvitch's dialectic — the desire to rid all concepts of dogma — has already been discussed. Gurvitch's general definition of dialectic was quite conventional: dialectic was the march of human society and its attempt to conceptualize this movement.[189] Nature was not dialectical in itself, though everything that human beings touched became dialectical by virtue of this contact. Dialectic existed as a method, as a movement, and as the object constructed by science. To use dialectic did not mean that sociology must become "committed" (*"engagé"*).[190] Neither must dialectic continue being the "fetishism of contradictions" that characterized it today, Gurvitch argued. Society could not be explained through one or even several basic contradictions. Society was far too complicated for such a simplistic approach. Indeed, besides the method of "the dialectic of polarization," Gurvitch distinguished four other dialectical methods: "dialectical complementarity," "mutual dialectical implication," "dialectical ambiguity," and "dialectical reciprocity of perspectives."[191] "Dialectical ambiguity" was a catch-all method that simply meant that all human reality is basically ambiguous. The other three methods spelled out, in different ways, the non-antagonistic relationship between two elements in a totality. "Dialectical complementarity" disclosed that two elements which seemed to be in contradiction were actually part of each other. "Mutual dialectical implication" covered instances in which two elements were not in a situation of polarity but intersected like two circles. "Reciprocity of perspectives," finally, was applicable in the case of an accentuated interpenetration of two elements which, at first sight, might seem to be in contradiction. Thus, Gurvitch's discourse on dialectic was directed against dogmatism ("dialectize the dialectic") and especially against the simplistic use of the concept of contradiction.

Gurvitch's attempt to rejuvenate sociology with the help of socialism did not impress bourgeois sociologists. To them, it was not a very interesting project. Some scholars, like Raymond Aron in France and René König in Germany, both of whom had been positive toward Gurvitch's sociology in the 1930's, now attacked him.[192] To König, Gurvitch's new sociology smelled of "totalitarianism of the left."[193] To Aron, Gurvitch's attempt to rehabilitate the class concept was nonsense; elites, rather than classes, were to Aron the crucial groups in "industrial society."[194] Among Marxists, the response was quite different. To them, Gurvitch's writings, especially his book on social class, became hot topics for discussion.[195]

The general attitude of the French Communist Party to sociology was, as we know, negative. The Party proclaimed sociology to be a bourgeois science and that usually ended the discussion. Gurvitch was consequently brushed aside at various times by the Party as an "ideologist of the bourgeoisie," "a bourgeois professor," and so on.[196] This position of unqualified dogmatism presented few problems in the 1940's and the early 1950's; after Stalin's death, however, it became increasingly difficult to maintain. Gurvitch's work around this time attracted the attention of several intellectuals in the Party who felt that official Marxism had become too dogmatic and that it could be revivified through sociology. As a result, Gurvitch became more or less the center of a vivid debate in the French Communist Party in 1953-1955 about the relationship between sociology and Marxism.[197]

This debate, into which Gurvitch was unwittingly drawn, was between some Marxists who felt increasingly disappointed with the French Communist Party's line and the official ideologists of the Party. Among the former were Jean Duvignaud and Henri Lefebvre; among the latter were Roger Garaudy and Jean Kanapa. Duvignaud felt that Gurvitch had made a good critique of dogmatic Marxism in his courses at the Sorbonne in 1954 and 1956.[198] Gurvitch's course on classes, according to Duvignaud, had made a strong impact on certain intellectuals in the Party: "It played, as I can testify to, a not negligible role in the general reevaluation of Marx that took place among certain intellectuals after Stalinism."[199] It was also this course on social classes that made Lefebvre become involved in a dispute about Gurvitch in the French Communist Party in 1954-1955. "All Marxists," Lefebvre said, "must agree that it is an important event that the Marxist theory of class has for the first time been exposed in detail at the Sorbonne and not in bad faith to belittle it but to accept it on several points."[200] Lefebvre felt so strongly about this that he and Gurvitch had a debate on the topic of social classes in January 1955 which was published in *Critique*.[201] Lefebvre stated that a "dialogue" with Gurvitch could be stimulating for Marxists since Gurvitch in many ways was close to "living Marxism." Gurvitch's work, with its emphasis on empirically testing Marx's ideas rather than on dogmatically accepting them, Lefebvre said, could perhaps awaken some Marxists from their "dogmatic slumber." The ideologists of the Party immediately reacted and attacked Lefebvre. Gurvitch, they argued, was of the same caliber as Aron and Merleau-Ponty and should be regarded, along with the others, as being part of an ideological offensive of the bourgeoisie whose aim was to lure the intellectuals away from a popular front with the working class. Garaudy, for instance, stated that "Every effort to blur the clear notion of 'class' expresses, in a philosophical, historical, or economic form, the dominant preoccupation of the bourgeoisie: to negate the fundamental thesis of Marxism-Leninism, i.e., the historical necessity of the dictatorship of the proletariat."[202] Lefebvre replied that "dialogues" with progressive social scientists were useful for communist intellectuals, but Garaudy and others were not impressed. Lefebvre, in his intellectual biography *La Somme et le Reste* (1959), has given a vivid picture of the discussions he had about Gurvitch in the Party in 1955:

The dogmatic:	You pretend that sociology exists and that it is a science. I hope you are right. I am not a sectarian. But show me; produce some sociological work.
Me:	That is exactly what I am trying to do. But it is not so easy, you know.
Him:	Give us your studies. We will publish them.
Me:	Studies on what?
Him:	For instance on the concentration of agricultural property. . . .
Me:	But that is not sociology; it is political economy.
Him:	There you see. It is you that says it. We want

something of value from you, something of political importance. Not descriptions like the Americans do.

Me: I am against that, too. You know my general thesis: "There is no worse abstraction than immediate experience."

Him: Okay. Do your work after those principles and the positions of the Party.

Me: What is that supposed to mean?

Him: What about your relations with Gurvitch? What about the things you publish in his journal, with him and about him?

Me: So?

Him: You have already abandoned the positions of the Party, the positions of the working class and without noticing it — that's the worst. Without you even noticing it, you have become opportunistic and side with the opponent.

Me: In what way?

Him: Gurvitch is an idealist.

Me: Gurvitch is not a materialist. Does that prove that his concepts are wrong?

Him: Yes, absolutely. You are underestimating philosophy and its fundamental problem. Concepts which are part of an idealistic attitude cannot be true.

Me: I don't agree. You talk of "concepts." You are thus aware of the fact that Gurvitch uses concepts. In that, he is different from empirical sociology, from American sociology. In the present situation, he is thus one of our allies. You should, from your point of view, see him as a sympathizer.

Him: That is opportunism! You confuse politics and ideology. Political sympathizers must not influence our ideology. Peaceful coexistence must not end up in a penetration into our ranks of the opponent's ideology. Peaceful coexistence does not mean an end to the ideological struggle. Sympathizers who try to smuggle in their trash among us — and you are a proof — must be deadly attacked on the ideological level. Exactly because they are close to us politically, in the present situation, while they are ideologically at the opposite end. Repeat to yourself: Gurvitch is an idealist and we are materialists.

Me: You think that our political sympathizers will stay with us if we attack them like that?

Him: They will. If they are honest.

Me: I assure you that the way Gurvitch uses concepts in general puts him on our side in the battle of knowledge.

Him: You are confused. Part idealist. You place the concept above the opposition of materialism and idealism. Above and beyond. There are idealist concepts and there are materialist ones.

Me: There are concepts which correspond to reality and there are those that don't.

Him: Only materialist concepts reflect reality and show that they reflect it.

Me: There are in Gurvitch concepts which correspond to an objective reality. He really has a feeling for the density of social reality which he calls depth sociology. He also speaks, in my opinion correctly, about micro- and macro-sociology. He insists on the multiplicity of social groups, on their relations, on their penetration and conflicts in global society at various levels or in their layers. His idea of multiple determinisms and of multiple acquired liberties appeals to me. I think in a similar vein about alienation: multiple alienations and multiple counter-attacks on them. He has a lot of ideas I disapprove of, but what do you want? I prefer people with plenty of ideas to those with none. Even if some of the ideas of those with plenty are contestable. I hesitate when it comes to Gurvitch's pluralism, but I think only a deep discussion . . . .

Him:	(Sternly) Pluralism? That is treason! What about the theory of different societies? There's socialism and capitalism; that's all. No third way. And what will become of classes in this sociology?
Me:	That's one of the questions! Even the class struggle is in question.
Him:	But is it a question from the point of view of the working class? You surprise me: materialism, political struggle, the struggle for power, the spirit of the party . . . .
Me:	What I have called class or party subjectivism.
Him:	You have already deserted the positions of the working class as Maurice [Thorez] says. Think about it. When you have done that, come back and see me. We will talk again . . . .[203]

Lefebvre, however, stuck to his guns despite a great number of attacks on him on this question. The same year, in an article published in *Cahiers Internationaux de Sociologie,* Lefebvre went so far as to say that "The situation of scientific sociology in France today is characterized by a certain meeting between the method of 'dialectical hyper-empiricism' and that of dialectical materialism. . . ."[204] He added, "This must not hide certain differences, especially in regard to the general theory of knowledge."[205]

Gurvitch's attempt to mediate between sociology and socialism in his works from 1953-1965 constitutes, to repeat, their most interesting aspect. For the first time since the early 1930's, Gurvitch tried to unite his scientific concerns with his belief in socialism. But he was not successful in this attempt. In an artificial way, Gurvitch tried to distill and isolate a "sociology" from the works of Saint-Simon, Marx, and Proudhon distinct from these thinkers' value judgments and political concerns. In each thinker, Gurvitch claimed, one could distinguish between a "sociology" and a "social philosophy" (*doctrine sociale*). Alienation, for instance, more appropriately belonged, according to Gurvitch, to Marx's "social philosophy" than to his "sociology," while Marx's class concept was in certain aspects "sociological" and in others "philosophical." The truth is, of course—and Gurvitch was often forced to admit this—that no such distinction between "sociology" and "social philosophy" exists in the works of Saint-Simon, Proudhon, and Marx.

Perhaps the most serious drawback to Gurvitch's arbitrary split of socialism into "sociology" and "philosophy" was the de-radicalization it entailed. Every time Marx or Proudhon explicitly attacked capitalism or defended the working class they became "philosophical," i.e. non-scientific, in Gurvitch's mind. A good example of Gurvitch's dilution of socialist thought is his concept of dialectic. Marx, in *Capital,* had described dialectic as "a scandal and abomination to bourgeoisdom and its doctrinaire professors," and Proudhon, in *La Création de l'Ordre dans l'Humanité,* had said that dialectic would *"explode all the canons of despotism and make all the Bastilles tremble."*[206] To Gurvitch, however, dialectic was just another neutral scientific tool that had no connection with philosophy or politics.

> We consider our effort to be a success if we have succeeded in making it clear that we do not, by tying the fate of sociology to that of dialectic, propose to engage sociology in another philosophical venture, i.e., tie it to a sinking ship. On the contrary, we propose to liberate sociology, as far as possible, from all ideological engagement, be it political or philosophical, by trying to minimize the social and historical coefficients of this science.[207]

As this quotation illustrates, Gurvitch hinted that sociology was part of social reality; it had some "social and historical coefficients"—that was all. Gurvitch explicitly rebuffed Goldmann's argument that value judgments and judgments of reality were inextricably united in Marxism.[208] As Gurvitch put it in a discussion about Proudhon and Marx some weeks before his death, the sociologist must "eliminate, as far as possible, value judgments and social philosophy [from sociology] in order to deal with social reality as such."[209]

On the level of class strategy, Gurvitch's enduring positivism meant that he never succeeded in breaking out of the ideological paralysis that characterized the progressive elements of the Western bourgeoisie from World War I on. Positivism thus prevented Gurvitch from putting all his energy behind his most important sociological discoveries: workers' self-management and the techno-bureaucratic menace. On each of those issues Gurvitch, with his brilliant mind and his profound knowledge, should have been able to produce works of long-lasting value. As it happened, it was only inadvertently that Gurvitch's sociological works in the 1953-1965 period became a positive force in the class struggle—as an inspiration to thinkers like Henri Lefebvre rather than as a force in their own right. Thus, Gurvitch's sociology was in the end a failure—a failure which was fundamentally that of the class strategy embodied in "twentieth century sociology."

AFTERWORD

This work has probed Gurvitch's thought in great detail and followed its very distinct development in the hope of doing it full justice. From my own point of view, Gurvitch's main contribution to social thought resides in his ideas on workers' self-management and in his magnificent work *L'Idée du Droit Social*. With this I differ from most sociologists; Gurvitch is first and foremost known as the author of *Vocation* and of some exciting works in the sociology of knowledge.

My analysis of Gurvitch's work has been conducted from a very specific angle — namely, that social thought may be conceived and understood as embodying a particular class strategy — and the present work is basically an attempt to show the validity of this perspective, using Gurvitch as an example.

To recapitulate, the basic theory governing this work is the following. Thought is inherent in human existence. Human beings live in groups and their survival implies cooperation. In capitalist society the main groups consist of classes, and each of these classes has a specific task to perform — the working class must produce surplus value and the capitalist class must assure the accumulation of capital. Capitalist society derives its essential nature from only two classes (*Capital*), but there are, of course, several classes, and each class contains separate fractions which usually struggle with each other. Even if the accumulation of capital is imperative to the capitalist system, there is always a great variety of problems facing each class and class fraction. To solve, indeed merely to confront one of these problems, one must first conceptualize it. Lawyers, authors, sociologists, etc. all have in common that they try to confront and, to some extent, solve problems. I suggest that one can see their analyses as embodying a distinct class strategy.

There are some who will raise objections to this perspective, but I think that creative thinking often demands single-mindedness. In order to say something useful in the social sciences one has, I think, to face difficulties and avoid an eclectic approach. As Simone de Beauvoir, in one of her autobiographical volumes, notes in this context:

> ... I have learned that, in order to make discoveries, the most essential thing is not merely to obtain a gleam of light here and there that other people have missed, but to drive straight for your goal, and damn everything else.[1]

In using the idea of social thought as class strategy on Gurvitch, I have found that, on the whole, it works well. Gurvitch's writings, which originally attracted me because of their idealism and their emphasis on justice and workers' self-management, gradually took on a new and what I felt to be a more substantive meaning when scrutinized through this perspective. I first tried to locate what Gurvitch's "problem" was as a young scholar. I found this to be his interest in voluntarism and in the relationship between the individual and the group. Then, by doing a class analysis of Russian society, I saw that this was not only Gurvitch's problem, but that of the whole Russian intelligentsia. It matters little that Gurvitch's theories were not the predominant ones of the time; what is essential is that he struggled with the same problem as the rest of the Russian intelligentsia. Moreover, the specific history of the Russian intelligentsia—its precarious position as an isolated progressive group in a society that was still essentially feudal—explains its great preoccupation with the problem of voluntarism. I feel very strongly that in order to understand Gurvitch one must never forget that he was and ultimately remained a representative of the progressive Russian intelligentsia.

That Gurvitch left the Soviet Union after the Russian Revolution and went to Germany, France, and the United States for a couple of years complicated the analysis considerably. However, I found that there was a parallel development of the liberal bourgeoisie, later to become part of the large middle class, in all of these countries and that Gurvitch easily fit into this trend. I have tried to illustrate this development by showing the process by which the originally progressive liberal bourgeoisie in France, Germany, and the United States became increasingly integrated into capitalism and by indicating that this process had already begun in Russia before 1917. Gurvitch's own development from a radical member of the Russian intelligentsia to a fairly conventional and positivistic sociologist is specifically interesting because he exemplifies the full course of this development, as opposed to, for instance, Weber, who only articulated the class strategy of the liberal bourgeoisie at a specific point.

Moreover, my study of the parallel development of the liberal bourgeoisie in Russia, France, and the United States, however schematic it might be, has led me to suggest a distinct historical reason for the predominance of positivistic and "value-free" sociology today. At the turn of the century the liberal bourgeoisie in these countries confronted the problem of a society torn by class struggles. It proposed, as a solution, a class compromise between the enlightened section of the capitalist class and the working class, and it tried to play the role of mediator in this compromise. Filled with hope for the success of this reformistic scheme, the members of the liberal bourgeoisie (Durkheim, Small, Mikhailovsky, etc.) merged ideals harmoniously with facts. But World War I put an end to this hope and in order to reorient itself to the post-war situation, the liberal bourgeoisie had to discard its ideals. Here, I suggest, began that destructive separation between values and facts that has become the hallmark of modern sociology. This, of course, is only a theory which perhaps can be refuted by a thorough historical analysis of the problem. Until such a historical analysis is done, however, this theory has a strong quality: it tries to explain the separation of values and facts in modern social science through direct historical experience—namely, the collapse of the dreams of the liberal bourgeoisie after World War I.

But as I have indicated, Gurvitch's exile did pose specific problems for the analysis. It was more difficult, for instance, to explain *Essais de Sociologie* through my perspective than his earlier works. Whether this was due to an inherent weakness in the theory or simply to my way of looking at the problem is difficult for me to say. It was not at all difficult to see that Durkheimian sociology and North American sociology in the 1940's, for instance, expressed distinct class strategies, but to characterize Gurvitch himself was a somewhat harder task. After having seen Gurvitch as part of Russia, after having seen his work as an organic part of the class struggle in his native country, I was more or less forced to see his later development as a *reflection* of the class struggle as it was expressed, for example, in Durkheimian sociology.* I felt that this was a reasonable assumption since Gurvitch's basic structure of thinking was set in the Russian class struggle, and I considered that it might be influenced but never totally changed by his experience of the class struggle in the other countries he lived in. Common sense, I feel, supports the idea that an exile (especially if he is an idealist like Gurvitch!) can never pick up the subtle multiple cultural influences of a new country and understand them as well as a native thinker. However, the fact remains that it has been somewhat unsatisfactory in the last chapters to describe Gurvitch's thought as being the result of several different class strategies. My conclusion—that Gurvitch failed as a sociologist in post-war France because he never clearly articulated a problem that a class faced—is perhaps one that merits thorough discussion.

There are some additional difficulties with the notion of class strategy that I have not been able to solve in a totally satisfactory way. The concept of "strategy," for instance, is somewhat ambivalent since it implies a level of consciousness that many sociologists would deny exists in society. My own position is that there is, indeed, behavior one can label as the particular strategy of a class, but I can see that there are difficulties involved in determining, for instance, a class's exact degree of awareness of a specific problem.

---

* A note on my use of "reflection." Mental activity in Marxist theory has been analyzed in essentially two ways: as part of a totality and as a reflection of social reality. Young Lukács and Goldmann are the main representatives of the former approach, while most Marxists support the latter approach. Those who see thought as an organic part of the totality tend to refer to Marx's concept of "praxis," while reflection theorists concentrate on the concept of "ideology."

Another difficulty with using the concept of class strategy concerns the determination of the institution which specifically outlines the strategy of a particular class. If, for instance, one looks at the capitalist class in the United States, one may ask: who elaborates its main strategy? It seems to me that only a thorough empirical study would satisfactorally answer this question and allow one to see whether or not the question has been wrongly conceptualized. However, until then, using the concept of class strategy certainly has its merits.

Some words in these concluding pages should also be said about the origin of the idea of social thought as class strategy. It originates, of course, in Marx himself, more precisely in his theses on Feuerbach. However, at this point of its development, Marxism contains the most divergent ideas and they all claim to go back to Marx. The real source of social thought as class strategy is Lukács' *History and Class Consciousness,* but it was Lucien Goldmann who first saw the great potential of Lukács' ideas. To my knowledge, however, Goldmann never used the concept, "class strategy."* Perhaps it would have struck him as a dogmatic label, since it might be utilized to characterize this or that author as, for instance, "expressing the class strategy of the petty bourgeoisie" and then serve as a reason to discard an important work.

This, however, is not my evaluation. I feel that the concept of class strategy, as applied to people's mental activities, is not in the least dogmatic but rather the opposite. A dogmatic approach is excluded if one takes into account the proper procedure that should be involved in an analysis—the painstaking work of establishing a thinker's central concern and then the careful placing of this concern into the context of a specific problem that a class or a class fraction faces. That dogmatic thinkers always get dogmatic results is a different issue.

A final consideration for using the concept of social thought as class strategy is the role it can play in the class struggle. For a Marxist this is a central question. I personally feel that this approach can play a progressive role in the change in orientation of socialist politics that is now taking place. The main impetus behind this reorientation has been the failure of the old communist strategy to gain the support of the masses in capitalist countries. It has gradually been realized that capitalism has deep cultural roots and that an attack on the state is not enough. One also has to triumph over the "cultural forces" that support capitalism. An analysis of these cultural forces would perhaps benefit from using the perspective of social thought as class strategy. Applying this perspective can help one to see more clearly how a seemingly neutral cultural idea—be it in the form of social theory, art, or literature—

* Henri Lefebvre, who is very interested in the concept of "strategy," occasionally uses the concept of thought as class strategy. In *Au-Delà du Structuralisme* (1971), for instance, he writes: "Partial logics, which abuse formal rigour by presenting themselves as proof, should be conceived as *class strategies*" (p. 9; emphasis in text).

actually helps to cement the links between various classes and class fractions. If the concept of social thought as class strategy can provide this valuable information, it will have more than fulfilled its promises: "Theory, my friend is grey; but green is the eternal tree of life." (Goethe's *Faust,* quoted by Lenin in *Letters on Tactics,* April 1917).[2]

NOTES

Introduction

[1]Don Martindale, *The Nature and Types of Sociological Theory* (Boston: Houghton Mifflin Company, 1960); Pitirim Sorokin, *Sociological Theories of Today* (New York: Harper & Row, 1966); Nicholas S. Timasheff, *Sociological Theory: Its Nature & Growth* (New York: Random House, 1955).

[2]Karl Marx and Frederick Engels, *The Holy Family, or Critique of Critical Criticism* (Moscow: Progress Publishers, 1975), pp. 225-226.

[3]Lucien Goldmann, *Marxisme et Sciences Humaines* (Paris: Gallimard, 1970), p. 62.

[4]Quoted by Lucien Goldmann in *The Hidden God: A Study of Tragic Vision in the Pensées of Pascal and the Tragedies of Racine,* trans. Philip Thody (New York: The Humanities Press, 1964), p. 265.

[5]Arthur Mitzman, *The Iron Cage: An Historical Interpretation of Max Weber* (New York: Alfred A. Knopf, 1970).

[6]Lucien Goldmann, *Recherches Dialectiques* (Paris: Gallimard, 1959), p. 51.

[7]Nicholas S. Mullins, with the assistance of Carolyn J. Mullins, *Theories and Theory Groups in Contemporary American Sociology* (New York: Harper & Row, 1973).

[8]Georg Lukács, *History and Class Consciousness: Studies in Marxist Dialectics,* trans. Rodney Livingstone (Cambridge, Mass: The MIT Press, 1968), p. 30.

[9]Lucien Goldmann, *The Hidden God,* p. 12.

[10]Terry Nichols Clark, *Prophets and Patrons: The French University and the Emergence of the Social Sciences* (Cambridge, Mass: Harvard University Press, 1973).

[11]Karl Marx and Frederick Engels, *The German Ideology* (Moscow: Progress Publishers, 1964), p. 388.

[12]Florian Znaniecki, *The Social Role of the Man of Knowledge* (New York: Columbia University Press, 1940).

Chapter One

[1]Karl Mannheim, *Ideology and Utopia* (London: Routledge & Kegan Paul Ltd, 1968), pp. 66-68.

[2]See, for instance, Lucien Goldmann, *Immanuel Kant,* trans. Robert Black (London: NLB, 1971), p. 32.

[3]Georges Gurvitch, "Mon itinéraire intellectuel," *Lettres Nouvelles,* 62 (Juillet-Août 1958), 65-83. See also the preface by Serge Jonas to the same article in *L'Homme et la Société,* 1 (1966), 3-12.

[4]Gurvitch, "My Intellectual Itinerary or 'Excluded From the Horde'," *Sociological Abstracts,* 17/2 (April 1969), p. i.

[5]*Ibid.,* p. ii.

[6]*Ibid.*

[7]*Ibid.*

[8]*Ibid.,* p. iii.

[9]*Ibid.*

[10]*Ibid.*

[11]*Ibid.,* p. iv.

[12]*Ibid.*

[13]*Ibid.*

[14]*Ibid.*

[15]*Ibid.*, pp. iv-v.

[16]*Ibid.*, p. i.

[17]*Ibid.*

[18]*Ibid.*, p. ii.

[19]*Ibid.*

[20]*Ibid.*, p. iii.

[21]*Ibid.*

[22]*Ibid.*, p. i.

[23]*Ibid.*, p. iv.

[24]*Ibid.*, pp. iii-iv.

[25]*Ibid.*, p. iii.

[26]*Ibid.*, p. ii.

[27]*Ibid.*, p. iv.

[28]*Ibid.*

[29]*Ibid.*, p. v.

[30]Jean Duvignaud, *Georges Gurvitch: Symbolisme Social et Sociologie Dynamique* (Paris: Editions Seghers, 1969).

[31]Gurvitch, "Intellectual Itinerary," p. iv.

[32]*Ibid.*

[33]Georges Gurvitch, "Kant und Fichte als Rousseau-Interpreten," *Kant-Studien,* 27 (1922), p. 159.

[34]*Ibid.*, p. 163.

[35]*Ibid.*, pp. 146-148.

[36]*Ibid.*, p. 153, n. 1. See also, Georges Gurvitch, *L'Idée du Droit Social* (Paris: Librairie du Receuil Sirey, 1932), p. 261.

[37]Gurvitch, *L'Idée du Droit Social,* p. 263.

[38]*Ibid.*, pp. 264-265.

[39]Cf. Antonio Gramsci, *Selections from the Prison Notebooks,* trans. Quintin Hoare and Geoffrey Nowell Smith (New York: International Publishers, 1975), pp. 5-23.

[40]Richard Pipes, *Russia Under the Old Regime* (London: Weidenfeld and Nicolson, 1974), pp. 171-190.

[41]Peter I. Lyashchenko, *History of the National Economy of Russia to the 1917 Revolution,* trans. L. M. Herman (New York: The Macmillan Company, 1949), p. 459.

[42]E. H. Carr, *The Bolshevik Revolution 1917-1923* (London: Penguin Books, 1972), II, p. 18.

[43]Pipes, *Russia,* pp. 221-245.

[44]Lyashchenko, *History,* pp. 403-407.

[45]V. I. Lenin, *The Development of Capitalism in Russia* (Moscow: Progress Publishers, 1974), pp. 179-183.

[46]Lyashchenko, *History,* p. 730.

[47]Theodore Dan, *The Origins of Bolshevism,* trans. Joel Carmichael (New York and Evanston: Harper & Row Publishers, 1964), pp. 14-23.

[48]Pipes, *Russia,* pp. 191-220.

[49]Carr, *The Bolshevik Revolution,* II, pp. 30-31.

[50]Lyashchenko, *History,* pp. 526, 533, 564.

[51]*Ibid.*, p. 746.

[52]J. L. H. Keep, *The Rise of Social Democracy in Russia* (Oxford: Clarendon Press, 1963).

[53]Lyashchenko, *History,* pp. 545-549.

[54]*Ibid.*, p. 646.

[55]See: Isaiah Berlin, "A Marvellous Decade I. 1838-1848: The Birth of the Russian Intelligentsia," *Encounter,* IV (June 1955), 27-39; Daniel R. Brower, "The Problem of the Intelligentsia," *Slavic Review* XXVI (1967), 638-647; Michael Confino, "On Intellectuals and Intellectual Traditions in Eighteenth and Nineteenth Century Russia," *Daedalus,* Spring 1972, 117-149; George Fischer, "The Intelligentsia and Russia," in Cyril E. Black, ed., *The Transformation of Russian Society: Aspects of Social Change Since 1861* (Cambridge, Mass.: Harvard University Press,

1960), pp. 253-274; George Fischer, *Russian Liberalism: From Gentry to Intelligentsia* (Cambridge, Mass.: Harvard University Press, 1958); Richard Hare, *Pioneers of Russian Thought* (New York: Vintage Books, 1964); Martin Malia, *Alexander Herzen and the Birth of Russian Socialism* (New York: The Universal Library, 1965); Vladimir C. Nahirny, "The Russian Intelligentsia: From Men of Ideas to Men of Convictions," *Comparative Studies in Society and History,* IV (1961-1962), 403-435; Richard Pipes, ed., *The Russian Intelligentsia* (New York: Columbia University Press, 1961); Alan P. Pollard, "The Russian Intelligentsia: The Mind of Russia," *California Slavic Studies,* IV (1964), 1-32; Philip Pomper, *The Russian Revolutionary Intelligentsia* (New York: Thomas Y. Crowell Company, 1970); Marc Raeff, *Origins of the Russian Intelligentsia: The Eighteenth-Century Nobility* (New York: Harcourt, Brace & World, Inc., 1966); Stuart Ramsey Tompkins, *The Russian Intelligentsia: Makers of the Revolutionary State* (Norman: University of Oklahoma Press, 1957); Franco Venturi, *Roots of Revolution: A History of Populist and Socialist Movements in Nineteenth Century Russia,* trans. Francis Haskell (New York: Alfred A. Knopf, 1960); Avraham Yarmolinsky, *Road to Revolution: A Century of Russian Radicalism* (New York: Collier Books, 1962).

[56]Yarmolinsky, *Road to Revolution,* p. 168.

[57]Venturi, *Roots of Revolution.*

[58]*Ibid.,* p. 411.

[59]T. H. Rigby, *Communist Party Membership in the U.S.S.R.* (Princeton: Princeton University Press, 1968), p. 63.

[60]Pollard, "The Russian Intelligentsia," *California Slavic Studies,* IV (1964), p. 16.

[61]George Plekhanov, *The Role of the Individual in History* (New York: International Publishers, 1940).

[62]Paul Mattick, "Préface" in Anton Pannekoek, *Lénine Philosophe,* trans. Daniel Saint-James et Claude Simon (Paris: Spartakus, 1970), p. 14.

[63]Jean Duvignaud, "Entretien avec Georges Gurvitch," *Lettres Nouvelles,* 1er Avril 1959, p. 24.

[64]Georges Gurvitch, "Marx et Proudhon," in *L'Actualité de Proudhon. Colloque des 24 et 25 Novembre 1965* (Bruxelles: Editions de l'Institut de Sociologie de l'Université Libre de Bruxelles, 1967), p. 96.

Chapter Two

[1]Georges Gurvitch, *Die Einheit der Fichteschen Philosophie-Personal und Gemeinschaftswert in der Ethik Fichtes. Eine Studie über Fichtes Lehre vom Sittlichen Ideal.I. Lieferung* (Berlin: Verlag Arthur Collignon, 1922) and *Fichtes System der Konkreten Ethik* (Tübingen: Verlag von J.C.B. Mohr (Paul Siebeck), 1924).

[2]See, for instance, Georg Lukács, *History and Class Consciousness,* pp. xxvii-xxviii.

[3]Gurvitch, *Fichtes System,* p. 375.

[4]Marx and Engels, *The German Ideology,* p. 451.

[5]See, for instance, Goldmann, *The Hidden God,* p. 17.

[6]See, for instance, Lucien Goldmann, *Marxisme et Sciences Humaines,* p. 44.

[7]See, for instance, Lukács, *History and Class Consciousness,* p. 5 and Goldmann, *Kant,* p. 127.

[8]Goldmann, *Kant,* pp. 38-39.

[9]See Nicos Poulantzas, *Political Power and Social Classes,* trans. Timothy O'Hagan (London: NLB and Sheld and Ward, 1973).

[10]V. I. Lenin, "The Tasks of the Youth Leagues (1920)" in Stefan Possony, ed., *Lenin Reader* (Chicago: Henry Regnery Company, 1966), p. 92.

[11]Frederick Engels, *Herr Eugen Dühring's Revolution in Science (Anti-Dühring)* (New York: International Publishers, 1966), p. 105.

[12]See, for instance, Karl Marx, "On the Jewish Question" in Karl Marx and Frederick Engels, *Collected Works* (New York: International Publishers, 1975), 3, pp. 146-175.

[13]Cf. Gurvitch, *Die Einheit* (38 pp.) and "Einleitung. Die Einheit der theoretischen Philosophie Fichtes," pp. 1-64 in *Fichtes System.*

[14]Gurvitch, *Die Einheit,* pp. 1-2 and *Fichtes System,* pp. 1-4.

[15]Gurvitch, *Die Einheit,* p. 2.

[16]Gurvitch, *Die Einheit,* pp. 2-4 and *Fichtes System,* pp. 4-8.

[17]Gurvitch, *Die Einheit,* pp. 4-10, 27-32 and *Fichtes System,* pp. 9-22.

[18]Gurvitch, *Die Einheit,* pp. 10-12, 27-33 and *Fichtes System,* pp. 22-28.

[19]Gurvitch, *Fichtes System,* p. 24.

[20]Gurvitch, *Die Einheit,* pp. 12-26, 33-38 and *Fichtes System,* pp. 29-64.

[21]Gurvitch, *Die Einheit,* p. 16.

[22]Gurvitch, *Fichtes System,* p. 44, n.3

[23]*Ibid.,* pp. 1, 65-76.

[24]*Ibid.,* pp. 76-110.

[25]*Ibid.,* pp. 110-137.

[26]*Ibid.,* pp. 137-214.

[27]*Ibid.,* pp. 215-231.

[28]*Ibid.,* pp. 231-284.

[29]*Ibid.,* pp. 284-294.

[30]*Ibid.,* pp. 294-375.

[31]*Ibid.,* pp. 294-375.

[32]Georges Gurvitch, *Les Tendances Actuelles de la Philosophie Allemande: E. Husserl. M. Scheler. E. Lask. N. Hartmann. M. Heidegger* (Paris: Librairie Philosophique J. Vrin, 1930) and *Morale Théorique et Science des Moeurs: Leurs Possibilités-Leurs Conditions* (Paris: P.U.F., 1937).

[33]See Martial Gueroult, *L'Evolution et la Structue de la Doctrine de la Science chez Fichte* (Strasbourg: Commission des Publications de la Faculté des Lettres de l'Université de Strasbourg, 1930), I, p. 153, n. 345.

[34]Nikolai Losskij, "Fichtes Konkrete Ethik im Lichte des Modernen Transcendentalismus," *Logos,* XV (1926), p. 357.

[35]Martial Gueroult, "Le Système de Morale Concrète d'après M. Gurwitsch," *Revue de Métaphysique et de Morale,* 33 (1926), p. 127.

[36]Gurvitch, "Intellectual Itinerary," p. v.

[37]Gurvitch, *Die Einheit,* p. 16.

[38]See, for instance, Alan P. Pollard, "The Russian Intelligentsia: The Mind of Russia," *California Slavic Studies,* IV (1964), pp. 24-26.

[39]See, for instance, V. I. Lenin, "Materialism and Empirio-Criticism" in *Collected Works,* 14, and G. Plekhanov, *The Development of the Monist View in History* (New York: International Publishers, 1972).

[40]N. O. Lossky, *History of Russian Philosophy* (New York: International Universities Press, 1951), pp. 59-64.

[41]Richard Pipes, "The Historical Evolution of the Russian Intelligentsia" in Richard Pipes, ed., *The Russian Intelligentsia,* pp. 55-56.

[42]Boris Jakowenko, "Dreissig Jahre russischer Philosophie (1900-1929)," *Russische Gedanke,* I (1930), p. 326.

[43]N. O. Lossky, *History of Russian Philosophy,* p. 175.

[44]Georges Gurvitch, "La Philosophie Russe du Premier Quart du XXe Siècle," *Monde Slave,* 3 (1926), p. 262.

[45]Struve quoted in Stuart Ramsey Tompkins, *The Russian Intelligentsia,* pp. 217 ff.

[46]Quoted in Tompkins, *The Russian Intelligentsia,* p. 214.

[47]Pipes, "The Historical Evolution of the Russian Intelligentsia," p. 56.

[48]Lenin, "Materialism and Empirio-Criticism," pp. 342, 358.

[49]V. I. Lenin, "Two Utopias" in *Collected Works,* 18, p. 386.

[50]V. I. Lenin, "Concerning *Vekhi*" in *Collected Works,* 10, pp. 123-124.

[51]Lenin, "Concerning *Vekhi,*" p. 124.

[52]Georges Gurvitch, "Fichte" in Edwin R. A. Seligman and Alvin Johnson, eds., *Encyclopaedia of the Social Sciences* (New York: The Macmillan Company, 1931), VI, p. 224.

[53]See Gurvitch, "Intellectual Itinerary," and V.V. Zenkovsky, *A History of Russian Philosophy* trans. George L. Kline (New York: Columbia University Press, 1967), II, pp. 702-704.

[54]Georges Gurvitch, "Structures Sociales et Systèmes de Connaissances," in *XXe Sémaine de*

Synthèse et Structure de la Connaissance, 18-27 Avril 1956 (Paris: Albin Michel, 1957), p. 341.

⁵⁵See also Gurvitch, "Intellectual Itinerary," and *Die Einheit,* p. 3 and *Fichtes System,* p. 2.

⁵⁶See Fichte's famous letter to Baggesen in April 1795: "My system is the first system of liberty. Just as the French nation will deliver mankind from its material chains, so shall my system deliver it from the yoke of the thing-in-itself . . . ." Quoted in Roger Garaudy, "Fichte et Marx" in *Annali (Instituto Giangiacomo Feltrinelli),* VII (1964/65), p. 138.

⁵⁷Georg Lukács, *Die Zerstörung der Vernuft* (Darmstadt und Neuwied: Luchterhand Verlag, 1973), I-III.

⁵⁸Lukács, *Die Zerstörung.*

⁵⁹Gurvitch, "Intellectual Itinerary," *Sociological Abstracts,* p. v.

⁶⁰For the utopian atmosphere among revolutionary intellectuals after the Russian Revolution, see, for instance, Lukács, *History and Class Consciousness,* pp. ix-xxxix, and for Gurvitch's revolutionary activities, for instance, Gurvitch, "Proudhon et Marx," *Cahiers Internationaux de Sociologie,* XL (1966), 7-16.

Chapter Three

¹Gurvitch, "Intellectual Itinerary," *Sociological Abstracts,* pp. v-vii.

²Georges Gurvitch, *L'Idée du Droit Social. Notion et Système du Droit Social. Histoire Doctrinale depuis le XVIIᵉ Siècle jusq'à la Fin du XIX Siècle* (Paris: Librairie du Recueil Sirey, 1932).

³See, for instance, Marcel Durry, "Georges Gurvitch," *Annales de l'Université de Paris,* 36 (1966), p. 184. For Gurvitch's 'left-wing' communism before 1917, see Jean Duvignaud, "Entretien avec Georges Gurvitch," *Lettres Nouvelles,* 1ᵉʳ Avril, 1959, p. 24.

⁴Lukács, "Preface to the New Edition (1967)" in *History and Class Consciousness,* pp. ix-xxxix.

⁵Georg Lukács, "Die neue Ausgabe von Lassalles Briefen," *Archiv für die Geschichte des Sozialismus und die Arbeiterbewegung,* XI (1925), 401-423 and "Moses Hess und die Probleme der Idealistischen Dialektik," *Archiv für die Geschichte des Sozialismus und die Arbeiterbewegung,* XII (1926), 105-155. See also *History and Class Consciousness,* pp. xxxiii-xxxiv.

⁶See, for instance, Georges Gurvitch "Otto v. Gierke als Rechtsphilosoph," *Logos,* XI (1922/23), 86-132, and *Le Temps Présent et l'Idée du Droit Social* (Paris: Librairie J. Vrin, 1932).

⁷"Juristen-Sozialismus," *Die Neue Zeit,* 5 (1887), 49-62. Reprinted in Karl Marx-Friedrich Engels, *Werke* (Berlin: Dietz Verlag, 1962), 21, 491-509.

⁸Georges Gurvitch, *L'Expérience Juridique et la Philosophie Pluraliste du Droit* (Paris: Editions A. Pedone, 1935).

⁹Gurvitch, *Le Temps Présent,* p. 294.

¹⁰Jean Duvignaud, "Georges Gurvitch: Une Théorie Sociologique de l'Autogestion," *Autogestion,* 1 (1966), p. 11.

¹¹Roger Bastide, "Georges Gurvitch (1894-1965)," *Année Sociologique,* 1965, p. ix and Jean Duvignaud, *Georges Gurvitch,* p. 184. It is customary to give 1932 as the printing year of *L'Idée du Droit Social.* The work, however, was published in 1931. See, for instance, Harold Laski's letter to Oliver Wendell Holmes in December 1931 in Mark de Wolfe, ed., *Holmes-Laski Letters. The Correspondence of Mr. Justice Holmes and Harold J. Laski 1916-1935* (Cambridge, Massachusetts: Harvard University Press, 1953), p. 1347.

¹²For general information concerning French doctoral theses in the social sciences and related questions, see Clark, *Prophets and Patrons.*

¹³Georges Gurvitch, "The Problem of Social Law," *Ethics,* LII (1941), 17-40.

¹⁴Roscoe Pound has the following to say on this question: "In the languages of Continental Europe the words used for the Latin *ius,* namely, *droit, derecho, diritto, Recht,* are entirely equivalents. To take the French word as representative, neither 'right' nor 'law' exactly translates *droit,* which often can only be rendered in English by an awkward phrase. Sometimes, indeed, it means what we should call law, that is, the body of authoritative guides to determination of controversies. Sometimes it is best rendered in English by 'what is right.' Sometimes it means 'a right.' In juristic discussion it usually must be rendered as 'what is right backed by politically organized society' or 'right plus law.' Often it means what an Anglo-American lawyer would have to express

by 'what we seek to bring about (or to maintain) through law.' Scotch writers in the last century often translated *ius* and its equivalents in modern languages by 'right' rather than by 'law.' In Anglo-American justice writing 'law,' as distinguished from 'a law,' usually means the system of authoritative materials for grounding or guiding judicial and administrative action recognized or established in a politically organized society. 'A law' is the equivalent of *loi.*" Roscoe Pound, "Sociology of Law" in Georges Gurvitch and Wilbert E. Moore, eds., *Twentieth Century Sociology* (New York: Philosophical Library, 1945), pp. 299-300. "Social constitution" would perhaps be the closest translation of *droit social.* It is, however, somewhat awkward.

[15]Gurvitch, *L'Idée du Droit Social,* pp. 15-46.

[16]*Ibid.,* pp. 46-95.

[17]*Ibid.,* pp. 95-169.

[18]*Ibid.,* pp. 171-710.

[19]*Ibid.,* p. 282.

[20]Louis Le Fur, "Préface," p. ix in *ibid.*

[21]Mark de Wolfe, ed., *Holmes-Laski Letters,* pp. 1347, 1364.

[22]For the reaction that social law was another version of natural law, see, for instance, G. Aillet, "Le Droit Social," *Revue de Métaphysique et de Morale,* 40 (1933), pp. 259-260; Sergius Hessen, "Zur Geschichte und Theorie des Sozialrechts," *Zeitschrift für Rechtsphilosophie,* 6 (1932/34), p. 265; Louis Le Fur, "Droit Individuel et Droit Social. Coordination, Subordination et Intégration," *Archives de Philosophie du Droit et de Sociologie Juridique,* 1 (1931), 279-309; R.G. Renard, "Thomisme et Droit Social," *Revue des Sciences Philosophiques et Théologiques,* 23 (Février 1934), p. 45; Ulrich Scheuner, Review of *L'Idée du Droit Social, Archiv für Rechts- und Wirtschaftsphilosophie,* XXVI (1932/33), p. 260. Gurvitch defends himself against this accusation in *L'Expérience Juridique,* pp. 118-137.

[23]Sergius Hessen, "Zur Geschichte und Theorie des Sozialrechts," *Zeitschrift für Rechtsphilosophie,* 6 (1932/34), pp. 251 ff; Ulrich Scheuner, Review, *Archiv für Rechts- und Wirtschaftsphilosophie,* XXVI (1932/33), pp. 261-262; N. S. Timasheff, "Gurvitch's Philosophy of Social Law," *Thought,* XVII (1942), p. 714.

[24]Ulrich Scheuner, Review, *Archiv für Rechts- und Wirtschaftsphilosophie,* XXVI (1932/33), pp. 261-262. Also Hugo Sinzheimer felt that Gurvitch underestimated the role of the state. See Hugo Sinzheimer, "Eine Theorie des sozialen Rechts," *Zeitschrift für Öffentliches Recht,* XVI (1936), pp. 45-57.

[25]N. S. Timasheff, "Gurvitch's Philosophy of Social Law," *Thought,* XVII (1942), p. 721, n. 25.

[26]G. Aillet, "Le Droit Social," *Revue de Métaphysique et de Morale,* 40 (1933), pp. 262-264.

[27]See, for instance, V. A. Tumanov's brief but sharp critique of Gurvitch's philosophy of law in *Contemporary Bourgeois Legal Thought: A Marxist Evaluation of the Basic Concepts* (Moscow: Progress Publishers, 1974), pp. 218-227.

[28]Karl Marx, "Report of the General Council on the Right to Inheritance (1869)" In Karl Marx, *On the First International,* ed. by Saul K. Padover (New York: McGraw-Hill Book Company, 1973), p. 111.

[29]Marx, *On the First International,* p. 110.

[30]Karl Marx, *A Contribution to the Critique of Political Economy* (New York: International Publishers, 1970), p. 21.

[31]V. I. Lenin, *Imperialism, The Highest Stage of Capitalism: A Popular Outline* (Peking: Foreign Languages Press, 1969). See, for instance, also Ernest Mandel, *Marxist Economic Theory,* trans. Brian Pears (New York and London: Modern Reader Press, 1968), chs. 12-13.

[32]Friedrich Engels, "Juristen-Sozialismus" in Kark Marx-Friedrich Engels, *Werke,* 21, 491-509. "Juristen-Sozialismus" was jointly written by Kautsky and Engels. Who wrote which part is not known according to *Werke,* 21, p. 617, n. 464.

[33]Marx-Engels, *Werke,* pp. 491-494.

[34]Karl Marx, "The Communist Manifesto" in *Collected Works,* 6, pp. 507-517.

[35]Gurvitch, "Intellectual Itinerary," p. iv.

[36]See, for instance, Richard Pipes, *Russia Under the Old Regime,* pp. 61-67, 104-105, 154, 288-299 and Max Laserson, "Die Russische Rechtsphilosophie," *Archiv für Rechts- und Wirtschaftsphilosophie,* XXVI (1932/33), pp. 289-293.

[37]See, for instance, Perry Anderson, *Lineages of the Absolute State* (London: NLB, 1974), pp. 195-220, 328-360.

[38]See, for instance, Pipes, *Russia,* pp. 305-307.

[39]See, for instance, E. Spektorsky, "Der Russische Anarchismus und Seine Stellung zum Rechtsproblem," *Philosophie und Recht,* II (1922/1923), pp. 63-80.

[40]See, for instance, Georges Gurvitch, "Übersicht der Neueren Rechtsphilosophischen Literatur in Russland," *Philosophie und Recht,* II (1922/1923), 111-125.

[41]Gurvitch, "Übersicht," p. 118 and Nicholas S. Timasheff in Leon Petrazycki, *Law and Morality,* trans. Hugh W. Babb (Cambridge, Massachusetts: Harvard University Press, 1955), p. xviii.

[42]Georges Gurvitch, "Die Zwei Grössten Russischen Rechtsphilosophen: Boris Tschitscherin und Wladimir Ssolowjew," *Philosophie und Recht,* II (1922/1923), 80-102.

[43]*Ibid.,* p. 95. Emphasis in text.

[44]Gurvitch, "Übersicht," p. 125. See also Laserson, "Die Russische Rechtsphilosophie," pp. 316-318.

[45]See Taranowsky's preface to Gurvitch's prize-winning essay on the origin of natural law in Russia: *"The Truth of the Monarch's Will" of Theophan Prokopovitch and Its Western-European Sources* (Dorpat: University of Dorpat, 1915) (in Russian). I thank Larry Nichols for having translated this preface for me.

[46]Gurvitch, "Übersicht," pp. 100-101 and "Die Zwei Grössten Russischen Rechtsphilosphen," pp. 118-120.

[47]Gurvitch, "Übersicht," pp. 119-120.

[48]Sergius Hessen, "Zur Geschichte des Sozialrechts," *Zeitschrift für Rechtsphilosophie,* 6 (1932/34), p. 73, and Robert Bierstedt, "Nicholas S. Timasheff, 1886-1970," *American Sociologist,* 5 (1970), p. 290.

[49]See, for instance, Gurvitch, "Übersicht," p. 112 and Laserson, "Die Russische Rechtsphilosophie," pp. 324-336.

[50]According to *L'Idée du Droit Social,* Petrazhitsky wanted to "reconcile . . . sociology and morality" (p. 338). Gurvitch wrote several articles on Petrazhitsky. See, for instance, "Une Philosophie Intuitionniste du Droit: Léon Petrasizky," *Archives de Philosophie du Droit et de Sociologie Juridique,* 1 (1931), 403-420.

[51]Leon Petrazycki, *Law and Morality,* p. 241.

[52]See, for example, George Fischer, *Russian Liberalism,* pp. 43-82 and Samuel Kucheron, *Courts, Lawyers and Trials under the Three Last Tsars* (New York: Frederick A. Praeger, 1953), pp. 302-316.

[53]Cf. N. O. Lossky in *Slavonic Religious Philosophy,* trans. Natalie Duddington (Unpublished Manuscript, Harvard University), p. 418: "Hessen's big work *The Problem of Legal Socialism* (Rechtssozialismus) deserves attention as an attempt to give a synthesis of the valuable aspects of the bourgeois-capitalist individualist social order with the valuable aspects of the Socialist ideal." Hessen's work was published in *Sovremenniya Zapiski* (Paris) during 1924-1928 according to N. O. Lossky, *History of Russian Philosophy,* p. 320.

[54]See, for instance, Myrtle Korenbaum, "Translator's Preface" in Gurvitch, *Spektrum,* p. xi.

[55]Gurvitch, *L'Idée du Droit Social,* pp. 327-406.

[56]"Justice is the central star which governs all societies, the pole around which the political world turns, and the principle and rule of each transaction." -P.-J. Proudhon, *Oeuvres Complétes* (Paris: Marcel Rivière, 1926), IV, p. 144.

[57]Gurvitch, *L'Idée du Droit Social,* p. 351.

[58]"The real meaning of socialism can only be grasped through a *pluralistic theory of law and society"* - Gurvitch, *L'Expérience Juridique,* p. 296. Emphasis in text. See also Celéstin Bouglé, *Bilan de la Sociologie Contemporaine* (Paris: Félix Alcan, 1938), pp. 102-103.

[59]See Franz Neumann, "The Change in Function of Law in Modern Society (1937)" in Franz Neumann, *The Democratic and the Authoritarian State: Essays in Political and Legal Theory* (New York: The Free Press, 1964), 24-68.

[60]For France, see Bouglé, *Bilan,* pp. 95-120.

[61]See Neumann, pp. 47-68.

[62]See, for instance, Edmond Laskine, "Die Entwicklung des Juristischen Sozialismus," *Archiv*

für die Geschichte des Sozialismus und der Arbeiterbewegung, III (1913), 17-70; Franz Neumann, *pp. 64-66; Tumanov, pp. 211-215.*

[63]Marx-Engels, *Werke,* 21, p. 502.

[64]Gurvitch, "Proudhon et Marx" in *L'Actualité de Proudhon,* p. 90, and Korenbaum, "Translator's Preface" in Gurvitch, *Spektrum,* p. x.

[65]Korenbaum in Gurvitch *Spektrum,* p. xi.

[66]See for instance, G.D.H. Cole, *A History of Socialist Thought* (New York: St. Martin's Press, 1955-1960).

[67]J.E.S. Hayward, "The Official Philosophy of the French Third Republic: Léon Bourgeois and Solidarism," *International Review of Social History,* VI (1961), p. 20, and Steven Lukes, *Emile Durkheim. His Life and Work. A Historical and Critical Study* (New York: Harper & Row, Publishers, 1972), p. 351.

[68]Gurvitch, *Le Temps Présent,* p. 12.

[69]*Ibid.,* pp. 294-315. See also *L'Expérience Juridique,* p. 235.

[70]Gurvitch, *Le Temps Présent.* See also, for instance, *L'Expérience Juridique,* p. 235.

[71]Gurvitch, *Le Temps Présent,* p. 181.

[72]See, for instance, "Manifesto of the Communist International to the Proletariat of the Entire World (1919)" and "Conditions of Admission to the Communist International Approved by the Second Comintern Congress (1920)'" in Jane Degras, ed., *The Communist International 1919-1943* (London: Oxford University Press, 1956), I, pp. 38-47, 166-172.

[73]Harold Laski, "Socialists and the League of Nations," *American Socialist Monthly,* 5 (March 1936), p. 8.

[74]See, for instance, E. H. Carr, *The Bolshevik Revolution,* III, pp. 206-208 and "Directives on the United Front of the Workers and on the Attitudes to Workers Belonging to the Second, Two-and-a-Half and Amsterdam International," in Helmut Gruber, ed., *International Communism in the Era of Lenin: A Documentary History* (New York: Doubleday & Company, Inc., 1972), pp. 318-327.

[75]Georges Gurvitch, *L'Expérience Juridique,* p. 235.

[76]Gurvitch, "L'Expérience Juridique," in *ibid.,* pp. 13-87.

[77]*Ibid.,* p. 66.

[78]*Ibid.,* p. 235.

Chapter Four

[1]The year of transition can be set, as Duvignaud says, in 1935. In that year Gurvitch published his first purely sociological study, "Remarques sur la Classification des Formes de la Sociabilité," *Archives de Philosophie du Droit et de Sociologie Juridique,* N⁰ 3-4, 1935, 43-91. *L'Expérience Juridique* (1935), according to its preface, was not only intended as an exposé of Gurvitch's method in the philosophy of law but was also an attempt to elaborate a "guide" for research in the sociology of law. Cf. Gurvitch, *Eléments de Sociologie Juridique,* p. 9; Jean Duvignaud, ed., *Anthologie des Sociologues Francais Contemporaine* (Paris: P.U.F., 1970), p. 38.

[2]Georges Gurvitch, *Eléments de Sociologie Juridique* (Paris: Aubier Editions Montaigne, 1940).

[3]Gurvitch was until his death a convinced socialist. See, for instance, Gurvitch, "Proudhon et Marx," *Cahiers Internationaux de Sociologie,* XL (1966), 7-16.

[4]Gurvitch, "Intellectual Itinerary," pp. vi-vii.

[5]*Ibid.,* pp. iii-iv.

[6]*Ibid.,* p. iv and Duvignaud, "Entretien avec Georges Gurvitch," pp. 23-25.

[7]Gurvitch, "Intellectual Itinerary," p. iv.

[8]For general information on Russian sociology, see, for instance, Howard Becker and Harry Elmer Barnes, *Social Thought from Lore to Science* (New York: Dover Publications, Inc., 1916), III. pp. 1029-1059; Julius Hecker, *Russian Sociology: A Contribution to the History of Sociological Thought and Theory* (New York: Columbia University Press, 1915); Pitirim Sorokin, "Die Russische Soziologie im zwanzigsten Jahrhundert," *Jahrbuch für Soziologie,* II (1926), 462-483; Alexander Vucinich, *Social Thought in Tzarist Russia: The Quest for a General Science of*

Society, 1861-1917 (Chicago: University of Chicago Press, 1976).

⁹For Mikhailovsky, see, for instance, Alexander Vucinich, *Social Thought in Tzarist Russia,* pp. 15-66.

¹⁰See, for instance, Becker and Barnes, *Social Thought,* III, pp. 1034-1041.

¹¹Pomper, *The Russian Revolutionary Intelligentsia,* pp. 108-109.

¹²Nicholas S. Timasheff, *Sociological Theory,* p. 126.

¹³V. I. Lenin, "What the 'Friends of the People' are and How They Fight the Social-Democrats" in *Collected Works,* I, 129-332.

¹⁴*Ibid.,* pp. 140, 145.

¹⁵*Ibid.,* p. 140.

¹⁶See, for instance, Barnes and Becker, *Social Thought,* III, pp. 1049-1059.

¹⁷See, for instance, the discussion of "Juristic Sociology" in Barnes and Becker, *Social Thought,* III, pp. 1053-1054 and Gurvitch, "Übersicht," 111-124.

¹⁸Pitirim Sorokin, "Die Russische Soziologie im Zwanzigsten Jahrhundert," *Jahrbuch für Soziologie,* II (1926), p. 473 and Pitirim Sorokin in letter to *Izvestia of the North Dvina Executive Committee* and quoted by V.I. Lenin, *Collected Works* (New York: International Publishers, 1945), XXIII, p. 303.

¹⁹For Lenin's analysis of Sorokin, see V.I. Lenin, "Pitirim Sorokin's Letter" and "Valuable Admissions by Pitirim Sorokin" in *Collected Works,* XXIII, pp. 303-304 and 305-313. For a description of one of Sorokin's "experiments" in which he proved communism to be inferior to individualism, see Pitirim Sorokin, "Die Russische Soziologie im Zwanzigsten Jahrhundert," pp. 474-475.

²⁰See, for instance, Gurvitch, *Eléments de Sociologie,* pp. 19, 23.

²¹See, for instance, *ibid.,* p. 20.

²²See, for instance, Gurvitch, *Morale Théorique,* pp. 144-158 and *Tendances Actuelles,* pp. 67-152. For Gurvitch's relation to Rauh, who took a similar position on this question, see, for instance, Gurvitch, *L'Expérience Juridique,* p. 41 and *L'Idée du Droit Social,* pp. 128-129.

²³See, for instance, Gurvitch, *Morale Théorique,* pp. 144-158 and *Tendances Actuelles,* pp. 67-152.

²⁴See, for instance, Gurvitch, *Essais de Sociologie,* pp. 97-112.

²⁵For a general analysis of German sociology during this time, see Volume Three of Lukács, *Zerstörung der Vernuft* entitled "Irrationalismus und Soziologie."

²⁶See, for instance, Wolfgang. J. Mommsen, *The Age of Bureaucracy: Perspectives on the Political Sociology of Max Weber* (Oxford: Basil Blackwell, 1974.)

²⁷*Ibid.,* pp. 96-97.

²⁸See, for instance, H. H. Gerth and C. Wright Mills, "Introduction: The Man and His Work," in *From Max Weber: Essays in Sociology,* trans. H. H. Gerth and C. Wright Mills (New York: Oxford University Press, 1972), pp. 49-50. Rosa Luxemburg wrote: "The German social scientists have always functioned as an extension of the police. While the latter act against Social Democracy with rubber truncheons, the former work with the intellect." See Peter Nettl, *Rosa Luxemburg* (London: Oxford University Press, 1969), pp. 139-142.

²⁹Mommsen, *The Age of Bureaucracy,* pp. 95-115. Others have noted the "sense of resignation" (Ringer) that characterized German sociology and have called it "the sociology of liberalism in despair" (Salomon) and "pessimistic bourgeois" (Horton). Cf. John Horton, "The Fetishism of Sociology" in J. David Colfax & Jack L. Roach, eds., *Radical Sociology* (New York: Basic Books, Inc., 1971) pp. 180-181; Fritz K. Ringer, *The Decline of the German Mandarins: The German Academic Community, 1890-1933* (Cambridge: Harvard University Press, 1969), p. 163; Albert Salomon, "German Sociology" in Georges Gurvitch and Wilbert E. Moore, eds., *Twentieth Century Sociology* (New York: Philosophical Library, 1945), p. 588.

³⁰Lukács, *Zerstörung der Vernuft,* III, p. 66.

³¹See, for instance, Martin Shaw, *Marxism and Social Science: The Roots of Social Knowledge* (London: Pluto Press Limited, 1975), pp. 72ff.

³²Lukács, *Zerstörung der Vernuft,* p. 63.

³³*Ibid.,* p. 63.

³⁴See Lucio Colletti, *From Rousseau to Lenin: Studies in Ideology and Science* (London: NLB, 1972), p. 233. Colletti adds: "In fact, reality is upside down. It is therefore not just a question of

criticizing the way in which economists and philosophers have depicted reality. It is necessary to overturn *reality* itself — to straighten it up and 'put it back on its feet.'" For a Marxist critique of Weber, see for instance, Lucio Colletti, "Weber and Aspects of Contemporary Sociology" in *From Rousseau to Lenin,* pp. 30-44; Georg Lukács, "Die Deutsche Sociologie der Wilhelminischen Zeit (Max Weber)" in *Zerstörung der Vernuft,* II, pp. 152-164; Martin Shaw, *Marxism and Social Science,* pp. 73-87.

[35]For a critique of Scheler, see Lukács, *Zerstörung der Vernuft,* II, pp. 152-164 and for an introduction to his work Gurvitch, *Tendances Actuelles,* pp. 67-152.

[36]See Leopold von Wiese, "Sociology is not a Normative Science" in *Systematic Sociology: On the Basis of the Beziehungslehre and Gebildlehre,* adopted and amplified by Howard Becker (New York: John Wiley & Sons, Inc., 1932), pp. 3-8. Von Wiese argues: ". . . the sociologist has no *value-judgments* to make" (p. 6).

[37]*Ibid.,* pp. 72-73. Quoted in Martindale, *The Nature and Types of Sociological Theory,* p.256.

[38]Gurvitch, "Intellectual Itinerary," p. ii.

[39]For the socialist beliefs of the Durkheimians, see, for instance, Göran Therborn, "The Sociologists and the Class Struggle" in *Science, Class and Society: On the Formation of Sociology and Historical Materialism* (London: NLB, 1976), pp. 135-144.

[40]Bouglé was the first person to try to resurrect Proudhon as a "sociologist." See, for instance, Celéstin Bouglé, "Proudhon Sociologue," *Revue de Métaphysique et de Morale* (1910), 614-648 and *Sociologie de Proudhon* (Paris: Librairie Armand Colin, 1911).

[41]See, for instance, Georges Bourgin, "Le Sociologue Marcel Mauss," *Revue Socialiste,* No 35 (Mars 1950), 220-227; Marie Granet, "Lucien Lévy-Bruhl, Socialiste," *Revue Socialiste,* No 110 (Octobre 1957), 274-280; for Halbwachs, see Terry Nichols Clark, *Prophets and Patrons,* pp. 188-189.

[42]Gurvitch, "Intellectual Itinerary," p.vi.

[43]See, for instance, Gurvitch, "Le Problème de Conscience Collective," in *Essais de Sociologie,* pp. 113-169 and *Eléments de Sociologie Juridique,* pp. 210-242.

[44]According to Terry Nichols Clark, "in the 1930's he [Gurvitch] worked through the legacy of the Durkheimians." Cf. Clark, *Prophets and Patrons,* p. 231.

[45]Gurvitch, *Morale Théorique* and "La Magie et le Droit" in *Essais de Sociologie,* pp. 171-277.

[46]See, for instance, Eva Metraux, "Trends in French Thought During the Third Republic," *Science & Society,* 5 (Summer, 1941), 207-221. Metraux argues that there is a "causal relation between the special character of monopoly capitalism in France and the ideological evolution of the intellectual elite between 1871 and 1914 (. . .)" (p. 207).

[47]For a general introduction to the history of the Third Republic, see, for instance, Theodore Zeldin, *France 1848-1945, I: Ambition, Love, Politics* (Oxford: The Clarendon Press, 1973) and David Thomson, *Democracy in France Since 1870* (New York: Oxford University Press, 1964).

[48]For Solidarism, see, for instance, Celéstin Bouglé, *Le Solidarisme* (Paris: Librairie-Editeur Marcel Giard, 1924); J.A.C. Scott, *Republican Ideals and the Liberal Tradition in France* (New York: Columbia University Press, 1951), pp. 157-186; Zeldin, *France 1848-1945,* pp. 640-682.

[49]See, for instance, Léon Bourgeois, *Solidarité* (Paris: Librairie Armand Colin, 1902).

[50]See, for instance, Bouglé, *Le Solidarisme,* pp. 177 ff.

[51]*Ibid.,* pp. 202-203.

[52]See, for example, J.E.S. Hayward, "The Official Philosophy of the French Third Republic: Léon Bourgeois and Solidarism," *International Review of Social History,* VI (1961), 19-48 and Alfred Croiset, ed., *Essai d'une Philosophie de la Solidarité* (Paris: Felix Alcan, 1907).

[53]Emile Durkheim, *The Division of Labor in Society,* trans. George Simpson (New York: The Free Press, 1964). For Durkheim's relation to Solidarism, see Steven Lukes, "Durkheim and Solidarism" in *Emile Durkheim,* pp. 350-354.

[54]Marcel Mauss, "Introduction" in Emile Durkheim, *Socialism,* trans. Charlotte Sattler (New York: Collier Books, 1967), p. 32. For an interpretation of Durkheim as a "conservative," see Robert Nisbet, "Conservatism and Sociology," *American Journal of Sociology,* LVII (July 1952 -March 1953), 167-175.

[55]Alfred Fouillée, *Le Socialisme et la Sociologie Réformiste* (Paris: Félix Alcan, 1909), pp. 357 ff.

[56]Emile Durkheim, *Suicide: A Study in Sociology,* trans. John A. Spaulding and George Simp-

son (New York: The Free Press, 1966).

[57]Durkheim, "Preface to the Second Edition" in *The Division of Labor in Society,* p. 28.

[58]For a Marxist analysis of the relation between Durkheim's sociology and the politics of the Third Republic, see Paul Nizan, *The Watchdogs: Philosophers of the Established Order,* trans. Paul Fittingoff (New York: Monthly Review Press, 1971), pp. 99-114.

[59]Emile Durkheim, "Value Judgments and Judgments of Reality" in *Sociology and Philosophy,* trans. D. F. Pocock (New York: The Free Press, 1974), p. 96.

[60]For Durkheim's analysis of economy, see, for instance, Lukes, *Durkheim,* pp. 499-500.

[61]For a Marxist critique of the idealism inherent in Durkheimian sociology, see Henri Lefebvre, "Marxisme et Sociologie," *Cahiers Internationaux de Sociologie,* IV (1948), pp. 48ff.

[62]For Durkheim's discussion of "collective effervescence," see, for instance, Emile Durkheim, *The Elementary Forms of the Religious Life,* trans. Joseph Ward Swain (New York: The Free Press, 1965) and *Sociology and Philosophy.*

[63]Emile Durkheim, *The Rules of Sociological Method,* trans. Sarah A. Solovay and John H. Mueller (New York: The Free Press, 1966).

[64]Celéstin Bouglé, *Leçons de Sociologie sur l'Evolution des Valeurs,* p. 36. Quoted by Georges Davy, *Sociologues d'Hier et d'Aujourd'hui* (Paris: Librairie Félix Alcan, 1931), pp. 12-13.

[65]Georges Davy, "La Sociologie Française de 1918 à 1925" in *Sociologues,* pp. 1-23.

[66]See, for instance, Davy, *Sociologues,* pp. 16-19 and Pierre Birnbaum, "Du Socialisme au Don," *L'Arc,* 48 (1972), 41-46.

[67]For the Durkheimians' attraction to the study of primitive society, see, for instance, W. Paul Vogt, "The Uses of Studying Primitives: A Note on the Durkheimians, 1890-1940," *History and Theory,* XV (1976), 33-44.

[68]See, for instance, Georges Friedmann, "Maurice Halbwachs" in Maurice Halbwachs, *Esquisse d'une Petite Psychologie des Classes Sociales* (Paris: Librairie Marcel Rivière et Cie, 1964), pp. 9-23.

[69]For a presentation of Simiand's ideas, see, for instance, Celéstin Bouglé, "Sociologie Economique" in *Bilan de la Sociologie Contemporaine* (Paris: Librairie Félix Alcan, 1938), pp. 121-157.

[70]Lucien Lévy-Bruhl, *La Morale et la Science des Moeurs* (Paris: Félix Alcan, 1902).

[71]Some of the reviewers of *L'Idée du Droit Social* raised this question. See, for instance, René Maunier in *Annales Sociologiques,* Série C. Fascicule 1 (1953), 102-105 and Hugo Sinzheimer, "Eine Theorie des Sozialen Rechts," *Zeitschrift für Offentliches Recht,* XVI (1936), pp. 45-49. G. Aillet summed up the problem in the following statement: "I think that Gurvitch both wants and does not want to be a sociologist at the same time". G. Aillet, "Le Droit Social," *Revue du Métaphysique et de Morale,* 40 (1933), p. 259.

[72]Gurvitch, "Intellectual Itinerary," p. viii.

[73]In *L'Idée du Droit Social,* for instance, there is one section which deals exclusively with sociology (pp. 124-128).

[74]Gurvitch, "Intellectual Itinerary," p. viii.

[75]Renato Treves points out the strong connection between the socialist ideal in Gurvitch's early legal works and his sociology of law in "La Sociologie du Droit de Georges Gurvitch," *Cahiers Internationaux de Sociologie,* XLV (1968), 51-66.

[76]Gurvitch also deals briefly with Durkheim in "Les Formes de la Sociabilité" in *Essais de Sociologie,* in *Morale Théorique* and in *Eléments de Sociologie Juridique.*

[77]"Les Formes de la Sociabilité" is a reworking of two of Gurvitch's earlier articles: "Remarques sur la Classification des Formes de la Sociabilité," *Archives de Philosophie du Droit et de Sociologie Juridique,* No 3-4 (1935), 43-91 and "Essai d'Une Classification Pluraliste des Formes de la Sociabilité," *Annales Sociologiques,* Série A, Fascicule 3 (1938), 1-48.

[78]Since the concept *conscience collective* is difficult to translate, the French term has been kept. Collective mind, collective conscience and collective consciousness all cover some aspects of the original meaning. See, for instance, Steven Lukes, "Conscience collective" in *Durkheim,* pp. 4-6.

[79]Most of the material on *conscience collective* is in Gurvitch's "Le Problème de la Conscience Collective dans la Sociologie de Durkheim" in *Essais de Sociologie,* pp. 113-169.

[80]See, for instance, Gurvitch, *Morale Théorique* where "reciprocity of perspectives" is directly related to Fichte's notion of *Gemeinde der Iche* (p. 77). Later Gurvitch claimed that it was Leibniz

who was the first to develop the notion of "reciprocity of perspectives." Cf. Gurvitch, "Réponse à une Critique. Lettre Ouverte au Professeur Léopold von Wiese," *Kôlner Zeitschrift für Soziologie,* 5 (1952/53), p. 102. See also, Gurvitch, *L'Idée du Droit Social,* pp. 16-17 and John Vincent Martin, *Depth Sociology and Microsociology, p. 168.* Claude Lévi-Strauss, in a review of *Essais de Sociologie,* said that Gurvitch, by not relying on the direct experience of experimental psychology, had created a "pseudo-solution." Cf. Claude Lévi-Strauss, Review of *Essais de Sociologie, Renaissance,* I., Fascicule II (Avril-Juin 1943), p. 324.

[81]See, especially Gurvitch, *Morale Théorique,* and "La Science des Faits Moraux et la Morale Théorique chez E. Durkheim" in *Essais de Sociologie,* pp. 277-306.

[82]Durkheim, "Preface to the Second Edition" (1902) in *The Division of Labor in Society,* p. xii.

[83]Gurvitch, *Morale Théorique,* p. 162.

[84]Gurvitch later wrote: "In 1948, while working on the second edition of my book (*Morale Théorique et Science des Moeurs*), I realized the fact that I had linked, without noticing it, the fate of the sociology of ethical life to a particular philosophical position. . . ." - "Intellectual Itinerary," pp. vii-viii.

[85]See Gurvitch, *Essais de Sociologie* and *Eléments de Sociologie Juridique,* pp. 1-32, 146-167, 179-191, 210-242.

[86]All translations of Gurvitch's French terms are from his *Sociology of Law,* which is the English expanded version of *Eléments de Sociologie Juridique* whose translation Gurvitch made himself. I have translated "société globale" as "global society," like Phillip Bosserman in *Dialectical Sociology: An Analysis of the Sociology of Georges Gurvitch* (Boston: Porter Sargent, 1968), rather than as "all-inclusive society" as Gurvitch suggested himself.

[87]In principle, this distinction was also present in *L'Idée du Droit Social.* The emphasis, however, was different. Gurvitch, *L'Idée du Droit Social,* p. 129.

[88]Gurvitch, following Scheler, used the notion of "negative value" to get out of this dilemma. This was another pseudo-solution like the reciprocity of perspectives.

[89]Gurvitch, "Remarques sur la Classification des Formes de la Sociabilité," *Archives de Philosophie du Droit et de Sociologie Juridique,* No 3-4 (1935), p. 67.

[90]Gurvitch, *Essais de Sociologie,* pp. 61-67 (Emphasis in text).

[91]For a discussion of German sociology from this perspective, see Lukács, *Zerstörung der Vernuft,* III.

[92]Leon Trotsky, *Whither France?* (London: New Park Publications, 1974). The book was originally published under the title *Où va la France?* in 1936.

[93]Celéstin Bouglé, the most politically interested of the Durkheimians, tried during the last years of the 1930's to orient himself and his students to the most important questions of the time. See, for example, Raymond Aron *et al, Inventaires II: L'Economie et le Politique* (Paris: Librairie Félix Alcan, 1937) and Raymond Aron *et al, Inventaires III: Classes Moyennes* (Paris: Librairie Félix Alcan, 1939). Maurice Halbwachs gave a famous course on social classes at the Sorbonne in 1938 and also contributed to Bouglé's *Inventaires.*

[94]Bouglé was the main editor of the section of *Annales Sociologiques* that dealt with general sociology. Simiand was the editor of one volume of the economic section. Halbwachs, at different times, was editor of several of the sections. J. Ray, finally, was the editor of the section that dealt with law and morality. Mauss, Fauconnet, and other Durkheimians were all on the editorial board of several sections. Cf. *Annales Sociologiques,* Série A. Fascicules 1-4 (1934-1941) (Sociologie Générale); Série B. Fascicules 1-4 (1939-40) (Sociologie Religieuse); Série C. Fascicules 1-3 (1935-1938) (Sociologie Juridique et Morale); Série D. Fascicules 1-4 (1934-1940) (Sociologie Economique); Série E. Fascicules 1-4 (1935-1942) (Morphologie Sociale, Language, Technologie Esthétique).

[95]Paul Nizan, *The Watchdogs,* p. 89.

Chapter Five

[1]See the chapter on *Ecole Libre* in Alvin Johnson, *Pioneer's Progress: An Autobiography* (New York: The Viking Press, MCMLII), pp. 366-375. Johnson saved many European scholars from fascism. He was careful, however, that no communist scholars got into the United States: "I

was just as anxious to keep Nazi and Communist propagandists out of the country as the [State Department's] committee was" (p. 370).

²Gurvitch summarized *L'Idée du Droit Social* in "The Problems of Social Law," *Ethics,* LII (1941-1942), 17-40 and *Eléments de Sociologie Juridique* in "Major Problems of the Sociology of Law," *Journal of Social Philosophy,* 6 (April 1941), 197-215. Parts of *Essais de Sociologie* appeared under the titles "Magic and Law," *Social Research,* 9 (1942), 104-122 and "Mass, Community, Communion," *Journal of Philosophy,* XXVIII (January - December 1941), 484-496. The basic ideas of *Morale Théorique et la Science des Moeurs* can be found in "Is Moral Philosophy a Normative Theory?" *Journal of Philosophy,* XL (January-December 1943), 141-148 and "Is the Antithesis of 'Moral Man' and 'Immoral Society' True?" *Philosophical Review,* LII (November 1943), 533-552.

³*Eléments de Sociologie Juridique* appeared in the United States under the title of *Sociology of Law.* Cf. Georges Gurvitch, *Sociology of Law,* with a Preface by Roscoe Pound (New York: Philosophical Library and the Alliance Book Corporation, 1942). In *Sociology of Law,* as opposed to *Eléments de Sociologie Juridique,* Gurvitch takes the American sociology of law into consideration. The differences between the two editions are analyzed by Renato Treves in "La Sociologie du Droit de Georges Gurvitch," *Cahiers Internationaux de Sociologie,* XLV (1969), 51-66.-Gurvitch also wrote two eulogies which were published as "The Sociological Legacy of Lucien Lévy-Bruhl," *Journal of Social Philosophy,* 5 (October 1939), 61-70 and "La Philosophie Sociale de Bergson," *Renaissance,* I (Janvier-Juin 1943), 81-94.

⁴Georges Gurvitch and Wilbert E. Moore, eds., *Twentieth Century Sociology* (New York: Philosophical Library, 1945), and *La Déclaration des Droits Sociaux* (New York: Editions de la Maison Francaise, Inc., 1944). Gurvitch published in 1946 an English translation of the latter under the title, *The Bill of Social Rights* (New York: International Universities Press, 1946). I will henceforth refer to the English version which, with some extremely minor differences, is identical to the original French edition. Note that Gurvitch here translates "droit social" as "social right," as opposed to his use of "social law" in *L'Idée du Droit Social.* Gurvitch explains the difference by claiming that in *La Déclaration des Droits Sociaux,* the emphasis is on the subjective rights of a people, while in *L'Idée du Droit Social,* the emphasis is on the objective regulation of society. Cf. Gurvitch, *The Declaration of Social Rights,* p. 70.

⁵Georges Gurvitch, "Democracy as a Sociological Problem," *Journal of Legal and Political Sociology,* 1-2,I (1942), 46-71; "Social Structure of Pre-War France," *American Journal of Sociology,* XLVIII (March 1943), 535-554; "Sovereignty and Its Fate in Post-War Society," *Journal of Legal and Political Sociology,* II (1943), 30-51.

⁶Gurvitch, "My Intellectual Itinerary," *Sociological Abstracts,* 17/2 (April 1969), vi-viii.

⁷Cf. Antonio Gramsci, *Selections From the Prison Notebooks.*

⁸Gurvitch was a good friend of Carlo Rosselli, the founder of *Giustizia e Libertà* who in 1937 was killed by fascist thugs. Gurvitch's and Rosselli's ideas converged in many aspects. Most important, both favored a reconciliation between liberalism and socialism. See Carlo Rosselli, *Socialisme Libérale,* trad. Stefan Priacet (Paris: Librairie Valois, 1930) and Celéstin Bouglé's eulogy over Carlo Rosselli in *Depêche de Toulouse,* June 28, 1937 which is reprinted in Gaetano Salvemini, *Carlo and Nelli Rosselli* (London: For Intellectual Liberty, 1937), pp. 69-71. For Gurvitch's relation to Rosselli and how he published one of his articles in the magazine *Giustizia e Libertà,* see Renato Treves "La Sociologie du Droit de Georges Gurvitch," *Cahiers Internationaux de Sociologie,* XLV (1969), pp. 65-66.

⁹Korenbaum in Gurvitch, *Spektrum,* p. xi.

¹⁰The quotation is from Engels' letter to Mrs. Wischnewetsky from June 3, 1886. Cf. Karl Marx and Frederick Engels, *Letters to Americans, 1848-1895: A Selection* (New York: International Publishers, 1969), p. 157. -For the general Marxist analysis of the United States, see Karl Marx and Frederick Engels, *The Civil War in the United States* (New York: International Publishers, 1940); Karl Marx and Frederick Engels, *Letters to Americans, 1848-1895: A Selection* (New York: International Publishers, 1969); *Lenin on the United States: Selected Writings by V.I. Lenin* (New York: International Publishers, 1970). A summary of the views of Marx and Engels can be found in Herbert M. Morais, "Marx and Engels on America," *Science & Society,* XII (1948), 3-21.

¹¹See, for instance, *Lenin on the United States,* pp. 50, 57.

[12]See, for instance, Rita James Simon, ed., *As We Saw the Thirties: Essays on Social and Political Movements of a Decade* (Urbana: University of Illinois Press, 1967).

[13]See, for instance, Tom Kemp, "The Intelligentsia of Modern Capitalism," *Science & Society,* XXVI (1962), pp. 314-316; Lewis A. Coser, *Men of Ideas: A Sociologist's View* (New York: The Free Press, 1970), pp. 180-187, 233-241; Max Schachtman, "Radicalism in the Thirties: The Trotskyist View" in Simon, ed., *As We Saw the Thirties,* pp. 35-42. ·

[14]Elton F. Guthrie, "Sociological Theory and Historical Materialism," *Sociology and Social Research,* XXI (March-April 1937), p. 342.

[15]See, for instance, George Novack, "Radical Intellectuals in the 1930's," *International Socialist Review,* March-April, 1968, 21-34.

[16]See, for instance, Paul Buhle, "Marxism in the United States" in Bart Grahl and Paul Piccone, eds., *Towards a New Marxism* (St. Louis: Telos Press, 1973), p. 204. -The few council communists in the United States, such as Paul Mattick and Karl Korsch, had a very small following.

[17]See, for instance, Seymour Martin Lipset, "Socialism and Sociology," in Irving Louis Horowitz, ed., *Sociological Self-Images: A Collective Portrait* (California: Sage Publications, 1969), pp. 143-176 and "The Biography of a Research Project: *Union Democracy,*" in Phillip E. Hammond, ed., *Sociologists at Work: Essays on the Craft of Social Research* (New York: Basic Books, 1964), pp. 96-120; Irving Kristol, "Memoirs of A Trotskyist," *New York Times Magazine,* January 23, 1977; Peter Blau, "The Research Process in The Study of *The Dynamics of Bureaucracy,*" pp. 16-49 in Hammond, ed., *Sociologists at Work.*

[18]See, for instance, Kemp, "The Intelligentsia and Modern Capitalism," *Science & Society,* XXVI (1962), pp. 314-316.

[19]See Barbara Heyt, "The Harvard 'Pareto Circle'", *Journal of the History of the Behavioral Sciences,* IV (1968), 316-334 and Talcott Parsons, "On Building Social System Theory: A Personal History," *Daedalus,* Fall 1970, 826-881.

[20]George C. Homans, "The Making of a Communist" (Review of *An American Testament* by Joseph Freeman), *The Saturday Review,* 1, XV (1936), p. 6.

[21]*Ibid.,* p. 6.

[22]See, for instance, Kenneth A. Thompson, "Introductory Essay," in Georges Gurvitch, *The Social Frameworks of Knowledge,* trans. Margaret A. Thompson and Kenneth A. Thompson (New York: Harper & Row, 1972), pp. ix-xxxviii; Nicholas S. Timasheff, *Sociological Theory: Its Nature and Growth* (New York: Random House, 1967), pp. 289-293; John Vincent Martin, *Depth Sociology and Microsociology,* pp. 258-259.

[23]See, for instance, Roscoe C. Hinkle, Jr. and Gisela Hinkle, *The Development of Modern Sociology* (New York: Random House, 1968) and Anthony Oberschall, "The Institutionalization of American Sociology" in Anthony Oberschall, ed., *The Establishment of Empirical Sociology: Studies in Continuity, Discontinuity, and Institutionalization* (New York: Harper & Row, 1972), pp. 187-251.

[24]Dusky Lee Smith, "Sociology and the Rise of Corporate Capitalism," *Science & Society,* XXIX (Fall, 1965), 401-418. For similarities between U.S. sociology and French sociology, see "The Parallels between Durkheim and the Americans," pp. 251-261 in Herman Schwendinger and Julia R. Schwendinger, *The Sociologists of the Chair: A Radical Analysis of the Formative Years of North American Sociology, 1883-1922* (New York: Basic Books, 1974).

[25]See, for instance, Hinkle and Hinkle, *Development of Modern Sociology,* pp. 16, 21, 22; Schwendinger and Schwendinger, *Sociologists of the Chair,* pp. 449-450; William Appleman Williams, *The Contours of American History* (Chicago: Quadrangle Books, 1966), pp. 420-425.

[26]The phrase "social bookkeeping" is Paul Lazarsfeld's. It gives associations to Weber's analysis of the role of accounting in early capitalism and is a suitable metaphor for the instrumental role of social knowledge in monopoly capitalism. Cf. Paul Lazarsfeld, "Foreword," in Oberschall, ed., *The Establishment of Empirical Sociology,* p. ix.

[27]See, for instance, Jürgen Habermas, "Technology and Science as 'Ideology'", in *Toward a Rational Society: Student Protest, Science and Politics,* trans. Jeremy J. Shapiro (Boston: Beacon Press, 1970), pp. 81-127.

[28]See, for instance, Hinkle and Hinkle, *Development of Modern Sociology,* pp. 1-17 and Oberschall, "The Institutionalization of Modern Sociology," pp. 187-232.

[29]Quoted in Hinkle and Hinkle, *The Development of Modern Sociology,* p. 10.

³⁰See, "Liberal Syndicalism as a Solution to the Neo-Hobbesian Problem" in Schwendinger and Schwendinger, *Sociologists of the Chair,* pp. 247-289.

³¹See Smith, "Sociology and the Rise of Corporate Capitalism," *Science & Society,* XXIX (Fall, 1965), pp. 411-418.

³²Early American sociologists had a superficial knowledge of Marxism and little respect for it. Small and Vincent wrote in *An Introduction to the Study of Society* (1894), "Sociology must be distinguished from Socialism . . . at present Socialism is related to Sociology much as Astrology was to the early history of Astronomy, or Alchemy to the beginnings of Chemistry" (p. 76). Quoted by Schwendinger and Schwendinger, *Sociologists of the Chair,* p. 240. Unlike later sociology, however, the founding fathers of sociology did not avoid the concept of class. Cf. Floyd Page, *Class and American Sociology: From Ward to Ross* (New York: Dial Press, 1940.)

³³Albion W. Small, "A Vision of Social Efficiency," *American Journal of Sociology,* 19 (January 1914), p. 440. Quoted by Schwendinger and Schwendinger, *Sociologists of the Chair,* p. 250.

³⁴Smith, "Sociology and the Rise of Corporate Capitalism," *Science & Society,* XXIX (Fall, 1965), p. 416.

³⁵Schwendinger and Schwendinger, *Sociologists of the Chair,* pp. xvii-xxviii, 86-95.

³⁶Albion W. Small, *Origins of Sociology* (Chicago: The University of Chicago Press, 1924), p. 6. See Also, Schwendinger and Schwendinger, p. 539.

³⁷Edward Alsworth Ross, *Social Control and the Foundations of Sociology* (Boston: Beacon Press, 1959).

³⁸See, for instance, Morris Janowitz, "Sociological Theory and Social Control," *American Journal of Sociology,* 81 (1975), 82-108.

³⁹Gabriel Kolko, *Main Currents in Modern American History* (New York: Harper & Row, 1976), p. 8.

⁴⁰Kolko, *Main Currents in Modern American History,* pp. 100-156 and Williams, *The Contours of American History,* pp. 425-438.

⁴¹Robert E. Park and Ernest W. Burgess, *Introduction to the Science of Sociology* (Chicago: The University of Chicago Press, 1925), p. 508.

⁴²*Ibid.*

⁴³*Ibid.,* p. 535.

⁴⁴Robert Ezra Park, "An Autobiographical Note" in *Race and Culture* (Glencoe: The Free Press of Glencoe, 1964), p. vii. "Progress is a terrible thing" is a quotation from William James.

⁴⁵Park and Burgess, *Introduction,* pp. 953-1001.

⁴⁶*Ibid.,* p. 1001, n.1.

⁴⁷*Ibid.,* p. 964.

⁴⁸*Ibid.,* pp. 953-1001.

⁴⁹Park and Burgess, *Introduction,* p. 43 and Hinkle and Hinkle, *Development of Modern Sociology,* pp. 23-24.

⁵⁰Park and Burgess, *Introduction,* p. 960.

⁵¹*Ibid.,* p. 961.

⁵²Gramsci, *Selections from the Prison Notebooks,* p. 426. The quotation is from Gramsci's review of Nikolai Bukharin's *Historical Materialism: A System of Sociology* (1921).

⁵³Park and Burgess, *Introduction,* p. 1001.

⁵⁴Robert E. L. Faris, *Chicago Sociology 1920-1932* (Chicago: The University of Chicago Press, 1970), p. 35.

⁵⁵Philip M. Hauser, "On Actionism in the Craft of Sociology," in Colfax and Roach, eds., *Radical Sociology,* pp. 434-435.

⁵⁶Faris, *Chicago Sociology,* p. 132.

⁵⁷Oberschall, "The Institutionalization of American Sociology" in Oberschall, ed., *The Establishment of Empirical Sociology,* p. 239 and Faris, *Chicago Sociology,* p. xiii.

⁵⁸See, for instance, Faris, *Chicago Sociology,* pp. 114-115; Hinkle and Hinkle, *Development of Modern Sociology,* pp. 24-28; Oberschall, "The Institutionalization of American Sociology" in Oberschall, ed., *The Establishment of Empirical Sociology,* pp. 236-238.

⁵⁹Everett C. Hughes, "Preface" in Park, *Race and Culture,* pp. xi-xiv.

⁶⁰For general information concerning this transformation, see, for instance, Oberschall, "The

Institutionalization of Modern Sociology" in Oberschall, ed., *The Establishment of Empirical Sociology,* pp. 187-251 and Robert W. Friedrichs, *A Sociology of Sociology* (New York: The Free Press, 1970). -The interchange between Everett C. Hughes and Talcott Parsons took place in 1958 at a national meeting for sociologists. See, Alvin W. Gouldner, "Anti-Minotaur: The Myth of A Value-Free Sociology," *Social Problems,* (Winter, 1962), 199-213.

[61]Gunnar Myrdal, *An American Dilemma* (New York: McGraw-Hill Book Company, 1964), II, p. 1042.

[62]William F. Ogburn, "The Folkways of a Scientific Sociology," *Publications of the American Sociological Society,* 24 (1930), 1-11.

[63]*Ibid.,* p. 2.

[64]*Ibid.,* p. 10.

[65]*Ibid.,* p. 2.

[66]*Recent Social Trends in the United States. Report of the President's Research Committee on Social Trends* (New York: McGraw-Hill Book Company, 1933), I-II. Hoover wanted, according to the preface, "to have a complete, impartial examination of facts" (p.v.).

[67]See, for instance, *An American Dilemma* in which Myrdal says that the attempt of American social science "to drive valuations underground" is part of the "Western culture" and can as much be found in "the man in the street" as in "the social scientist" (p. 1046).

[68]Loren Baritz, *The Servants of Power: A History of the Use of Social Science in American Industry* (Middletown: Wesleyan University Press, 1960).

[69]See, for instance, Lazarsfeld, "An Episode in the History of Social Research" in Donald Fleming and Bernard Bailyn, eds., *The Intellectual Migration: Europe and America, 1930-1960* (Cambridge, Mass.: Harvard University Press), pp. 270-337 and Morton M. Hunt, "Profiles: Robert K. Merton (*New Yorker,* January 28, 1961)," *Sociological Abstracts,* 20 (July 1972), xvii-xxiv.

[70]Lazarsfeld, "An Episode in the History of Social Research" in Fleming and Bailyn, eds., *The Intellectual Migration,* p. 276.

[71]According to Adorno, he does not remember whether it was he or Lazarsfeld who coined the term. Lazarsfeld, however, used it to denote his own research. Cf. Theodor W. Adorno, "Scientific Experiences of A European Scholar in America" in Fleming and Bailyn, eds., *The Intellectual Migration,* pp. 342-343.

[72]William F. Ogburn, Shelby M. Harrison and Malcolm M. Willey, "Foreword" in Samuel A. Stouffer and Paul F. Lazarsfeld, *Research Memorandum on the Family in the Depression* (New York: Social Science Research Council, 1937), p. v.

[73]See also Robert E. L. Faris, "American Sociology" in Gurvitch and Moore, eds., *Twentieth Century Sociology,* p. 559.

[74]From the very beginning of his career Parsons was interested in "capitalism as a social system." Cf. Talcott Parsons, "On Building Social System Theory: A Personal History," *Daedalus,* Fall 1970, pp. 827, 852.

[75]See, for instance, Edward Shils, "Tradition, Ecology, and Institution in the History of Sociology," *Daedalus,* Fall 1970, pp. 785, 789 and Talcott Parsons, *The Structure of Social Action: A Study in Social Theory with Special Reference to A Group of Recent European Writers* (New York: The Free Press, 1968), I-II.

[76]See, for instance, Morris Janowitz, "Sociological Theory and Social Control," *American Journal of Sociology,* 81 (1975), 82-108.

[77]Robert K. Merton, "The Sociology of Knowledge"; Talcott Parsons, "The Present Position of Prospects of Systematic Theory in Sociology"; and Florian Znaniecki, "Social Organization and Institutions" in Gurvitch and Moore, eds., *Twentieth Century Sociology,* pp. 42-69, 172-217, 366-405.

[78]R. Derathé, review of *Twentieth Century Sociology,* in *Revue de Métaphysique et de Morale,* 55 (1950), 89-90.

[79]Claude Lévi-Strauss, "French Sociology" and Albert Salomon, "German Sociology" in Gurvitch and Moore, eds., *Twentieth Century Sociology,* pp. 503-537 and 586-614.

[80]See, for instance, Huntington Cairns, "Sociology and the Social Sciences," p. 7; Max Laserson, "Russian Sociology," p. 678; Robert E. L. Faris, "American Sociology," pp. 548-550; Alfredo Mendizabal, "Spanish Sociology," p. 655; Joachim Wach, "Sociology of Religion," pp. 406-407;

James W. Woodard, "Social Psychology," pp. 221, 238, 249, 255. -For a different opinion see Znaniecki, "Social Organization and Institutions," pp. 172-217 and especially Jerome Hall, "Criminology," pp. 342-365.

[81] James W. Woodard, "Social Psychology," p. 221.

[82] Ernest W. Burgess, "Research Methods in Sociology," p. 23.

[83] Robert E.L. Faris, "American Sociology," p. 548.

[84] Ibid.

[85] Parsons, "The Present Position and Prospects of Systematic Theory in Sociology," p. 54 and Sorokin, "Sociocultural Dynamics and Evolution," p. 101.

[86] See, for instance, Parsons, "The Present Position and Prospects of Systematic Theory in Sociology," p. 51; Sorokin, "Sociocultural Dynamics and Evolution," pp. 113 ff.; Laserson, "Russian Sociology," p. 684.

[87] See, for instance, Sorokin, "Sociocultural Dynamics and Evolution," p. 101 and Wilbert E. Moore, "Sociology of Economic Organization," pp. 456-458.

[88] Robert Morrison MacIver, "Social Causation and Change," pp. 121-138.

[89] Parsons, "The Present Position and Prospects of Systematic Theory in Sociology," pp. 42, 54.

[90] Lévi-Strauss, "French Sociology," pp. 503-537; Merton, "Sociology of Knowledge," pp. 366-405; Parsons, "The Present Situation and Prospects of Systematic Theory in Sociology," pp. 42-69; Znaniecki, "Social Organization and Institutions," pp. 172-217.

[91] Merton, "Sociology of Knowledge," pp. 368-369.

[92] Ibid., p. 368.

[93] Lévi-Strauss, "French Sociology," p. 520.

[94] Ibid., p. 518.

[95] The preface is only three pages long but was later expanded into a thirty-page long chapter entitled "Les faux problèmes de la sociologie au XIXe siècle" in Georges Gurvitch, La Vocation Actuelle de la Sociologie-Vers Une Sociologie Différentielle (Paris: P.U.F., 1950), pp. 19-48. From this chapter in La Vocation Actuelle de la Sociologie — as well as from Gurvitch's article on social control in Twentieth Century Sociology — it is clear that Gurvitch strongly supported every statement in the preface.

[96] Gurvitch and Moore, "Preface," p. i.

[97] Ibid.

[98] Ibid.

[99] Georges Gurvitch, "Social Control," pp. 267-296.

[100] Ibid., p. 269.

[101] Ibid., pp. 269 ff.

[102] Ibid., p. 273.

[103] For a general analysis of the technocratic implications of many sociological concepts, including that of social control, see Theodor Adorno, "Is Marx Obsolete?" Diogenes, Winter 1968, 1-16.

[104] Georges Gurvitch, "Social Structure of Pre-War France," American Journal of Sociology, XLVIII (March 1943), 535-554.

[105] Gurvitch himself always regarded his sociology of law, etc., as empirical. Here, however, empirical sociology is understood as sociology in which the subject matter determines the theory and not vice versa.

[106] Gurvitch's patriotism occasionally lapsed into imperialistic chauvinism: "The predominance of the rationalistic attitude with its faith in universally valid principles, was very characteristic of French international and colonial policy; it was a faith that the democratic principles of the French Revolution could be applied in all countries, which led also to the humanitarian treatment of natives in the colonies and the refusal to countenance any ethnic discrimination" (p. 550).

[107] For Gurvitch's analysis of fascism, see "Democracy as a Sociological Problem" Journal of Legal and Political Sociology, 1-2, I (1942), pp. 50, 53-54; Eléments de Sociologie Juridique, pp. 12, 177, 204, 213, 227, 240, 242, 248; "Liberalisme et Communisme," Esprit, 1er Juin 1934, 448-452; "The Problem of Social Law," Ethics, LII (1941-1942), pp. 20, 24, 29, 30, 37. For the inconsistency of Gurvitch's analysis of fascism, see especially, The Bill of Social Rights, p. 47 and Eléments de Sociologie Juridique, p. 240.

[108]Compare, for instance, such emigré magazines as *Social Research* and *Studies in Philosophy and Social Science* with the two most prestigious American sociological magazines, *American Journal of Sociology* and *American Sociological Review*. There were very few articles on fascism in the latter two magazines and hardly any have withstood the test of time. Among the exceptions are Theodore Abel, "Is a Psychiatric Interpretation of the German Enigma Necessary?" *American Sociological Review*, 10 (1945), 457-464 and Hans Gerth, "The Nazi Party, Its Leadership and Composition," *American Journal of Sociology*, 45 (1939-40), 517-541.

[109]See, for instance, H. Stuart Hughes, *The Sea Change: The Migration of Social Thought, 1930-1965* (New York: Harper & Row, 1975). In the chapter called "The Critique of Fascism" Hughes says that the major works on fascism are the following: Gaetano Salvemeni, *Under the Axe of Fascism* (1936), Franz Neumann, *Behemoth* (1942), Hannah Arendt, *The Origins of Totalitarianism* (1951), Ernst Nolte, *Three Faces of Fascism* (1963), and Karl Dieter Bracher, *The German Dictatorship* (1969). Not being a Marxist, Hughes leaves out a series of excellent works on fascism by Antonio Gramsci, Daniel Guérin, Nicos Poulantzas, and others.

[110]MacIver's attitude is characteristic. During World War II, MacIver made some speeches concerning fascism. "These and related activities," as he put it, "blocked any progress in my more professional studies." -Robert M. MacIver, *As A Tale Is Told: The Autobiography of R.M. MacIver* (Chicago: University of Chicago Press, 1968), p. 142.

[111]For a discussion of the intellectual affinities between European sociology and fascism, see Georg Lukács, *Die Zerstörung der Vernuft. Band III. Irrationalismus und Soziologie,* and Svend Ranulf, "Scholarly Forerunners of Fascism," *Ethics,* L (1939-40), 16-34. The spread of irrationalism in American sociology has not been studied, but it was especially apparent in the interest shown toward Pareto in the 1930's. No doubt the emphasis on value neutrality also passified American sociologists just as the irrational *Lebensphilosophie* had passified German intellectuals. See, for instance, Georg Lundberg's statement, "The services of *real* social scientists would be as indispensable to Fascists as to Communists and Democrats just as are the services of physicists and physicians." -Georg Lundberg, *Can Science Save Us?* (New York: Longmans, Green and Co., 1947), pp. 47-50. Quoted by Don J. Hager, "German Sociology under Hitler, 1933-1941," *Social Forces*, 28 (October, 1949), pp. 18-19, n. 23.

[112]See, for instance, Theodore Abel, "The Pattern of A Successful Political Movement," *American Sociological Review,* II (1937), 347-352 and *Why Hitler Came Into Power: An Answer Based on the Original Life Stories of Six Hundred of His Followers* (New York: Prentice-Hall, Inc., 1938); Harry Elmer Barnes, *Social Institutions in an Era of World Upheaval* (New York: Prentice-Hall, Inc., 1942); Howard Becker, *German Youth: Free or Bond* (New York: Oxford University Press, 1946); Hadley Cantril, *The Psychology of Social Movements* (New York: Wiley & Sons, 1941); Everett C. Hughes, "Good People and Dirty Work (1948/1962)," pp. 87-97 in *The Sociological Eye: Selected Papers* (Chicago & New York: Aldine-Atherton, 1971); Talcott Parsons, "Democracy and Social Structure in Pre-Nazi Germany (1942)," and "Some Sociological Aspects of the Fascist Movements (1942)" in *Essays in Sociological Theory* (New York: The Free Press, 1964), pp. 104-123 and 124-141. -For a summary of later works, see the bibliography to Herbert Blumer, "Collective Behavior" in Joseph B. Gittler, ed., *Review of Sociology: Analysis of a Decade* (New York: John Wiley & Sons, Inc., 1957), pp. 151-158.

[113]H. Stuart Hughes, *The Sea Change*, pp. 132-133.

[114]C. Wright Mills, who wrote an interesting review of *Behemoth* for *Partisan Review* in 1942, was to write later in *The Sociological Imagination* (1959): "It is curious, I think, that we do not yet happen to have a definite work on the causes of this war [World War II]. . . ." Cf. C. Wright Mills, "The Nazi Behemoth" in *Power, Politics, and People: The Collected Essays of C. Wright Mills* (New York: Ballantine Books, 1963), pp. 170-178 and *The Sociological Imagination* (New York: Grove Press, Inc., 1961), p. 53.

[115]Gurvitch, "My Intellectual Itinerary," *Sociological Abstracts,* 17/2 (April 1969), pp. vi-vii.

[116]*Ibid.,* p. vi.

[117]*Ibid.,* p. vii. For an attempt to unite values and facts, see Georges Gurvitch, "Democracy as a Sociological Problem," *Journal of Legal and Political Sociology,* 1-2, I (1942), 46-71. Gurvitch, however, was totally unsuccessful since he did not consider a discussion of the values of democracy as belonging to the competence of sociology.

[118]See, for instance, Phillip Bosserman, *Dialectical Sociology* and René Toulemont, *Sociologie*

et Pluralisme Dialectique: Introduction à l'OEuvre de Georges Gurvitch (Louvain: Nauwelaerts, 1955).

[119]No Name, *American Sociological Review,* 12 (1947), p. 131.

[120]Duvignaud, *Gurvitch,* p. 185. Emphasis added.

[121]Balandier, *Gurvitch,* p. 8. Emphasis added.

[122]See, for instance, G.D.H. Cole, *Europe, Russia and the Future* (London: The MacMillan Company, 1942); Harold Laski, *Where Do We Go From Here?* (New York: Viking, 1940); Anton Pannekoek, *De Arbeidersraden (The Workers' Councils)* (Amsterdam, 1946); Karl Mannheim, *Man and Society in an Age of Reconstruction* (London: K. Paul, Trench, Trubner & Co, 1940). -As director for the sociological section of *Ecole Libre des Hautes Etudes* in New York during 1942-1945, Gurvitch organized a section on "The Problems of the Reconstruction of France" (1943-1944) and "The Large Social Problems of Post-War Society" (1944-1945). He also devoted several issues of his magazine *Journal of Legal and Political Sociology* to these questions. See, "Chroniques," *Cahiers Internationaux de Sociologie,* I (1946), pp. 190-194.

[123]Theodor W. Adorno, "The Sociology of Knowledge and Its Consciousness (1953)" in *Prisms,* trans. Samuel and Shierry Weber (London: Neville Spearman, 1967), p. 37.

[124]Adorno wrote, "Accepted along with elite theory is its specific colouration. Conventional notions are joined by naive respect for that which they represent. Mannheim designated 'blood, property, and achievement' as the selection principles of the elites. His passion for destroying ideologies does not lead him to consider even once the legitimacy of these principles; he is actually able, during Hitler's lifetime, to speak of a 'genuine blood-principle,' which is supposed to have formerly guaranteed 'the purity of aristocratic minority stocks and their traditions.'" -"The Sociology of Knowledge and Its Consciousness" in *Prisms,* p. 39. -Also Paul Mattick has pointed out how Mannheim's respect for the elites made him come dangerously close to fascism. See *Mass und Wert,* October 1937, p. 113 where Mannheim says, "The fascistic labor camps, though not a pleasant solution for the crisis under which the permanently unemployed suffer, are nevertheless, from the viewpoint of social technique, a better method if compared with those of liberalism which tried to solve the social-psychological problem of unemployment by way of the dole." Quoted by Paul Mattick, "Man and Society in an Age of Reconstruction," *Living Marxism,* 4, IV (Spring 1941), pp. 40-41.

[125]Anton Pannekoek, *The Workers' Councils* (Melbourne: Excelsior Printing Works, 1950). The main part of the English version was written during the war and published in Dutch in 1946.

[126]Gurvitch, *The Bill of Social Rights,* p. 21.

[127]*Ibid.,* pp. 118-119.

[128]See also, Georges Gurvitch, "Sovereignty and Its Fate in Post-War Society," *Journal of Legal and Political Sociology,* II (1943), 30-51.

[129]See, for instance, Gurvitch, *The Bill of Social Rights,* pp. 59, 73, 88, 89 and also Nicola Chiaromonte, "Social Law, After Proudhon," *Politics,* January 1945, 25-28.

Chapter Six

[1]See, for instance, Seymour Leventman, "The Rationalization of American Sociology," pp. 348-364 in Edward Tiryakian, ed., *The Phenomenon of Sociology: A Reader in the Sociology of Sociology* (New York: Meredith Corporation, 1971) and C. Wright Mills, *The Sociological Imagination* (New York: Oxford University Press, 1959).

[2]Talcott Parsons, "On Building Social System Theory: A Personal History," *Daedalus,* Fall 1970, p. 842.

[3]See Gabriel Kolko, *The Politics of War: The World and United States Foreign Policy, 1943-1945* (New York: Random House, 1968).

[4]See Joyce Kolko and Gabriel Kolko, *The Limits of Power and the United States Foreign Policy, 1945-1954* (New York: Harper & Row, 1972).

[5]Kolko, *Main Currents in Modern American History,* p. 225.

[6]See, for instance, "Avant-Propos," *Année Sociologique (1940-1948),* I (1949), p. ix; Georges Bourgin, "Le Sociologue Marcel Mauss," *Revue Socialiste,* No. 35 (Mars 1950), pp. 220-227; François Bourricaud, "La Sociologie Francaise," pp. 24-25 in *Transactions of the Fourth World*

Congress of Sociology. Milan and Stresa, 8-15 September, 1959 (London: International Sociological Association, 1959), I; Alain Girard, "Entwicklungstendenzen der Soziologie in Frankreich," *Soziale Welt*, 8 (1957), p. 13; Raymond Polin, "La Sociologie Française Pendant la Guerre," *Synthèse*, V (1946), 117-129.

⁷Georges Gurvitch, "La Vocation Actuelle de la Sociologie," *Cahiers Internationaux de Sociologie*, I (1946), 3-22 and *La Vocation Actuelle de la Sociologie: Vers Une Sociologie Différentielle* (Paris: P.U.F., 1950). *Vocation* contained a theoretical part (pp. 1-348) and a section called "Antécédents and Perspectives" (pp. 349-602). The latter part contained the following articles: "The Problem of *Conscience Collective* in Durkheim's Sociology," "Magic, Religion and Law," "The Science of Moral Facts and Moral Theory in E. Durkheim," "Bergson's Sociological Theory," and "The Sociology of Young Marx."

⁸Henri Michels, *The Shadow War: European Resistance 1939-1945* (New York: Harper & Row, 1972), pp. 135 ff. and Gordon Wright, *The Reshaping of French Democracy* (New York: Reynal & Hitchcock, 1948), p. 169.

⁹The program of the National Council of Resistance can be found in, for instance, David Thomson, *Democracy in France Since 1870* (New York: Oxford University Press, 1964), pp. 322-324.

¹⁰Shepard B. Clough, "Economic Planning in a Capitalist Society: France from Monnet to Hirsh," *Political Science Quarterly*, LXXI (1956), 539-552.

¹¹Adolf Sturmthal, "Nationalization and Workers' Control in Britain and France," *Journal of Political Economy*, LXI (February-December, 1953), 43-79.

¹²Kolko, *The Politics of War*, pp. 33-34, 80, 85-86, 92, 436.

¹³Kolko, *The Limits of Power*, pp. 156, 440, 465, 640-641.

¹⁴*Ibid.*, pp. 153-156, 450 ff.

¹⁵Fernando Claudin, *The Communist Movement: From Comintern to Cominform*, trans. Brian Pearce and Francis MacDonaugh (Middlesex: Penguin Books, 1975), pp. 316-343.

¹⁶*Ibid.*, p. 321.

¹⁷Russell E. Planck, "Public Opinion in France after the Liberation, 1944-1949," pp. 227-230 in Mirra Komarovsky, ed., *Common Frontiers of the Social Sciences* (Glencoe: The Free Press, 1957). According to a study made in 1947 by the French Institute for Public Opinion (I.F.O.P.), forty-nine percent of all voters favored a "strong man." The majority of the supporters of M.R.P. and P.R.F. — as opposed to those who voted communist — were for a "strong man."

¹⁸Paul Lafargue, "Le Socialisme et la Science Sociale," *Devenir Social*, 2 (1896), p. 1048.

¹⁹Paul F. Lazarsfeld, "The Sociology of Empirical Social Research," *American Sociological Review*, 27 (December, 1962), p. 761.

²⁰Paul F. Lazarsfeld, *Main Trends in Sociology* (New York: Harper & Row, 1970), p. 65.

²¹Bernard Lécuyer and Anthony R. Oberschall, "Sociology: The Early History of Social Research," pp. 36-63 in David L. Sills, ed., *International Encyclopaedia of the Social Sciences*, 15 and Jean Stoetzel, "Sociology in France: An Empiricist View," pp. 632-657 in Howard Becker and Alvin Boskoff, eds., *Modern Sociological Theory in Continuity and Change* (New York: The Dryden Press, 1957).

²²J. I. Roubinski, "La Théorie de la 'Technocratie' en France," *Cahiers du Communisme*, N⁰ 3 (Mars 1961), 522-539.

²³David Caute, *Communism and the French Intellectuals 1914-1960* (New York: Macmillan, 1960), p. 160.

²⁴Kolko, *Politics of War*, p. 94.

²⁵*Ibid.*, p. 156.

²⁶Claudin, *The Communist Movement*, pp. 326-327.

²⁷Gramsci, *Selections from the Prison Notebooks*, pp. 229-239.

²⁸Kolko, *Politics of War*, p. 94.

²⁹Claudin, *The Communist Movement*, p. 467.

³⁰*Ibid.*, p. 472.

³¹See, for instance, René Maublanc, "French Teachers in the Resistance Movement," *Science & Society*, XI (Winter, 1947), 38-52.

³²Roger Garaudy and Georges Cogniot, *Les Intellectuels et la Renaissance Francaise* (Paris: Editions du Parti Communiste Francais, 1945). Cogniot repeated this appeal in 1947 and 1950 ac-

cording to Caute, *Communism and the French Intellectuals 1914-1960,* p. 50.

[33]Garaudy said, "The first duty of a communist artist is to be a great artist." The limits of his vision, however, can be seen in his labelling of Sartre and Gide as "decadent" and in his praise of Picasso and Pignon for painting the portraits of Thorez and Duclos. Cf. Garaudy and Cogniot, *Les Intellectuels et la Renaissance Francaise,* pp. 4, 7-8.

[34]J.-P. Sartre, David Rousset, Gerard Rosenthal, *Entretiens sur la Politique* (Paris: Gallimard, 1949), p. 75.

[35]Edgar Morin, *Autocritique* (Paris: Rene Juillard, 1959), pp. 63-76.

[36]See, for instance, Morin, *Autocritique,* p. 97 and K. A. Jelinski, "The Literature of Disenchantment," *Survey,* 41 (April 1962), 115-118.

[37]Caute, *Communism and the French Intellectuals 1914-1960,* pp. 28, 54, 182.

[38]*Ibid.,* p. 28.

[39]Maurice Merleau-Ponty, "For the Sake of Truth," p. 155 in *Sense and Non-Sense,* trans. Hubert L. Dreyfus and Patricia Allen Dreyfus (Chicago: Northwestern University Press, 1964). Originally published in *Les Temps Modernes* in 1946.

[40]Merleau-Ponty, *Sense and Non-Sense,* p. 170.

[41]Morin, *Autocritique,* p. 101.

[42]*Ibid.*

[43]J.-P. Sartre, "Le Réformisme et les Fétiches," *Les Temps Modernes,* Nº 122 (Février 1956), p. 1159.

[44]Henri Lefebvre, *La Somme et le Reste* (Paris: Belibaste, Editeur, 1973), pp. 201-204 and Serge Mallet, "Marxisme et Sociologie," pp. 40-41 in J. M. Vincent, ed., *Marxisme et Sociologie* (Paris: Les Cahiers d'Etudes Socialistes, 1963).

[45]Lefebvre, *La Somme et le Reste,* pp. 201-204.

[46]See especially Henri Lefebvre, *Critique de la Vie Quotidienne* (Paris: Editions Grasset, 1947).

[47]See, for instance, the discussion of Lefebvre's work in Paul Kahn, "Marx et le Marxisme," *Année Sociologique (1940-1948),* 1949, 262-268. Kahn refers to the following works by Lefebvre: *Matérialisme Dialectique* (2nd ed., 1947), *Critique de la Vie Quotidienne* (1947), and *Pour Connaitre la Pensée de Karl Marx* (1947).

[48]Henri Lefebvre, "Marxisme et Sociologie," *Cahiers Internationaux de Sociologie,* IV (1948), 48-74.

[49]*Ibid.,* p. 49.

[50]Henri Lefebvre, "La Sociologie Marxiste," *Cahiers Internationaux de Sociologie,* XXVI (1959), pp. 92-94.

[51]Pierre Fougeyrollas, "De la Psychotechnique à la Sociologie Policière," *Nouvelle Critique,* Nº 28 (Juillet-Août 1951), 25-46.

[52]*Ibid.,* p. 44.

[53]See Tom Kemp, "The Intelligentsia and Modern Capitalism," *Science & Society,* XXVI (1962), p. 311; René Maublanc, "French Teachers in the Resistance Movement," *Science & Society,* XI (Winter, 1947), 38-52; Henri Michel, *The Shadow War: European Resistance 1939-1945,* pp. 138-139.

[54]J.-P. Sartre, "Merleau-Ponty," pp. 258-259 in *Situations,* trans. Benita Eisler (New York: George Braziller, 1965).

[55]Planck, "Public Opinion in France After the Liberation, 1944-1949," pp. 184-241 in Komarovsky, ed., *Frontiers of the Social Sciences.*

[56]Sartre, "Merleau-Ponty" in *Situations* and *What Is Literature?* trans. Bernard Frechtman (New York: Harper & Row, 1965), pp. 155-291.

[57]Simone de Beauvoir, *Force of Circumstance.* Quoted in Michel-Antoine Burnier, *Choice of Action: The French Existentialists on the Political Frontline,* trans. B. Marchand (New York: Random House, 1968), p. 43.

[58]Sartre, "Merleau-Ponty," pp. 259-260 in *Situations.*

[59]Merleau-Ponty, "For the Sake of Truth," p. 171 in *Sense and Non-Sense.*

[60]Sartre, "Merleau-Ponty," p. 295 in *Situations.*

[61]*Ibid.,* p. 261.

[62]Sartre, "Materialism and Revolution," p. 107 in Georg Novack, ed., *Existentialism versus Marxism: Conflicting Views on Humanism* (New York: Dell Publishing Co., 1966).

[63]Merleau-Ponty, *Humanism and Terror: An Essay on the Communist Problem,* trans. John O'Neill (Boston: Beacon Press, 1969), p. xxi.

[64]Merleau-Ponty, "The War Has Taken Place," pp. 139-152 in *Sense and Non-Sense.*

[65]*Ibid.,* p. 151.

[66]Merleau-Ponty, *Humanism and Terror,* p. 34.

[67]*Ibid.,* p. xxxii.

[68]Simone de Beauvoir, *Force of Circumstance,* trans. Richard Howard (New York: G.P. Putnam's Sons, 1965), p. 22.

[69]Sartre, *What is Literature?,* p. 285.

[70]Simone de Beauvoir, *The Ethics of Ambiguity,* trans. Bernard Frechtman (New Jersey: The Citadel Press, 1972), p. 65.

[71]J.-P. Sartre, "Présentation," *Temps Modernes,* 1 (October 1945), p. 19.

[72]Sartre, "Materialism and Revolution," p. 108 in Novack, ed., *Existentialism versus Marxism.*

[73]Sartre, *What Is Literature?,* p. 256.

[74]Merleau-Ponty, "For the Sake of Truth," pp. 167-168 in *Sense and Non-Sense.*

[75]Georges Gurvitch, "La Réprésentation Ouvrière et le Problème des Nationalisations- 'Conseils de Contrôle' et 'Conseils de Gestion'", *Esprit* 14 (1er Janvier 1946), 107-112, and "Vers l'Unité Ouvrière," *Esprit,* 14 (1er Février 1946), 270-279.

[76]Georges Gurvitch, "La Technocratie est-elle un Effet Inévitable de l'Industrialisation?" pp. 179-199 in *Industrialisation et Technocratie* (Paris: Librairie Armand Colin, 1949).

[77]See Henri Lévy-Bruhl, "Le Centre d'Etudes Sociologiques," *Synthèse,* V (1946), 130-132; "Centre d'Etudes Sociologiques," *Cahiers Internationaux de Sociologie,* I (1946), 177-180; *Centre d'Etudes Sociologiques* (Paris: Centre National de la Recherche Scientifique, 1964). Gurvitch was the director of the center from 1945 to 1949.

[78]The work of the *Annales* school is in many aspects sociological, and their magazine *Annales. Economies. Sociétés. Civilizations.* should be mentioned.

[79]Gurvitch became "maître de conferences" in October 1948 and "professeur" in October 1952. Cf. "Rapport sur la Vie de la Faculté des Lettres de l'Année scolaire 1947-1948," *Annales de l'Université de Paris,* 19 (1949), p. 65 and "Rapport de M. Georges Davy, Doyen de la Faculté des Lettres, Maître de l'Institut, sur l'activité et les travaux de cette Faculté pendant l'Année scolaire 1952-1953," *Annales de l'Université de Paris* 26 (1956), p. 86. For the courses Gurvitch taught at the Sorbonne, from 1949 onward, see *Université de Paris. Livret de l'Etudiant.*

[80]See, for instance, Paul Kahn, "Les quatre premiers Volumes de la 'Bibliothèque de Sociologie Contemporaine'", *Cahiers Internationaux de Sociologie,* IX (1950), 156-174.

[81]Armand Cuvillier, *Où va la Sociologie Francaise?* (Paris: Librairie Marcel Rivière et Cie, 1953), pp. 102-160 and Lucien Goldmann, *Sciences Humaines et Philosophie* (Paris: P.U.F., 1952).

[82]See, for instance, Timasheff, who writes, "The Dean of the School of Letters at the Sorbonne remarked to me in 1955 that Gurvitch was *the* French sociologist."—Nicholas S. Timasheff, *Sociological Theory: Its Nature and Growth* (New York: Random House, 1967), p. 289, n.1.

[83]Georges Davy, "Inauguration du Centre d'Etudes Sociologiques," *Revue Philosophique de la France et de l'Etranger,* CL (1960), p. 87.

[84]Lucien Goldmann, "Preface (1966)," p. 10 in *The Human Sciences & Philosophy,* trans. Hayden V. White and Robert Anchor (London: Jonathan Cape, 1973).

[85]Gurvitch, "My Intellectual Itinerary," *Sociological Abstracts,* 17/2 (April 1969), p. xi.

[86]*Ibid.*

[87]*Ibid.*

[88]*Ibid.,* p. vii.

[89]Gurvitch, "La Réprésentation Ouvrière et le Problème des Nationalisations—'Conseils de Contrôle' et 'Conseils de Gestion'", *Esprit,* 14 (1er Janvier 1946), pp. 107-112 and "Vers l'Unité Ouvrière," *Esprit,* 14 (1er Février 1946), 270-279.

[90]Gurvitch, "La Réprésentation Ouvrière et le Problème des Nationalisations—'Conseils de Contrôle' et 'Conseils de Gestion'", *Esprit,* 14 (1er Janvier 1946), pp. 107-112.

[91]*Ibid.,* p. 108.

[92]*Ibid.,* p. 111.

[93]*The Bill of Social Rights* contains vague allusions to a spontaneous uprising by the workers in

which they would seize control of the factories and immediately start to run the factories themselves. Cf. Gurvitch, *The Bill of Social Rights,* p. 96.

⁹⁴Roy Pierce, *Contemporary French Political Thought* (London: Oxford University Press, 1966), p. 40. During 1944 and 1945 *Esprit* published several articles on this topic.

⁹⁵Jean Puillon, "Un Souhait Etrange: 'La Révolution par Loi'", *Temps Modernes,* 1 (Octobre 1945), 189-190. This opinion was shared by the rest of the people at *Temps Modernes,* according to Burnier, *Choice of Action,* p. 22.

⁹⁶Etienne Fajon, "Un Projet de Constitution Démocratique de la République Francaise," *Cahiers du Communisme,* 13 (Décembre 1945), 91. The Communist Party's policy toward a new constitution was laid out by Cogniot in *Cahiers du Communisme* in 1944. Cf. Gordon Wright, *The Reshaping of French Democracy* (New York: Reynal & Hitchcock, 1948), pp. 38-40.

⁹⁷Wright, *The Reshaping of French Democracy,* p. 157.

⁹⁸The preamble to the constitution of the Fourth Republic said "Everybody must work and has the right to be employed. . . . Every worker participates via his delegates in the collective determination of the conditions of work as well as in the management of the companies . . . [each] monopoly in fact must become the property of the collective." "Constitution de la République Francaise," *Journal of Legal and Political Sociology,* IV (Summer 1946/Winter 1947), p. 156.

⁹⁹Gurvitch, "Vers l'Unité Ouvrière," *Esprit* 14 (1ᵉʳ Février 1946), p. 279.

¹⁰⁰Gurvitch, *La Vocation Actuelle de la Sociologie: Vers une Sociologie Différentielle* (Paris: P.U.F., 1950), p. 9.

¹⁰¹See, for instance, *ibid.,* p. vii.

¹⁰²*Ibid.,* p. 8.

¹⁰³*Ibid.,* pp. 20-48.

¹⁰⁴*Ibid.,* p. 48.

¹⁰⁵*Ibid.,* pp. 55-95.

¹⁰⁶See, for instance, Bosserman, *Dialectical Sociology,* p. 121 and John Vincent Martin, *Depth Sociology and Microsociology: A Critical Analysis of the Basic Concepts of Georges Gurvitch* (Unpublished Ph.D-thesis, Harvard University, 1957), p. 51.

¹⁰⁷Gurvitch, *Vocation,* p. 99.

¹⁰⁸See Chapter IV, entitled "Microsociologie et Sociométrie," pp. 236-268 in *Vocation.* The chapter was published in an English translation in *Sociometry,* XII (February-August, 1949), 1-31.

¹⁰⁹Gurvitch, *Sociology of Law,* pp. 231-241. Briefly, Gurvitch's classification included the following sub-categories: scope (particular and inclusive groups), duration (temporary and stable groups), function (for instance, kinship groups and locality groups), attitude (divisive and unifying groups), ruling organizational principle (unorganized and organized groups), form of constraint (groups with conditional and unconditional constraint), and degree of unity (unitary, federalist and confederated groups). Cf. Chapter Four for a more complete discussion of Gurvitch's classification system.

¹¹⁰Gurvitch, *Vocation,* pp. 292-338. Gurvitch's sub-categories of the new categories were the following: size (small, medium, large), time rhythm (slow, medium, accelerated), degree of dispersion (non-assembled groups, groups with artificial contact, groups periodically united, and groups permanently assembled), basis of foundation (voluntary, forced, *de facto*), mode of admission (open, closed, conditional entry), degree of externalization (unorganized and unstructured, unorganized and structured, partially organized, totally organized), degree of penetration by the global society (groups totally submissive to penetration, groups partially submissive, and groups which resist penetration), and degree of compatibility between similar groups which are totally compatible, partially compatible, and not compatible; exclusive groups.

¹¹¹Gurvitch, *Vocation,* pp. 338-348.

¹¹²*Ibid.,* pp. 340-345.

¹¹³Georges Gurvitch, "Réponse à une Critique," *Kölner Zeitschrift für Soziologie,* 5 (1952/53), p. 104.

¹¹⁴Georges Gurvitch, "A Sociological Analysis of International Tensions," pp. 243-256 in Hadley Cantril, ed., *Tensions That Cause War: Common Statements and Individual Papers by a Group of Social Scientists Brought Together by UNESCO* (Urbana: University of Illinois Press, 1950).

¹¹⁵Alexander Szalai, p. 249 in Cantril, ed., *Tensions That Cause War.*

[116]Szalai, pp. 253-254 in *ibid.*

[117]Horkheimer, pp. 251-252 in *ibid.*

[118]Horkheimer, p. 255 in *ibid.*

[119]Gurvitch, *Vocation,* p. 83.

[120]Ibid., pp. 102-103, 339.

[121]*Ibid.,* pp. 82-83. Durkheim wrote in 1911 in "Value Judgments and Judgments of Reality": "It is, in fact, at such moments of collective ferment that are born, the great ideals upon which civilization rests. The periods of creation or renewal occur when men for various reasons are led into a closer relationship with each other, when reunions and assemblies are most frequent, relationships better maintained and the exchange of ideas most active. Such was the great crisis of Christendom, the movement of collective enthusiasm which, in the twelfth and thirteenth centuries, bringing together in Paris the scholars of Europe, gave birth to Scholasticism. Such were the Reformation and Renaissance, the revolutionary epoch and the Socialist upheavals of the nineteenth century." Emile Durkheim, trans. D. F. Pocock, *Sociology and Philosophy* (New York: The Free Press, 1974), pp. 91-92.

[122]According to *Essais de Sociologie* (1938), p. 1, Gurvitch was preparing a book called *Déterminisme Social et Libre Arbitre.*

[123]Georges Gurvitch, "Les Degrés de la Liberté Humaine," *Cahiers Internationaux de Sociologie,* XI (1951), 3-20.

[124]*Ibid.,* p. 5.

[125]Georges Gurvitch, "La Sociologie du Jeune Marx," *Cahiers Internationaux de Sociologie,* IV (1948), 3-47. Reprinted in *Vocation,* pp. 568-602.

[126]Georges Gurvitch, "La Technocratie est-elle un Effet Inévitable de l'Industrialisation?", pp. 179-199 in Gurvitch, ed., *Industrialisation et Technocratie.*

[127]For Burnham and the effect of his book, see "The Cerebral Communist: James Burnham" and "Social Theory and the Cold War: Burnham," pp. 169-198, 303-337 in John P. Diggens, *Up from Communism: Conservative Odysseys in American Intellectual History* (New York: Harper & Row, 1975).

[128]The first traces of this conviction are to be found in *The Bill of Social Rights,* p. 47.

[129]Gurvitch, "La Technocratie est-elle un Effet Inévitable de l'Industrialisation?", *Industrialisation et Technocratie,* p. 165.

[130]*Ibid.,* p. 96.

[131]See Max Weber, "Politics as a Vocation" and "Science as a Vocation," pp. 77-128 and 129-156 in H. H. Gerth and C. Wright Mills, eds., *From Max Weber: Essays in Sociology,* trans. H. H. Gerth and C. Wright Mills, (New York: Oxford University Press, 1972).

[132]Gurvitch, "La Technocratie est-elle un Effet Inévitable de l'Industrialisation?", *Industrialisation et Technocratie,* p. 182.

[133]*Ibid.,* p. 187.

[134]Georges Gurvitch, "La Technocratie est-elle un Effet Inévitable de l'Industrialisation?", pp. 440 in *La Vocation Actuelle de la Sociologie. Tome. Second. Antécédents et Perspectives* (Paris: P.U.F., 1969). This edition is identical to the one published in 1963.

[135]See Gurvitch, "La Sociologie du Jeune Marx," *Cahiers Internationaux de Sociologie,* IV (1948), p. 23.

[136]Gurvitch, "La Technocratie est-elle un Effet Inévitable de l'Industrialisation?", *Industrialisation et Technocratie,* p. 194.

[137]Among the positive reviews of *Vocation,* see especially Georges Balandier, *Critique,* IX (1952), 93-96 and Paul Kahn, "Les Quatre Premiers Volumes de la 'Bibliothèque de Sociologie Contemporaine'", *Cahiers Internationaux de Sociologie,* IX (1950), 156-174.

[138]Fougeyrollas, "De la Psychotechnique à la Sociologie Policière," *Nouvelle Critique,* 28 (Juillet-Août 1951), 25-46.

[139]Goldmann, *The Human Sciences & Philosophy;* J. W. Lapierre, "Vers une Sociologie Concrète," *Esprit,* 184 (Novembre 1951), 720-730; Jean-Paul Sartre, *The Communists and Peace with a Reply to Claude Lefort,* trans. Martha H. Fletcher and Philip P. Berk (New York: George Braziller, 1968), pp. 90-100.

[140]Armand Cuvillier, *Où va la Sociologie Francaise?* and Fernand Braudel, "Georges Gurvitch ou la Discontinuité du Social," *Annales. Economies. Sociétés. Civilisations,* 8 (1953), 347-361.

[141]Fougeyrollas, "De la Psychotechnique à la Sociologie Policière," *Nouvelle Critique,* 28 (Juillet-Août 1951), 25-46.

[142]Cuvillier, *Où va la Sociologie Francaise?* and Braudel, "Georges Gurvitch ou la Discontinuité du Social," *Annales. Economies. Sociétés. Civilisations,* 8 (1953), 347-361.

[143]Here, as elsewhere, Cuvillier repeated von Wiese's critiques of *Vocation.* See L.V. Wiese, "Gurvitch's Beruf der Soziologie," *Kölner Zeitschrift für Soziologie,* 4 (1951/52), 365-374.

[144]Braudel, "Georges Gurvitch ou la Discontinuité du Social," *Annales. Economies. Sociétés. Civilisations,* 8 (1953), 347-361.

[145]"La longue durée" and "l'événementiel" can be translated as "long-term" and "short-term." See, for instance, Peter Burke, ed., *Economy and Society in Early Modern Europe: Essays from Annales* (New York: Harper & Row, 1972).

[146]Goldmann, *The Human Sciences & Philosophy;* Sartre, *The Communists and Peace.* J.W. Lapierre's review of *Vocation* in *Esprit* was generally positive to Gurvitch but refused to accept the distinction between value judgments and judgments of reality. Cf. J.W. Lapierre, "Vers Une Sociologie Concrète," *Esprit,* No 184 (Novembre 1951), p. 729.

[147]Sartre, *The Communists and Peace,* p. 94.

[148]Goldmann, *The Human Sciences & Philosophy.*

[149]Goldmann, *Sciences Humaines & Philosophie,* p. 71.

Chapter Seven

[1]See bibliography of Gurvitch's work at the end of this work.

[2]Georges Gurvitch, *Déterminismes Sociaux et Liberté Humaine-Vers l'Etude Sociologique des Cheminements de la Liberté* (Paris: P.U.F., 1958-1960, 1962); ed., *Traité de Sociologie,* I-II (Paris: P.U.F., 1958-1960, 1963); *Les Cadres Sociaux de la Connaissance* (Paris: P.U.F., 1966).

[3]Georges Gurvitch, *La Vocation Actuelle de la Sociologie* (Paris: P.U.F., 1957, 1963).

[4]Georges Gurvitch, *La Concept de Classes Sociales de Marx à Nos Jours* (Paris: C.D.U., 1955); *Les Fondateurs Français de la Sociologie Contemporaine: Saint-Simon et P. J. Proudhon* (Paris: C.D.U., 1955); *La Sociologie de Karl Marx* (Paris: C.D.U., 1959). For some of the other courses that Gurvitch taught during these years, see bibliography.

[5]*Université de Paris. Livret de l'Etudiant 1949-1950* (Paris: P.U.F., 1949), p. 191.

[6]*Université de Paris. Livret de l'Etudiant 1951-1952* (Paris: P.U.F., 1951), p. 192.

[7]Gurvitch, "My Intellectual Itinerary," *Sociological Abstracts,* 17/2 (April 1969), p. x. For Serge Jonas' account of his conversation with Gurvitch, see Gurvitch "Mon Itineraire Intellectual," *L'Homme et la Société,* 1 (1966), p. 3.

[8]Georges Gurvitch, "Hyper-Empirisme Dialectique. Ses Applications en Sociologie," *Cahiers Internationaux de Sociologie,* XV (1953), 3-33; "Les Voies de la Démocratisation Industrielle," *Esprit,* Juin 1953, 964-972.

[9]Perry Anderson, *Considerations on Western Marxism* (London: NLB, 1976), p. 46.

[10]Henri Lefebvre, *La Survie du Capitalisme: La Reproduction des Rapports de Production* (Paris: Editions Anthropos, 1973), p. 154.

[11]Joyce and Gabriel Kolko, *The Limits of Power.*

[12]*Ibid.,* p. 708.

[13]See, for instance, Michel Branciard, *Société Francaise & Luttes de Classes, tome II. 1914/1967* (Paris: Chronique Sociale de France, 1967), pp. 195 ff., and David Thomson, *Democracy in France Since 1870* (New York and London: Oxford University Press, 1964), p. 298.

[14]John and Anne-Marie Hachet, *Economic Planning in France* (Cambridge, Mass.: Harvard University Press, 1963), pp. 20-27.

[15]See, for instance, Daniel Bell, *The Coming of Post-Industrial Society: A Venture in Social Forecasting* (New York: Basic Books, Inc., 1973), p. 78, and J. I. Roubinsky, "La Théorie de la Technocratie en France," *Cahiers du Communisme,* 37 (Mars 1961), 522-539.

[16]Francois Fejtő, *The French Communist Party and the Crisis of International Communism* (Cambridge, Mass.: The MIT Press, 1967), p. 40.

[17]*Ibid.*

[18]Kingsley Davis, "The Myth of Functional Analysis as a Special Method in Sociology and An-

thropology," *American Sociological Review,* 24 (December 1959), 755-772. See also Don Martindale, "American Sociology Since World War Two," *International Journal of Contemporary Sociology,* 11 (1974), 165-173.

[19]For conflict theory, see, for instance, Lewis Coser, *Continuities in the Study of Social Conflict* (New York, The Free Press, 1967), and Martindale, *The Nature and Types of Sociological Theory,* pp. 125-207.

[20]For Marxism, see, for instance, J. David Colfax and Jack L. Roach, eds., *Radical Sociology* (New York: Basic Books, Inc., 1971); Jack L. Roach, "The Radical Sociology Movement: A Short History and Commentary," *American Sociologist,* 5 (August 1970), 224-233; Schwendinger and Schwendinger, *Sociologists of the Chair,* pp. 561 ff. The first North American sociological magazine which is socialist, *Insurgent Sociologist,* exists since 1970.

[21]See, for instance, M. Crozier, "The Cultural Revolution: Notes on the Changes in the Intellectual Climate in France," in Stephen Graubard, ed., *A New Europe* (Boston: Houghton Mifflin Company, 1964), pp. 602-630.

[22]See, for instance, *"Die Gegenwärtige Situation der fransösichen Soziologie,"* in Gottfried Eisermann, ed., *Die Gegenwärtige Situation der Soziologie* (Stuttgart: Ferdinand Enke Verlag, 1967) pp. 60 ff. and René Laurou, "Sociology and Politics in 1968," in Charles Posner, ed., *Reflections on the Revolution in France* (Hammondsworth: Penguin, 1972), pp. 228, 235.

[23]See, for instance, Pierre Bourdieu and Jean-Claude Passeron, "Sociology and Philosophy in France since 1945: Death and Resurrection of A Philosophy without Subject," *Social Forces,* 34 (1967), pp. 185-186. According to Lefebvre, Western social science during 1950-1970 expressed the "strategy" of "neo-capitalism." See Henri Lefebvre, *La Survie du Capitalisme,* pp. 151, 154.

[24]See, for instance, Pierre de Bie, *Les Sciences Sociales dans l'Enseignement Supérieur: Sociologie, Psychologie Sociale et Anthropologie Culturelle* (Paris: UNESCO, 1954), p. 217 ff., and François Bourricaud, "La Sociologie Française," in *Transactions of the Fourth World Congress of Sociology. Milan and Stresa,* 8-15 September, 1959, Volume I (London: International Sociological Association, 1959), pp. 23-32.

[25]See, for instance, Clark, *Prophets and Patrons,* pp. 234-244.

[26]See, for instance, Lourau, "Sociology and Politics in 1968," in Posner, ed., *Reflections on the Revolution in France,* p. 232.

[27]Friedmann's main journal was *Sociologie du Travail* and his foremost student is Alain Touraine. For a short sketch of Friedmann's interesting career, see *Une Nouvelle Civilization: Hommage à Georges Friedmann* (Paris: Editions Gallimard, 1973), pp. 475-491.

[28]Lucien Goldmann, "Preface to the New Edition (1966)," in *The Human Sciences & Philosophy,* pp. 9 ff, and "Structuralisme, Marxisme, Existentialisme," *L'Homme et la Société,* 2 (Octobre-Décembre 1966), p. 120.

[29]See Aron's own discussion of this in his *The Industrial Society: Three Essays on Ideology and Development* (New York: Simon and Schuster, 1968).

[30]Raymond Aron, *La Lutte des Classes: Nouvelles Lecons sur les Sociétés Industrielles* (Paris: Gallimard, 1964) and *Main Currents in Sociological Thought,* I-II, trans. Richard Howard and Helen Weaver (New York: Doubleday & Company, Inc., 1968).

[31]Raymond Aron, *The Opium of the Intellectuals,* trans., Terence Kilmartin (New York: W.W. Norton & Company, Inc., 1962), p. 322. That Aron was despised by the French left can be seen in, for instance, Annie Besse, "Moniseur Aron Bouleverse la Science," *Nouvelle Critique,* 7 (Juillet-Août 1955), 92-109.

[32]It is generally considered that structuralism replaced existentialism as the ideology à la mode in the 1950's. See, for instance, Goldmann, *The Human Sciences & Philosophy,* pp. 9 ff.; H. Stuart Hughes, *The Obstructed Path: French Social Thought in the Years of Desperation 1930-1960* (New York: Harper & Row, 1969), pp. 261 ff.; Adam Schaff, "Le Structuralisme en tant que Courant Intellectuel," *L'Homme et la Société,* 24-25 (Avril-Septembre 1972), pp. 94 ff.

[33]Claude Lévi-Strauss, *Tristes Tropiques,* trans. John and Doreen Weightman (New York: Atheneum, 1974), p. 58.

[34]See, for instance, Henri Lefebvre, "Réflections sur le Structuralisme et l'Histoire," *Cahiers Internationaux de Sociologie,* XXXV (1963), 3-24, and Jean-Paul Sartre, "Replies to Structuralism: An Interview (1906)," *Telos,* 9 (Fall 1971), 110-116.

[35]Henri Lefebvre, "Claude Lévi-Strauss et le Nouvel Eléatisme (suite)," *L'Homme et la Société,*

2 (Octobre-Décembre 1966), p. 81.

[36]Lévi-Strauss, noting the similarities between functionalism and structuralism, called the former a "rudimentary version of structuralism." See Lévi-Strauss, *Structural Anthropology,* p. 328.

[37]For the similarities between structuralism and the *Annales* school with its emphasis on "unconscious history" (Braudel), see Robert D'Amico, "The Contours and Coupures of Structuralist Theory," *Telos,* 17 (Fall 1973), 70-97.

[38]Louis Althusser, *For Marx,* trans. Ben Brewster (New York: Vintage Books, 1970), p. 229.

[39]Claude Lévi-Strauss, *The Savage Mind,* trans. George Werdenfeed (Chicago: University of Chicago Press, 1966), p. 247.

[40]Michel Foucault, *The Order of Things* (New York: Vintage Books, 1973), p. 387.

[41]Lucien Goldmann, *Cultural Creation in Modern Society,* introduction by William Mayrl and translation by Bert Grahl (Saint Louis: Telos Press, 1976), p. 112.

[42]Claude Lévi-Strauss, *Tristes Tropiques,* trans. John Russel (New York: Atheneum, 1969), pp. 60-61.

[43]Author's interview with Henri Lefebvre, February, 1975. For Duvignaud, see Jean Duvignaud, *Gurvitch* and "France: The Neo-Marxists," in Leopold Labedz, ed., *Revisionism: Essays in the History of Marxist Ideas* (New York: Praeger, 1962), pp. 316-317.

[44]For *Temps Modernes,* see this magazine between 1953-1965. Morin, Duvignaud and Kriegel all left the French Communist Party around the middle of the 1950's. For the intellectuals who left the Party, see Caute, *Communism and the French Intellectuals,* pp. 179, 181, 227 ff., 272, and Jean Duvignaud, "La Sociologie est un Humanisme," *L'Homme et la Société,* 1 (1967), p. 35.

[45]Duvignaud and Morin were among the founders of *Arguments* (1956-1962). Among the other neo-Marxist magazines of this period, special mention should be made of *Socialisme ou Barbarie* (1949-1961) and *l'Internationale Situationniste* (1958-1969). See Edgar Morin, "Arguments," *Survey: A Quarterly for Pluralist Socialism,* 6 (October 1960), 86-87; Paul Cardan (Cornelius Castoriadis), "Socialisme ou Barbarie," *Survey: A Quarterly for Pluralist Socialism,* 6 (October 1960), 96-97; Guy Debord, "La Question de l'Organisation pour l'I.S.," *L'Internationale Situationniste,* 12 (Septembre 1969), 112-114.

[46]Jean-Paul Sartre, *The Ghost of Stalin,* trans. Martha H. Fletcher (New York: George Braziller, 1968), p. 27.

[47]*Ibid.,* p. 28.

[48]For the vivid debate about the dialectic in the early 1960's, see Predrag Vranicki, "Die Diskussion über die Dialektik," in Volume Two of *Geschichte des Marxismus* (Frankfurt am Main: Suhrkamp Verlag, 1970) pp. 930-934.

[49]Maurice Merleau-Ponty, *Adventures of the Dialectic,* trans. Joseph Bien (Evanston: Northwestern University Press, 1973), pp. 32, 35.

[50]For Goldmann, see especially "Structuralisme, Marxisme, Existentialisme," *L'Homme et la Société,* 2 (Octobre-Décembre 1966), 105-124 and Lefebvre's articles against structuralism as collected in *Au-Dèla du Structuralisme.*

[51]For Goldmann, see for instance, Goldmann-Mallet, "Débat sur l'Autogestion" *Autogestion,* 7 (Décembre 1968), 57-75 and for Lefebvre, see for instance, *Vers le Cybernanthrope* (Paris: Denoël, Gonthier, 1971).

[52]According to Jean Bancal and Yvon Bourdet, the term "autogestion" was introduced in France in 1960. See Jean Bancal, *Proudhon: Pluralisme et Autogestion* (Paris: Aubier Montaigne, 1970), p. 18, n. 1 and Yvon Bourdet, *Pour l'Autogestion* (Paris: Editions Anthropos, 1974), pp. 49, 159. Also according to Lucien Goldmann, the concept of "autogestion" is very new. Cf. Goldmann-Mallet, "Débat sur l'autogestion," *Autogestion,* 7 (Décembre 1968), p. 58.

[53]See, for instance, Perry Anderson, *Considerations on Western Marxism,* pp. 24-48.

[54]Henri Lefebvre, *La Vallée de Campan: Etude de Sociologie Rural* (Paris: P.U.F., 1963); André Gorz, *Stratégie Ouvrière et Néocapitalisme* (Paris: Editions du Seuil, 1964); Serge Mallet, *La Nouvelle Classe Ouvrière* (Paris: Editions du Seuil, 1963).

[55]For the French Communist Party's attitude to sociology, see especially the section *"Sur la Sociologie,"* in Henri Lefebvre, *La Somme et le Reste* (Paris: Belibaste, Editeur, 1973), pp. 201-210. See also Edgar Morin and Serge Mallet in J.M. Vincent, ed., *Marxisme et Sociologie* (Paris: Les Cahiers de Centre d'Etudes Socialistes, 1963).

[56]Henri Lefebvre, *The Sociology of Marx*, trans. Norbert Guterman (New York: Vintage Books, 1969), p. 22.

[57]Lucien Goldmann, "Y a-t-il une Sociologie Marxiste?" in *Recherches Dialectiques* (Paris: Gallimard, 1959), pp. 280-302.

[58]Lefebvre, *Le Somme et le Reste*, pp. 201-210. Althusser brushes aside sociology in *For Marx*, p. 171.

[59]Author's conversation with Annie Kriegel, February 18, 1977.

[60]Vranicki, *Geschichte des Marxismus*, p. 887. Vranicki's book contains a section on Marxism in France, pp. 887-948.

[61]Cf. "Appel, " *Temps Modernes*, 7 (1961), 624-628. Gurvitch thought that his apartment had been bombed because of his protests against police brutality, according to the information he gave Myrtle Korenbaum (Letter to author February 27, 1976). The bomb attack caused Gurvitch to have his first heart attack; his wife was also severely traumatized. Cf. Jean Duvignaud, *Gurvitch*, p. 186.

[62]"Collegue de L'Association Internationale des Sociologues de Langue Francaise," *L'Homme et la Société*, 1 (1966), p. 122.

[63]"Après le Colloque de Royaument: Les Sociologues Francophones et la Décolonisation," *Le Monde*, 7-8 Novembre, 1965, p. 15.

[64]Letter from Gurvitch to Duvignaud, November 4, 1961. Cf. Duvignaud, *Gurvitch*, p. 113.

[65]See, for instance, Georges Gurvitch, "L'Effondrement d'un Mythe Politique: Joseph Staline," *Cahiers Internationaux de Sociologie*, XXXIII (1962), 5-18.

[66]See, for instance, Georges Gurvitch, "Libéralisme et Communisme: *Une Réponse à M. Ramon Fernandez,*" *Esprit*, No 21 (1er Juin 1934), 448-452.

[67]Georges Gurvitch, "Perspectives du Socialisme: Le Sort des Structures Sociales Actuelles," in *Quel Avenir Attend l'Homme?-Rencontre Internationale de Royaument, 17-20 Mai 1961* (Paris: P.U.F., 1961), p. 164.

[68]See especially Georges Gurvitch, "Les Voies de la Démocratisation Industrielle," *Esprit*, Juin 1953, 964-972 and "Three Paths to Self-Management" (1957), in Branko Horvat *et al*, eds., *Self-Governing Socialism: A Reader. Volume Two. Sociology and Politics, Economics* (New York: International Arts and Sciences Press, Inc., 1975), pp. 20-28.

[69]Gurvitch, "Les Voies de la Démocratisation Industrielle," *Esprit*, Juin 1953, 964-972.

[70]*Ibid.*, p. 966. *"La démocratie industrielle sera révolutionnaire ou ne sera pas."*

[71]*Ibid.*

[72]Georges Gurvitch, "Les Oeuvres de la Civilisation et les Structures Sociales Sont-Elles Menacées par le Déchaînement Actuel des Techniques?" *Revue de Sociologie*, No 1-2/1961, p. 280.

[73]Gurvitch, "Three Paths to Self-Management," in Horvat *et al*, eds., *Self-Governing Socialism*, pp. 26-27. Gurvitch visited Yugoslavia twice, in 1957 and 1963. Information on his first trip to Yugoslavia can be found in *Anali Pravnog fakulteta u Beogradu*, br. 3, 1958, 275-285; *Filozofia- Sociologija*, br. 1-2, 1958, 66-77. In *Pregled*, br. 2, 1958, pp. 99-107 is Gurvitch's article "Radnicki savjeti (workers' councils). "All the information on Gurvitch's trips to Yugoslavia comes from Dr. Miodrag Rankovic, who has written a work in Yugoslavian on *The Structure and Typology of Global Societies in G. Gurvitch* (Belgrade, 1970) (Letter to author, February 29, 1976).

[74]"I don't think one can find the ideal of workers' self-management in Marx" — Henri Lefebvre, "Une Interview d'Henri Lefebvre Realisée par Y. Bourdet et O. Corpet, 16 Février 1976," *Autogestion et Socialisme*, No 33-34 (Janvier-Mars 1976), p. 123.

[75]Conversation with author, February 1975. Cf. Yvon Bourdet and O. Corpet, "Une Interview d'Henri Lefebvre," *Autogestion*, 33-34 (Janvier-Mars 1976), p. 123. According to Daniel Guérin, "Gurvitch's work has very little influence on the *Autogestion* movement in France today. . . ." (Letter to author, January 23, 1976).

[76]See, for instance, Jean Duvignaud's fine study *Change at Shebika: Report from a North African Village*, trans. Frances Freyaye (New York: Pantheon Books, 1970).

[77]"La revue Autogestion, comme on le sait, a été le réalisation posthume d'un projet de Georges Gurvitch" — Yvon Bourdet, "Anarchistes et Marxistes," *Autogestion et Socialisme*, 18-19 (Janvier-Avril 1972), p. 3. -Gurvitch's role in the founding of *Autogestion* is fully documented in "Sommaire: 1966-1976. Traces, contradictions, projects," *Autogestion et Socialisme*, Nos 37-38 (Avril 1977), 3-73.

⁷⁸Letter to author from Yvon Bourdet, January 9, 1976. On the question of whether Gurvitch was the first sociologist to study self-management, Bourdet replied: ". . . the first sociologist to study self-management was, in my opinion (even if the word sociologist did not exist), Karl Marx and then Anton Pannekoek. Don't forget Rosa Luxemburg, Georges Sorel, the anarchists, etc., (also *Socialisme ou Barbarie*). In any case, the 'sportlike' notion of 'who did it first' is both unsolvable and secondary."

⁷⁹See, for instance, Gurvitch, "Perspectives du Socialisme. Le Sort des Structures Sociales Actuelles," in *Quel Avenir Attend l'Homme?* pp. 151-160. Gurvitch's political analyses of technocracy, as opposed to those of self-management, often coincided with his work in sociology. See, for instance, Georges Gurvitch, "Société, Technique et Civilisation," *Cahiers Internationaux de Sociologie*, XLV (1968), 5-16.

⁸⁰Gurvitch, "Les Oeuvres de la Civilisation et les Structures Sociales Sont-Elles Menacées par le Dechaînement Actuel des Techniques," *Revue de Sociologie*, Nᵒ 1-2/ 1961, p. 274.

⁸¹Bell, *The Coming of Post-Industrial Society*, p. 78.

⁸²Georges Gurvitch, "Proudhon et Marx," *Cahiers Internationaux de Sociologie*, XL (1966), 7-16.

⁸³*Ibid.*, p. 16.

⁸⁴See, for instance, Armand Cuvillier, *Sociologie et Problèmes Actuels* (Paris: Librairie Philosophique J. Vrin, 1958), p. 42; Steven Lukes, "Cataloguing the Concrete: A Review of Georges Balandier's *Gurvitch,"* *Times Literary Supplement*, September 12, 1975, p. 1019; Maxime Rodinson, "M. Gurvitch, Le Déterminisme, les Classes et l'Avenir du Proletariat," *Pensée*, Nᵒ 67, Mai-Juin 1956, 122-130; Fernand Braudel, "Georges Gurvitch ou la Discontinuité du Social," *Annales. Economies. Sociétés. Civilisations,*, 8(1953), p. 358.

⁸⁵Joseph B. Ford, Review of *Déterminismes Sociaux* (1955), *American Sociological Review*, 20 (1955), p. 599; Pitirim A. Sorokin, *Sociological Theories of Today* (New York and London: Harper & Row, 1966), p. 481.

⁸⁶R. Martin Goodridge, "Georges Gurvitch and the Sociology of Knowledge," *Inquiry*, 16 (1973), p. 240.

⁸⁷Maurice Merleau-Ponty, "The Philosopher and Sociology," p. 108 in *Signs*.

⁸⁸For Gurvitch and Lévi-Strauss' relationship, see, for instance, Claude Lévi-Strauss, *Structural Anthropology*, pp. 324-345 and Gurvitch, *La Vocation Actuelle de la Sociologie*, (1963), pp. 414 ff. Gurvitch's strongest attack on Parsons is in Gurvitch's "On Some Deviations in the Interpretation of the Concept of Social Structure," *Sociometry*, 18 (1955), pp. 508 ff. In an interview the author had with Parsons, Parsons brushed aside Gurvitch's work as insignificant: "He did not leave many traces behind" — July 18, 1976.

⁸⁹Similarities between Gurvitch and Parsons' theories have been noted by, for instance, John Vincent Martin. Cf. J.V. Martin, "Microsociology and Pattern Variables: The Possibilities of Theoretical Convergence," in *Depth Sociology and Microsociology: A Critical Analysis of the Basic Concepts of Georges Gurvitch*, pp. 239-257.

⁹⁰Sartre, *Critique de la Raison Dialectique*, p. 117.

⁹¹Georges Gurvitch, "Discussion," *Cahiers Internationaux de Sociologie*, XXVI (1959), p. 73.

⁹²Gurvitch, *The Social Frameworks of Knowledge*, pp. 115-228. Since *The Social Frameworks of Knowledge* was Gurvitch's last work, it contains his most polished version of global societies.

⁹³*Ibid.*, pp. 137-228.

⁹⁴*Ibid.*, pp. 123-136.

⁹⁵*Ibid.*, p. 118. Gurvitch now described his typology of global societies in *Sociology of Law* as "a mistake." He noted, "to establish a multitude of global societies (based on different human activities such as economy, religion, etc.) would be to ruin their character as total social phenomena; and who would deny that in the case of global societies one has to deal with the total social phenomenon par excellence so-to-speak?" — Gurvitch, *Déterminismes Sociaux et Liberté Humaine* (Paris: P.U.F., 1955), p. 197. Many of the global societies that Gurvitch outlined in *Déterminismes Sociaux et Liberté Humaine*, however, were quite similar to the ones in *Sociology of Law*.

⁹⁶See, for instance, Fernand Braudel, "L'Apport de l'Histoire des Civilisations," *Encyclopédie Francaise*, XX (1959), 20.10.11-20.12.14. For a critique of Gurvitch's analysis of global society, see François Bourricaud, "Les Trois Méthodes d'Analyse dans la 'Sociologie en Profendeur' de Georges Gurvitch," *Critique*, XII (1956), pp. 241-243, and Pitirim A. Sorokin, *Sociological*

Theories of Today, pp. 492 ff. According to another critic, Gurvitch's analysis of global societies lacks the ethnocentrism of "modernization" theories. Cf. Maria Isaura De Queiroz, "La Sociologie de Développment et la Pensée de Georges Gurvitch," *Cahiers Internationaux de Sociologie,* LI (1971), 213-236.

[97]See especially Georges Gurvitch, "Continuité et Discontinuité en Histoire et en Sociologie," *Annales. Economies. Sociétés. Civilisations,* 12 (1957), 73-84, and "Philosophie et Sociologie," *Encyclopédie Francaise,* XIX (1957), 19.26-15-19.28-4.

[98]See Georges Gurvitch, *Les Cadres Sociaux de la Connaissance; Déterminismes Sociaux et Liberté Humaine; La Multiplicité des Temps Sociaux* (Paris: Centre de Documentation Socials, 1954); "Réflexions sur la Sociologie de la Vie Morale," *Cahiers Internationaux de Sociologie,* XX-IV (1958), 3-17; "Problèmes de la Sociologie de la Vie Morale" and "Problèmes de Sociologie du Droit," in *Traité,* II (1968), pp. 137-172, 173-206; *"La Variation des Perceptions Collectives des Etendues,"* *Cahiers Internationaux de Sociologie,* XXXVII (1964), 79-106.

[99]Gurvitch, *La Multiplicité des Temps Sociaux* (Paris: C.D.U., 1958).

[100]Gurvitch, *The Spectrum of Social Time,* pp. 13-14.

[101]Gurvitch, "Réflexions sur la Sociologie de la Vie Morale," *Cahiers Internationaux de Sociologie,* XXIV (1958), p. 15.

[102]Gurvitch, *Déterminismes Sociaux et Liberté Humaine* (1955), pp. 103-147, 148-161.

[103]*Ibid.,* pp. 163-177, 178-190, 191-282.

[104]Georges Gurvitch, "La Crise de l'Explication en Sociologie," *Cahiers Internationaux de Sociologie,* XXI (1956), 3-18. The various elements in Gurvitch's system were dialectically inter-related. See, for instance, Gurvitch, "My Intellectual Itinerary," *Sociological Abstracts,* 17/2 (April 1969), p. ix.

[105]Gurvitch, *The Social Frameworks of Knowledge,* pp. 43-56, 57-85, 87-114, 115-228.

[106]*Ibid.,* pp. 22-37.

[107]*Ibid.,* pp. 37-41.

[108]*Ibid.,* pp. 124-127. The hierarchy of knowledge within this type of global society is the following: (A) perceptual knowledge of the external world, (B) technical knowledge, (C) political knowledge, knowledge of the Other and the We, and common-sense knowledge. This does not make very much sense like so many of Gurvitch's other lists of types of knowledge in global societies.

[109]*Ibid.,* pp. 65-67, 96-100.

[110]Myrtle Korenbaum, "Translator's Preface," in Gurvitch, *The Spectrum of Social Time,* p. xii.

[111]See, for instance, Gurvitch, "Avertissement," in *La Sociologie au XXe Siècle, I. Les Grands Problèmes de la Sociologie* (Paris: P.U.F., 1947), p. vii and "Psychologie Collective et Psychologie de la Connaissance," *Année Sociologique,* 1951 (1948-1949), p. 175.

[112]See, for instance, Gurvitch, "La Crise de l'Explication en Sociologie," *Cahiers Internationaux de Sociologie,* XXI (1956), 3-18, and "Philosophie et Sociologie," *Encyclopédie Française,* XIX (1957), 19.26.15-19.28.4.

[113]Gurvitch, "Philosophie et Sociologie," *Encyclopédie Française,* XIX (1957), 19.26.15-19.28.4.

[114]See, for instance, Gurvitch, "Les Cadres Sociaux de la Connaissance Sociologique," *Cahiers Internationaux de Sociologie,* XXVI (1959), 165-172. The concepts "quantophrenia" and "testomania" come from Sorokin's work, *Fads and Foibles in American Sociology* to which Gurvitch wrote the preface when it appeared in French translation in 1959.

[115]Gurvitch, "La Crise de l'Explication en Sociologie," p. 467 in *La Vocation Actuelle de la Sociologie. Tome Second. Antécédants et Perspectives* (Paris: P.U.F., 1969).

[116]See, for instance, "Fondation de l'Association des Sociologues de Langue Francaise," *Cahiers Internationaux de Sociologie,* XXV (1958), 178 and Balandier, *Gurvitch,* p. 10.

[117]See, for instance, Balandier, *Gurvitch,* pp. 10-11.

[118]See especially Gurvitch, *Déterminismes Sociaux et Liberté Humaine* (1955, 1963) which has as a subtitle, "Vêrs l'Etude Sociologique des Cheminements de la Liberté."

[119]Gurvitch, *La Vocation Actuelle de la Sociologie* (1957), p. 9.

[120]See also, Gurvitch, "Continuité et Discontinuité en Histoire et en Sociologie," *Annales, Economies. Société. Civilisations,* 12 (1957), 73-84.

[121]Gurvitch, *La Vocation Actuelle de la Sociologie* (1957), pp. 16. 19. *Emphasis in text.*

[122]Gurvitch,"Réflections sur la Sociologie de la Vie Morale," *Cahiers Internationaux de Sociologie,* XXIV (1958), p. 16, and *Spectrum of Social Time,* pp. 14, 33.

[123]See, for instance, Roger Bastide, Review of *Déterminismes Sociaux, Cahiers Internationaux de Sociologie,* XVIII (1955), pp. 173-174.

[124]Gurvitch, *Dialectique et Sociologie,* p. 5.

[125]Raymond Ledrut, Review of *Dialectique et Sociologie, Critique,* XVIII (1962), p. 874.

[126]See, for instance, Balandier, *Gurvitch,* p. 12, and Duvignaud, *Gurvitch,* p. 12.

[127]See, for instance, Bosserman, *Dialectical Sociology,* pp. 275 ff., and Sorokin, *Sociological Theories of Today,* pp. 462-496.

[128]Duvignaud described Gurvitch's sociology as "subversive" in Duvignaud, *Gurvitch,* p. 75, and Balandier approvingly quotes this in Balandier, *Gurvitch,* p. 49.

[129]Gurvitch, *Dialectique et Sociologie,* p. 13.

[130]See, for instance, Gurvitch, "Le Concept de Structure Sociale," *Cahiers Internationaux de Sociologie,* XIX (1955), 3-44, and "Le Concept de Structure Sociale," in *La Vocation Actuelle de la Sociologie* (1957), pp. 400-442.

[131]Gurvitch's critique of U.S. sociologists and their concepts of social structure was reprinted in English in "On Some Deviations in the Interpretation of Social Structure," *Sociometry,* XVIII (1955), 501-518.

[132]Gurvitch, *La Vocation Actuelle de la Sociologie* (1957), p. 417.

[133]*Ibid.,* p. 418. Many of Gurvitch's works from this period contain bitter remarks about Lévi-Strauss' work. See, for instance, *Déterminismes Sociaux et Liberté Humaine* (1963), p. 225; *Dialectique et Sociologie* (1962), p. 201; *The Social Frameworks of Knowledge* (1966), pp. 120-126; *Traité de Sociologie* (1967), I, pp. 211-212.

[134]Lévi-Strauss devoted one angry postscript in *Anthropologie Structural* to some of his critics, among them Gurvitch. See Claude Lévi-Strauss, *Structural Anthropology,* pp. 324-345.

[135]Gurvitch, *The Social Frameworks of Knowledge,* n. 1., p. 46.

[136]Gurvitch, *La Vocation Actuelle de la Sociologie* (1957), p. 422.

[137]Georges Gurvitch, "Structures Sociales et Systèmes de Connaissances," in *XXe Sémaine de Synthèse. Notion de Structure et Structure de la Connaissance,* 18-27 Avril 1956 (Paris: Editions Albin Michel, 1957), p. 320.

[138]Gurvitch, *La Vocation Actuelle de la Sociologie* (1957), p. 403.

[139]*Ibid.,* p. 404.

[140]Gurvitch, "Problèmes de Sociologie Générale," in *Traité de Sociologie, Tome Premier* (Paris: P.U.F., 1967), p. 214.

[141]Gilles Granger, "Evènement et Structure dans les Sciences de l'Homme," *Cahiers de l'Institut de Science Economique Appliquée,* No 96 (Décembre 1959), p. 173.

[142]See Jean Piaget, *Structuralism,* trans. Chaninah Maschler (New York: Harper & Row, 1970), and Maurice de Gandillac *et al.,* eds., *Entretiens sur les Notions de Genèse et de Structure* (Paris and Le Hague: Mouton & Co., MCMLXV), pp. 9-10.

[143]See, for instance, Goldmann, "Structuralisme, Marxisme, Existentialisme," *L'Homme et la Société,* 2 (Octobre-Décembre 1960), 105-124.

[144]Georges Davy, "Discussion," in Gurvitch, "Structures Sociales et Systèmes de Connaissances," pp. 327-333. Davy made a similar critique of Gurvitch in 1950. Cf. Cuvillier, *Où va la Sociologie Française?* p. 130.

[145]Jean Cazeneuve, "La Sociologie de Georges Gurvitch," *Revue Française de Sociologie,* VII (1966), p. 7.

[146]Henri Lefebvre, "Réflexions sur le Structuralisme et l'Histoire," *Cahiers Internationaux de Sociologie,* XXXV (1963), pp. 19 ff.

[147]Pierre-Maxime Schuhl, "Georges Gurvitch (1894-1965)," *Revue Philosophique de la France et de l'Etranger,* CLVII (1967), p. 331.

[148]Duvignaud, "Entretiens Avec Georges Gurvitch," *Lettres Nouvelles,* 1er Avril 1959, p. 25.

[149]Gurvitch, *Déterminismes Sociaux et Liberté Humaine* (1963), p. 3.

[150]*Ibid.,* pp. 7-8.

[151]See, for instance, Nicola Abbagnano, "La Sociologie de la Liberté: Georges Gurvitch,"

Revue de Métaphysique et de Morale, 61 (1956), 74-86.

[152]T. B. Bottomore, Review of *Déterminismes Sociaux* (1955), *British Journal of Sociology,* 6 (1955), 386-388. Bottomore was in close contact with Gurvitch in the 1950's (Letter to author, August, 1975).

[153]Georges Balandier, "Georges Gurvitch ou la Sociologie Combattante," *Le Nouvel Observateur,* No 58 (22-28 Décembre 1965), 32-33, and Jean Duvignaud, "Mort de Georges Gurvitch," *Nouvel Observateur,* No 57 (16-21 Décembre 1965), 45.

[154]See Henri Lefebvre, *Au-Dèla du Structuralisme,* p. 254, and *Vers le Cybernanthrope,* pp. 112-113, 145.

[155]See Martin, *Depth Sociology and Microsociology,* pp. 98, 262 ff. and George J. Stack, "Gurvitch and Sartre's Dialectic," *Modern Schoolman,* LII (May 1975), 341-375.

[156]Stack, "Gurvitch and Sartre's Dialectic," *Modern Schoolman,* LII (May 1975), pp. 341, 355, 357.

[157]Gurvitch, *Déterminismes Sociaux et Liberté Humaine* (1963), p. 92.

[158]See, for instance, Gurvitch, *Le Concept de Classes Sociales* (Paris: C.D.U., 1954); *Les Fondateurs Français de la Sociologie Contemporaine: Saint-Simon et P.J. Proudhon* (Paris: C.D.U., 1955); *La Sociologie de Karl Marx* (Paris: C.D.U., 1959); *Dialectique et Sociologie* (Paris: Flammarion, 1962).

[159]C.-H. de Saint-Simon, *La Physiologie Sociale, Oeuvres Choisies avec Introduction et Notes de Georges Gurvitch* (Paris: P.U.F., 1965); Gurvitch ed., *Proudhon, Sa Vie, Son Oeuvre avec un Exposé de Sa Philosophie* (Paris: P.U.F., 1965).

[160]See, for instance, Georges Gurvitch, "Brève Esquisse de l'Histoire de la Sociologie," in *Traité de Sociologie, Tome Premier,* (Paris: P.U.F., 1967), pp. 28-64.

[161]Gurvitch maintained that Durkheim was one of the finest sociologists but showed no interest in his work. Comte was, as in *L'Idée du Droit Social,* seen as an authoritarian and poor scientist. Spencer only interested Gurvitch insofar as he was a predecessor to structural-functionalism. Cf. Georges Gurvitch, "Pour le Centenaire de Durkheim," *Cahiers Internationaux de Sociologie,* XXVII (1959), 3-10; *Pour le Centenaire de Comte* (Paris: C.D.U., 1957); "Une Source Oubliée des Concepts de 'Structure Social,' 'Fonction Social' et 'Institution': Herbert Spencer," *Cahiers Internationaux de Sociologie,* XXII (1957), 111-121.

[162]Raymond Aron's course exists in English translation under the title *Main Currents in Sociological Thought,* I-II (New York: Doubleday & Company, 1968).

[163]Gurvitch, *Les Fondateurs Français de la Sociologie Contemporaine, I. Saint-Simon: Sociologue,* p. 50.

[164]*Ibid.,* p. 45.

[165]*Ibid.,* pp. 26-27.

[166]Saint-Simon, *La Physiologie Sociale,* pp. 34-35.

[167]Gurvitch, *Les Fondateurs Français,* p. 42, n.1 and Bosserman, *Dialectical Sociology,* p. 261, n.1.

[168]See, for instance, C.-H. de Saint-Simon, *La Physiologie Sociale,* pp. 34-35.

[169]The theme of a synthesis between Marx and Proudhon first emerged in Gurvitch's work in 1946. It was more fully developed during the 1950's and 1960's and was the topic of Gurvitch's last public speech. See Gurvitch, "Vers l'Unité Ouvrière," *Esprit,* 14(1er Février 1946), pp. 274 ff; *Pour Le Centenaire de la Mort de Pierre-Joseph Proudhon: Proudhon et Marx: Une Confrontation;* "Proudhon et Marx," *Cahiers Internationaux de Sociologie,* XL (1966), 7-16.

[170]See, for instance, Gurvitch, *Les Fondateurs Francais de la Sociologie Contemporaine. II. P.J. Proudhon,* pp. 26-27, 81; *Pour le Centenaire de Pierre-Joseph Proudhon,* p. 26.

[171]See Celéstin Bouglé, *Sociologie du Proudhon* (Paris: A. Colin, 1911). Bouglé had outlined his ideas the year before in "Proudhon Sociologue," *Revue de Métaphysique et de Morale,* (1910), 614-648.

[172]For an articulate expression of the opposite opinion, see especially the work of Pierre Ansart who was himself influenced by Gurvitch. See, for instance, Pierre Ansart, *Sociologie de Proudhon* (Paris: P.U.F., 1967).

[173]Karl Marx, *The Poverty of Philosophy: Answer to the "Philosophy of Poverty" by M. Proudhon* (Moscow: Progress Publishers, 1966). This edition also contains the older Marx's opinion of Proudhon as expressed in his letter of January 24, 1865 to J. B. Schweitzer.

[174]Gurvitch, "La Sociologie de Karl Marx," in *Vocation* (1969), p. 222.

[175]Gurvitch, *Pour le Centenaire de la Mort d'Auguste Comte (1857-1957). Trois Chapitres d'Histoire de la Sociologie: Auguste Comte-Karl Marx-Herbert Spencer* (Paris: C.D.U., 1967), p. 51.

[176]Gurvitch, "La Sociologie de Karl Marx," in *Vocation,* (1969), p. 226.

[177]*Ibid.,* pp. 223 ff., 227 ff.

[178]*Ibid.,* p. 270.

[179]See, for instance, Gurvitch, *Pour le Centenaire,* p. 76.

[180]See Gurvitch, *Vocation* (1950), pp. 338-348.

[181]Georges Gurvitch, *Etudes Sur les Classes Sociales: L'Idée de Classe Sociale de Marx à Nos Jours* (Paris: Editions Gonthier, 1966), p. 15.

[182]Gurvitch, *Etudes Sur les Classes Sociales,* p. 234.

[183]*Ibid.,* p. 111.

[184]Gurvitch, *Dialectique et Sociologie,* p. 11.

[185]Gurvitch criticized in *Dialectique et Sociologie* his own analysis of the dialectic in *Fichtes System der Konkreten Ethik.* See Gurvitch, *Dialectique et Sociologie,* pp. 58-59.

[186]Gurvitch, *Dialectique et Sociologie,* p. 92.

[187]*Ibid.,* p. 97.

[188]*Ibid.,* p. 158; Sartre, *Critique de la Raison Dialectique,* p. 670.

[189]Gurvitch, *Dialectique et Sociologie,* p. 28.

[190]*Ibid.,* p. 27.

[191]*Ibid.,* pp. 189-220.

[192]Raymond Aron, *La Lutte de Classes. Nouvelles Lecons sur les Sociétés Industrielles* (Paris: Gallimard, 1964); René König, "On Some Recent Developments in the Relation between Theory and Research," in *Transactions of the Fourth World Congress of Sociology. Milan and Stresa 8-15 September, 1959. Volume II* (London: International Sociological Association, 1959) pp. 275-289. For Aron's earlier view of Gurvitch, see his reviews of *Essais de Sociologie* and *L'Expérience Juridique* in *Annales Sociologiques,* Série A, 4(1938), 117-119, and *Zeitschrift für Sozialwissenschaft,* V(1936), 118-119. For König's earlier opinion of Gurvitch, see Rene König, *Kritik der historisch-existentialistischen Soziologie: Ein Beitrag zur Begründung einer objektiven Soziologie* (München: R. Piper & Co., 1975), pp. 11-12, 18.

[193]René König, "On Some Recent Developments in the Relation between Theory and Research," in *Transactions of the Fourth World Congress of Sociology,* p. 287. König's argument that the concept of "totality" in Gurvitch comes from Marx is wrong. It comes from Marcel Mauss who forged it in conscious opposition to Marxist theory. Cf. Marcel Mauss, "Appréciation Sociologique du Bolchevisme," *Revue de Métaphysique et de Morale,* 3 (1924), p. 122.

[194]Aron, *La Lutte de Classes,* pp. 91, 104-108, 110, 123-125. Gurvitch answered Aron's critique in, for example, Georges Gurvitch, "Avant-Propos," *Cahiers Internationaux de Sociologie,* XXXVIII (1965), pp. 6-7.

[195]Gurvitch's course on dialectics stirred up less of a discussion. On the whole, both old time Marxists and neo-Marxists disapproved of Gurvitch's concept of dialectics. See, for instance, Ileana Bauer, Review of the German translation of *Dialectique et Sociologie, Deutsche Zeitschrift für Philosophie,* 14 (1966), 900-906; Pierre Fougeyrollas, "Réflexions sur la Sociologie de M. Georges Gurvitch," *Nouvelle Critique,* No 56 (Juin 1954), 73-90; Adolf Gucinski, Review of German translation of *Dialectique et Sociologie, Telos,* 1 (Spring 1968), 49-52. Henri Lefebvre, in the earlier mentioned interview with the author in February, 1975, said that he found Gurvitch's concept of the dialectic very subjectivistic and in the Fichtean tradition. George Lichtheim stressed that Gurvitch's concept of dialectic was directed at the distortions of the Marxist dialectic: "George Gurvitch's 'Dialectique et Sociologie' performs the interesting feat of turning positivism into a critical weapon against both Hegel and Marx" — George Lichtheim, "Western Marxist Literature 1953-1963," *Survey,* 50 (January 1964), 119-128.

[196]See, for instance, E. Bottigelli, "Le Chemin de Marx," *Nouvelle Critique,* No 71 (Janvier 1956), p. 80, and "Quel Avenir Attend l'Humanité? La Rencontre Internationale de Royaumont," *Nouvelle Revue Internationale,* 4 (Novembre 1961), pp. 92-94. The official Marxist opinion of Gurvitch can be found in the Russian Philosophical Encyclopaedia of 1960. There Gurvitch is described as a "reactionary" sociologist and a "bourgeois sociologist-idealist" who, however, "sided

with the proponents of peace in the world." See *Filosofskaia Encyclopedia* (Moscow: Institute of Philosophy of the USSR Academy of Sciences, 1960), I., p. 419. (The author is grateful to Professor Alex Simirenko for this information).

[197]See especially Roger Garaudy, "La Lutte Idéologique chez les Intellectuels," *Cahiers du Communisme*, N<small>OS</small> 7-8 (Juillet-Août 1955), 891-905; "Réponse à Henri Lefebvre: Sur les Fondaments Idéologiques et les Problèmes de l'Unité," *Cahiers du Communisme*, N<small>O</small> 10 (Octobre 1955), 1216-1237; Jean Kanapa, "Situation de l'Intellectuel: Introduction" *Nouvelle Critique*, N<small>O</small> 68 (1955), 19-32; Henri Lefebvre, "Une Lettre de Henri Lefebvre à Roger Garaudy," *Cahiers du Communisme*, N<small>O</small> 10 (Octobre 1955), 1207-1215; Maxime Rodinson, "M. Gurvitch, le Déterminisme, les Classes et l'Avenir du Prolétariat," *Pensée*, N<small>O</small> 67 (Mai-Juin 1956), 122-130.

[198]Jean Duvignaud, "France: The Neo-Marxists," in Leopold Labedz, ed., *Revisionism: Essays in the History of Marxist Ideas* (New York: Frederick A. Praeger, 1962), p. 317.

[199]Jean Duvignaud, Review of *Etudes sur les Classes Sociales, L'Homme et la Société*, 2 (1966), p. 185.

[200]Henri Lefebvre-Georges Gurvitch, "Le Concept de Classes: *Un Dialogue Entre Georges Gurvitch et Henri Lefebvre*," *Critique*, XL (1955), p. 560.

[201]*Ibid.*, 558-569.

[202]Garaudy, "La Lutte Idéologique chez les Intellectuels," *Cahiers du Communisme*, N<small>O</small> 7-8, (Juillet-Août 1955), p. 895.

[203]Henri Lefebvre, *La Somme et le Reste* (Paris: Belibaste, Editeur, 1973), pp. 206-208.

[204]Henri Lefebvre, "La Notion de Totalité dans les Sciences Sociales," *Cahiers Internationaux de Sociologie*, XVIII (1955), p. 65.

[205]*Ibid.*

[206]Karl Marx, *Capital: A Critique of Political Economy*, trans. Samuel Moore and Edward Aveling (New York: The Modern Library, 1965), pp. 10-12; Proudhon, *La Création de l'Ordre dans l'Humanité* (1843), p. 461. The quote by Proudhon is from Gurvitch, *Pour le Centenaire de Pierre-Joseph Proudhon*, p. 27.

[207]Gurvitch, *Dialectique et Sociologie*, p. 239.

[208]See, for instance, Gurvitch, ed., *Traité de Sociologie*, (1967), p. 38; *Vocation* (1969), p. 227.

[209]Gurvitch, "Proudhon et Marx," in *L'Actualité de Proudhon*, pp. 130-131.

Notes to Afterword

[1]Simone de Beauvoir, *The Prime of Life*, trans. Peter Green (New York: Lancer Books, 1973), p. 46.

[2]V. I. Lenin, "Letters on Tactics" in *April Thesis* (Moscow: Progress Publishers, 1970), p. 14.

BIBLIOGRAPHY

Works by Georges Gurvitch

All items in the following bibliography have been personally inspected by the author unless preceded by (*). Translations of Gurvitch's work into foreign languages have been disregarded unless they contained changes by Gurvitch in the text. Since it has been impossible to check the various editions of *Centre de Documentation Sociale,* these have generally been disregarded.

Information on courses taught by Gurvitch can usually be found in the bulletins of the school. This is, for instance, the case with the Sorbonne (*Université de Paris, Livret de l'Etudiant*), Harvard University and the New School For Social Research. According to Jean Cazeneuve, there are several unpublished courses and speeches by Gurvitch (cf. Jean Cazeneuve, "La Sociologie de Georges Gurvitch," *Revue Française de Sociologie,* VII (1966), p. 11). Information on some of Gurvitch's trips to various conferences is available in *Annales de l'Université de Paris* (see, for instance, 1935, 1950, and 1957).

1915a   *'The Truth of the Monarch's Will' of Theophan Prokopovich and Its Western-European Sources.* Edited and with a Preface by Professor F. W. Taranowsky. (Reprinted from *Studies of the Imperial University of Yurev*). Yurev: K. Mattisen, 1915. (In Russian.)

1918a(*)   *Rousseau and the Declaration of Rights: The Idea of Man's Inalienable Rights in the Political Doctrine of Rousseau.* Petrograd: Wolf, 1918. (In Russian.)

1921a(*)   "The Idea of Man's Inalienable Rights in the Political Doctrine of the 17th and 18th Centuries" in *Works of Russian Scholars Abroad,* I (Berlin, 1921).

1922a   *Die Einheit der Fichteschen Philosophie. Personal und Gemeinschaftswert in der Ethik Fichtes. Eine Studie über Fichtes Lehre vom sittlichen Ideal. I. Lieferung.* Berlin: Verlag Arthur Collignon, 1922.

1922b   "Kant und Fichte als Rousseau-Interpreten," *Kant-Studien,* 27(1922), 138-164. Reprinted in a French translation in *Revue de Métaphysique et de Morale,* 76(1971), 385-405.

1922c(*)   *Otto v. Gierke als Rechtsphilosoph.* Tübingen: J.C.B. Mohr, 1922.

1922d   "Übersicht der Neueren Rechtsphilosophischen Literatur in Russland," *Philosophie und Recht,* II(1922/23), 111-125. - Gurvitch edited this number of *Philosophie und Recht* with Paul Nowgorodzeff.

1922e   "Die Zwei Grössten Russischen Rechtsphilosophen: Boris Tschitscherin und Wladimir Ssolowjew," *Philosophie und Recht,* II (1922/23), 80-102.

1923a(*)   *Introduction to A General Theory of International Law.* Prague: The Faculty of Russian Law, 1923. (In Russian.)

1923b   "Otto v. Gierke als Rechtsphilosoph," *Logos,* XI(1922/23), 86-132.

1924a   *Fichtes System der Konkreten Ethik.* Tübingen: J.C.B. Mohr (Paul Siebeck), 1924.

1925a(*)   "The State and Socialism," *Sovremennva Zapiski,* 1925. (In Russian.)

1926a(*)   "Morality and Religion," *Sovremennva Zapiski,* 1926. (In Russian.)

1926b   "La Philosophie Russe du Premier Quart du XXᵉ Siècle," *Monde Slave,* 3(1926), 254-272.

1926c(*)   "Proudhon and Modernity," *Sovremennva Zapiski,* 1926. (In Russian.)

1926d(*)   "Socialism and Property: Review of Sergius Hessen's *The Problem of Legal Socialism,*" *Sovremennva Zapiski,* 1926-1930. (In Russian.)

1927a(*)   "The Future of Democracy," *Sovremennva Zapiski,* 1927. (In Russian.)

1927b   "La Philosophie du Droit de Hugo Grotius et la Théorie Moderne du Droit Interna-
            tional (A l'Occasion du Tricentenaire du *De jure belli ac pacis,* 1625-1925)," *Revue de
            Métaphysique et de Morale,* 34(1927), 365-391.

1928a   "(*Discussion:*) L'Intuitivisme Russe et le Réalisme Anglo-Saxon," *Bulletin de la
            Société Francaise de Philosophie,* 28(1928), 167-171, 172.

1928b   "La Philosophie Phénoménologique en Allemagne: I.-Edmund Husserl," *Revue de
            Métaphysique et de Morale,* 35(1928), 353-397.

1928c   "Proudhon und die Gegenwart," *Archiv für Rechts- und Sozialphilosophie,*
            XXI(1927/28), 537-562.

1929a   "Phénoménologie et Criticisme (Une Confrontation entre les Deux Courants dans la
            Philosophie d'Emile Lask et de Nikolai Hartmann)," *Revue Philosophique de la
            France et de l'Etranger,* CXVIII(1929), 235-284.

1929b   "Le Principe Démocratique et la Démocratie Future," *Revue de Métaphysique et de
            Morale,* 36(1929), 403-431.

1930a   "Chicherin, Boris Nikolayevitch (1828-1904)," in Edwin R. A. Seligman and Alvin
            Johnson, eds., *Encyclopaedia of the Social Sciences,* III(1930), 372. New York: The
            Macmillan Company, 1930.

1930b   "Kritische Bemerkungen über die Philosophie M. Heideggers," *Der Russische
            Gedanke,* I(1930), 234-237.

1930c   "Socialisme et Propriété," *Revue de Métaphysique et de Morale,* 37(1930), 113-147.

1930d   *Les Tendances Actuelles de la Philosophie Allemande. E. Husserl. M. Scheler. E.
            Lask. N. Hartmann. M. Heidegger.* Préface de Léon Braunschvicg. Paris: Librairie
            Philosophique J. Vrin, 1930.

1931a   "Fichte, Johann Gottlieb (1762-1814)" in Edwin R. A. Seligman and Alvin Johnson,
            eds., *Encyclopaedia of the Social Sciences,* IV(1931), 223-225. New York: The Mac-
            millan Company, 1931.

1931b   "Les Idées-Maîtresses de Maurice Hauriou," *Archives de Philosophie du Droit et de
            Sociologie Juridique,* 1(1931), 156-194.

1931c(*)   "Petrazhitsk," *Sovremennva Zapiski,* 1931. (In Russian.)

1931d   "Une Philosophie Intuitioniste du Droit: Léon Petrasizky," *Archives de Philosophie
            du Droit et de Sociologie Juridique,* 1(1931), 403-420.

1931e   "La Philosophie Sociale de Chr. Fr. Krause (A Suivre)," *Der Russische Gedanke,*
            II(1931), 151-160. Cf. 1932g.

1931f   "*Review:* J. Delos.-*La Société Internationale et les Principes de Droit Public,* 1929
            (édition Pedone)," *Archives de Philosophie du Droit et de Sociologie Juridique,*
            1(1931), 264-266.

1931g   "*Review:* L. Le Fur.-*Le Saint-Siège et le Droit des Gens.* 1930 (Recueil Sirey)," *Ar-
            chives de Philosophie du Droit et de Sociologie Juridique,* 1(1931), 256-259.

1931h   "*Review: OEuvres Complètes de Proudhon.-* Nouvelle Edition Publiée avec des Notes
            et des Commentaires. *De la Justice dans la Révolution et dans l'Eglise.* 1 vol. Introduc-
            tion par G. Guy-Grad, Etude de Gabriel Séailles, Notes de C. Bouglé et J.-l. Puech
            (1930, Edition Rivière)," *Archives de Philosophie du Droit et de Sociologie Juridique,*
            1(1931), 241-242.

1932a   "Gradovsky, Alexander Dmitrievich (1841-1889)" in Edwin R. A. Seligman and Alvin
            Johnson, eds., *Encyclopaedia of the Social Sciences,* VII(1932), 134-135. New York:
            The Macmillan Company, 1932.

1932b   *L'Idée du Droit Social. Notion et Système du Droit Social. Histoire Doctrinale Depuis
            le XVIIe Siècle Jusqu'à la Fin du XIXe Siècle.* Préface de Louis Le Fur. Paris:
            Librairie du Recueil Sirey, 1932.

1932c   "Justice" in Edwin R. A. Seligman and Alvin Johnson, eds., *Encyclopaedia of the
            Social Sciences,* VIII(1932), 509-515. New York: The Macmillan Company, 1932.

1932d   "Kistiakovsky, Bogdan Alexandrovich (1868-1920)" in Edwin R. A. Seligman and
            Alvin Johnson, eds., *Encyclopaedia of the Social Sciences,* VIII(1932), 575-576. New
            York: The Macmillan Company, 1932.

1932e   "Korkunov, Nikolay Mikhaylovich (1853-1904)" in Edwin R. A. Seligman and Alvin

Johnson, eds., *Encyclopaedia of the Social Sciences,* VIII(1932), 591-592. New York: The Macmillan Company, 1932.

1932f   "Une Philosophie Antimonique du Droit—Gustav Radbruch," *Archives de Philosophie du Droit et de Sociologie Juridique,* 2(1932), 530-563.

1932g   "La Philosophie Sociale de Chr. Fr. Krause," pp. 9-27 in *Festschrift N. O. Losski j zum 60. Geburtstage.* Bonn: Friedrich Cohen, 1932. Cf. 1931e.

1932h   "*Review:* C. Bouglé.-*Socialismes Francais.* Du 'Socialisme Utopique' à la 'Démocratie Industrielle', Paris, 1932, éd. Armand Colin, pp. 200," *Archives de Philosophie du Droit et de Sociologie Juridique,* 2(1932), 298-739.

1932i   "*Review:* Maxime Leroy-*La Société des Nations. Guerre ou Paix?,* Paris, 1932, éd. A. Pedone, pp. 237," *Archives de Philosophie du Droit et de Sociologie Juridique,* 2(1932), 288-290.

1932j   "*Review:* Scelle-*Précis de Droit des Gens. Principes et Systematique.* Première Partie. Introduction. Le Milieu Intersocial, Ed. du Recueil Sirey, 1932, pp. 312," *Archives de Philosophie du Droit et de Sociologie Juridique,* 2(1932), 279-286.

1932k   *Le Temps Présent et l'Idée du Droit Social.* Préface de Maxime Leroy. Paris: Librairie Philosophique J. Vrin, 1932.

1933a   "Droit Naturel ou Droit Positif Intuitif?," *Archives de Philosophie du Droit et de Sociologie Juridique,* N⁰ 3-4(1933), 55-90.

1933b   "L'Evolution de la 'Doctrine de la Science' chez Fichte, d'après M. Gueroult (M. Gueroult, *L'Evolution et la Structure de la Doctrine de la Science chez Fichte,* t. I et II, Paris, 1930, édition Les Belles-Lettres," *Revue de Métaphysique et de Morale,* 40(1933), 119-128.

1933c   "Menger, Anton (1841-1906)" in Edwin R. A. Seligman and Alvin Johnson, eds., *Encyclopaedia of the Social Science,* X(1933), 310-313. New York: The Macmillan Company, 1933.

1933d   "*Review:* Adolfo Posada-*Les Fonctions Sociales de l'Etat,* (Bibliothèque Sociologie Internationale, sous la Direction de Gaston Richard). Paris, 1929, p. 227, éd. Girard," *Archives de Philosophie du Droit et de Sociologie Juridique,* 3(1933), 223-226.

1933e   "*Review:* Alexander and Eugen Kulischer-*Kriegs und Wanderzúge. Weltqeschichte als Vôlkerbewegung,* Berlin, 1932, pp. 230, éd. Walter de Gruyter et C⁰," *Archives de Philosophie du Droit et de Sociologie Juridique, 3(1933), 247-249.*

1933f   "*Review:* Eugène Dupréel-*Traité de Morale,* I et II vol. (Travaux de la Faculté de Philosophie et Lettres de l'Université de Bruxelles), Bruxelles, 1932, pp. 705," *Archives de Philosophie du Droit et de Sociologie Juridique,* 3(1933), 219-223.

1933g   "*Review:* Friedrich Darmstaedter-*Rechtsstaat oder Machtstaat?* Eine Frage nach der Geltung der Weimarer Verfassung, Berlin, 1932, p. 160, éd. W. Rotschild," *Archives de Philosophie du Droit et de Sociologie Juridique,* 3(1933), 246-247.

1933h   "*Review:* Giorgio Del Vecchio, *La Société des Nations au Point de Vue de la Philosophie du Droit International* (Académie du Droit International), 1932, Paris, éd. Sirey, p. 105," *Archives de Philosophie du Droit et de Sociologie Juridique,* 3(1933), 228-232.

1933i(*)   "Les Syndicats et l'Interêt Générale," *L'Homme Réel,* 1(1933), 13-19.

1933j   (*Together with Paul Léon:*) "*Review:* Emmanuel Lévy-*Les Fondements du Droit,* Paris, 1933, éd. Alcan," *Archives de Philosophie du Droit et de Sociologie Juridique,* N⁰ 3-4, 3(1933), 266-270.

1934a   (*Discussion:*) *Annuaire de l'Institut International de Philosophie du Droit et de Sociologie Juridique. 1934-1935. Travaux de la Première Session. Le Problème des Sources du Droit Positif.* Paris: Librairie du Recueil Sirey, 1934. Pp. 71-72, 80, 112-113, 130-131, 186, 208.

1934b   "Les Fondements et l'Evolution du Droit d'Après Emmanuel Lévy," *Revue Philosophique de la France et de l'Etranger,* CXVII(1934), 104-138.

1934c   "Libéralisme et Communisme—*Une Réponse à M. Ramon Fernandez,*" *Esprit,* 2(1ᵉʳ Juin 1934), 448-452.

1934d   "Petrazhitsky, Lev Iosifovich (Petrazycki, Leon) (1867-1931)," in Edwin R. A. Seligman and Alvin Johnson, eds., *Encyclopaedia of the Social Sciences,* XII(1934),

103-104. New York: The Macmillan Company, 1934.

1934e   *"Reviews:* Edouard Lambert-*Une Fuite dans les Institutions de Paix.* Le Libre Jeux
          des Représailles et l'Embargo Punitif sur les Marchandises. Lyon, 1934, pp. 71, édit.
          de la Revue de l'Université.-Le même. *Un Parère de Jurisprudence Comparative.* 1.
          Dettes Contractées en Monnaie Etrangère; Règles du Droit International sur Leur
          Paiement. 2. Le Rôle de la Clause Compromissoire dans les Marchés du Commerce
          International (Bibliothèque de l'Institut de Droit Comparé de Lyon, tome 33), Paris,
          1934, pp. 221, éd. M. Giard," *Archives de Philosophie du Droit et de Sociologie
          Juridique,* 4(1934), 261-263.

1934f   *"Review:* Otaka Tomoo-*Grundlegung der Lehre vom Socialen Verband.* Wien, 1932,
          éd. I. Springer, 279 pp.," *Archives de Philosophie du Droit et de Sociologie Juridique,*
          4(1934), 264-266.

1934g   "Théorie Pluraliste des Sources du Droit Positif," pp. 114-130 in Georges Gurvitch,
          ed., *Le Problème des Sources du Droit Positif. Annuaire de l'Institut International de
          Philosophie du Droit et de Sociologie Juridique.* Paris: Librairie du Recueil Sirey,
          1934. – See also "Discussion du Rapport de M. Gurvitch," pp. 130-131.

1935a   *L'Expérience Juridique et la Philosophie Pluraliste du Droit.* Paris: Editions A.
          Pedone, 1935.

1935b   "Natural Law" in Edwin R. A. Seligman and Alvin Johnson, eds., *Encyclopaedia of
          the Social Sciences,* XI(1935), 284-290. New York: The Macmillan Company, 1935.

1935c   "Remarques sur la Classification des Formes de la Sociabilité – Analyse Critique des
          Doctrines en Présence," *Archives de Philosophie du Droit et de Sociologie Juridique,*
          NO 3-4, 5(1935), 43-91.

1935d   *"Review: Recueil d'Etudes sur les Sources du Droit, en l'Honneur de Francois Gény.*
          Tome I. *Aspects Historiques et Philosophiques.* Tome II. *Les Sources Générales des
          Systèmes Juridiques Actuels.* Tome III. *Les Sources des Diverses Branches du Droit.*
          Publié par M. Edouard Lambert, Directeur de l'Institut de Droit Comparé de
          l'Université de Lyon. Paris, Sirey, 1934, 3 vol., pp. 1428," *Archives de Philosophie du
          Droit et de Sociologie Juridique,* 5(1935), 288-289.

1935e   "Secrétan, Charles (1815-95)," in Edwin R. A. Seligman and Alvin Johnson, eds., *En-
          cyclopaedia of the Social Sciences,* XIII(1934), 623-624. New York: The Macmillan
          Company, 1934.

1936a   "(*Discussion:*) *IIᵉAnnuaire de l'Institut de Philosophie du Droit et de Sociologie
          Juridique. 1935-1936, Travaux de la Seconde Session. Droit, Morale, Moeurs.* Paris:
          Librairie du Recueil Sirey, 1936. Pp. 81-82, 219-220, 233-234, 248-249.

1936b   *"Review:* C. Bouglé-*Bilan de la Sociologie Francaise Contemporaine,* Paris, 1935.
          (*Nouvelle Encyclopédie Philosophique,* Paris, 1935. (*Nouvelle Encyclopédie
          Philosophique,* sous la Direction de M. Henri Delacroix), éd. Alcan," *Archives de
          Philosophie du Droit et de Sociologie Juridique,* 6(1936), 212-213.

1936c   *"Review:* Carl Schmitt-*Légalité et Légitimité.* Traduction et Introduction par William
          Gueydan de Roussel, Paris 1936, Librairie Générale de Droit et de Jurisprudence, pp.
          102," *Archives de Philosophie du Droit et de Sociologie Juridique,* 6(1936), 235-236.

1936d   *"Review:* E. Halévy, R. Aron, G. Friedmann, E. Bernard, R. Marjolin, E. Dennery et
          C. Bouglé.-*Inventaires. La Crise Sociale et les Idéologies Nationales,* avec un Avant-
          Propos de M. C. Bouglé, 1936, Paris, éd. Alcan, 233 pages," *Archives de Philosophie
          du Droit et de Sociologie Juridique,* 6(1936), 230-232.

1936e   *"Review:* L. Le Fur-*Règles Générales du Droit de la Paix.* Paris, 1936, p. 306 (Extrait
          du Recueil des Cours de l'Academie du Droit International de la Haye)," *Archives de
          Philosophie du Droit et de Sociologie Juridique,* NO 3-4, 6(1936), 229-231.

1936f   *"Review:* Marcel Prélot-*L'Empire Fasciste. Les Origines, les Tendances et les Institu-
          tions. De la Dictature et du Corporatisme Italien. (Bibliothèque Constitutionelle et
          Parlamentaire Contemporaine,* volume 8.) Paris, éd. de Recueil Sirey, 1936, 258
          pages," *Archives de Philosophie du Droit et de Sociologie Juridique,* 6(1936),
          232-235.

1936g   *"Review:* R. Aron-*La Sociologie Allemande Contemporaine,* Paris, Alcan, 1935, 176
          pages (*Nouvelle Encyclopédie Philosophique*)," *Archives de Philosophie du Droit et*

de Sociologie Juridique, 6(1936), 213-214.

1937a   *Morale Théorique et Science des Moeurs. Leurs Possibilités-Leurs Conditions.* Paris: Librairie Félix Alcan, 1937.

1937b   "*Review: Inventaires II* par C. Bouglé, R. Aron, V. Obolensky-Ossinski, L. Rosenstock-Frank, P. Vaucher, R. Polin, G. Prache, G. Lefranc, M. Déat, Paris, 1937, pp....," *Archives de Philosophie du Droit et de Sociologie Juridique,* Nᵒ 3-4, 7(1937), 250.

1937c   "*Review:* Jean Lacroix-*Itinéraire Spirituel* (Cahiers de la Nouvelle Journée, nᵒ 35, Paris, 1937)," *Archives de Philosophie du Droit et de Sociologie Juridique,* Nᵒ 3-4, 7(1937), 233-234.

1937d   "*Review:* Robert Leroux-*Guillaume de Humbold. La Formation de sa Pensée Jusqu'en 1794* (Publications de la Faculté des Lettres de l'Université de Strasbourg, 1932)," *Archives de Philosophie du Droit et de Sociologie Juridique,* Nᵒ 3-4, 7(1937), 236-237.

1937e   "La Science des Faits Moraux et la Morale Théorique chez E. Durkheim," *Archives de Philosophie du Droit et de Sociologie Juridique,* 7(1937), 18-44.

1937f   "La Théorie des Valeurs de Heinrich Rickert," *Revue Philosophique de la France et de l'Etranger,* CXXIV(1937), 80-88.

1937g(*)   "Les Variations de l'Expérience Morale Immédiate," pp. 39-44 in *Travaux du IX Congrès Internationale de Philosophie.* Paris: Hermann, 1937.

1938a   (*Ed.*:) *Le But du Droit: Bien Commun, Justice, Securité. IIIᵉ Annuaire de l'Institut International de Philosophie du Droit et de Sociologie Juridique. Tome III. 1937-1938. Travaux de la Troisième Session.* Paris: Librairie du Recueil Sirey, 1938.

1938b   "Essai d'une Classification Pluraliste des Formes de Sociabilité," *Annales Sociologiques,* Séries A. 3(1938), 1-48.

1938c   *Essais de Sociologie.-Les Formes de la Sociabilité. Le Problème de la Conscience Collective. La Magie et le Droit. La Morale de Durkheim.* Paris: Librairie du Receuil Sirey, 1938.

1938d   "Le Problème de la Conscience Collective dans la Sociologie d'Emile Durkhiem," *Archives de Philosophie du Droit et de Sociologie Juridique,* 8(1938), 119-173.

1938e   "*Review:* Gaston Richard-*La Conscience Morale et l'Expérience Morale; les Lois Morales, les Lois Naturelles et les Lois Sociales,* 1937, Paris, éd. Hermann," *Archives de Philosophie du Droit et de Sociologie Juridique,* 8(1938), 276-278.

1938f   "*Review:* Maxime Leroy-*Les Tendances du Pouvoir et de la Liberté en France au XXᵉ Siècle.* 1937, Paris, éd. du Recueil Sirey," *Archives de Philosophie du Droit et de Sociologie Juridique,* 8(1938), 280-282.

1939a   "*Review:* René Hubert-*Essais d'une Doctrine de la Moralité.* Paris, 1938, éd. Vrin, p. 387," *Archives de Philosophie du Droit et de Sociologie Juridique,* 9(1939), 258-259.

1939b   "The Sociological Legacy of Lucien Lévy-Bruhl," *Journal of Social Philosophy,* 5(October 1939), 61-70.

1939c   "La Sociologie Juridique de Montesquieu," *Revue de Métaphysique et de Morale,* 46(1939), 611-626.

1940a   *Eléments de Sociologie Juridique.* Paris: Aubier-Editions Montaigne, 1940.

1940b   "*Review:* Prélot (Marcel)-*L'Evolution Politique du Socialisme Francaise (1789-1934),* Paris, Editions Spès, 1939, 296 pages," *Archives de Philosophie du Droit et de Sociologie Juridique,* 10(1940), 248-249.

1940c   "*Review:* Timasheff (N.S.)-*Introduction à la Sociologie Juridique,* Paris, 1939, Editions Pedone, 345 pages," *Archives de Philosophie du Droit et de Sociologie Juridique,* 10(1940), 249-250.

1941a   "Major Problems of the Sociology of Law," *Journal of Social Philosophy,* 6(April 1941), 197-215.

1941b   "Mass, Community, Communion," *Journal of Philosophy,* XXXVIII(January-December 1941), 485-496.

1941c   "The Problem of Social Law," *Ethics,* LII(1941), 17-40.

1942a   "Democracy as a Sociological Problem," *Journal of Legal and Political Sociology,* I(1942), 46-71.

1942b   "Magic and Law," *Social Research,* 9(1942), 104-122.
1942c   *"Review: The Managerial Revolution,* by James Burnham, New York, 1941, pp. 285.
           The John Day Company," *Journal of Legal and Political Sociology,* I(1942), 163-165.
1942d   *"Review: Social Causation,* by R. M. MacIver, New York; Ginn and Company, 1942,
           pp. 410," *Journal of Legal and Political Sociology,* I(1942), 152-155.
1942e   *"Review: Theory of Legal Science,* by Huntington Cairns. Chapel Hill, 1941, The
           University of North Carolina Press, pp. 155," *Journal of Legal and Political
           Sociology,* 1-2, I(1942), 160-162.
1942f   *Sociology of Law.* With a Preface by Roscoe Pound. New York: Philosophical
           Library and Alliance Book Corporation, 1942.-An index is supplied in the later edi-
           tions published by Routledge & Kegan Paul Ltd., London.
1943a   "Is Moral Philosophy A Normative Theory?" *Journal of Philosophy,* XL(January-
           December 1943), 141-148.
1943b   "Is the Antithesis of 'Moral Man' and 'Immoral Society' True?" *Philosophical Review,*
           LII (November 1943), 533-552.
1943c   "La Philosophie Sociale de Bergson," *Renaissance,* I(1943), 81-95.
1943d   *"Review: Europe, Russia and the Future,* by G. D. H. Cole, London and New York,
           The Macmillan Company, 1942, pp. 234," *Journal of Legal and Political Sociology,*
           I(1943), 155-157.
1943e   *"Review: Religion in Soviet Russia,* by N. S. Timasheff, New York, Sheed and Ward,
           pp. 171," *Journal of Legal and Political Sociology,* I(1943), 166-168.
1943f   *"Review: Sociocultural Causality, Space, Time,* A Study of Referential Principles of
           Sociology and Social Science, by Pitirim A. Sorokin, Duke University Press,
           Durham, 1943, pp. 246," *Journal of Legal and Political Sociology,* II(1943), 174-178.
1943g   "Social Structure of Pre-War France," *American Journal of Sociology,* XLVIII(1943),
           535-554.
1943h   "Sovereignty and Its Fate in Post-War Society," *Journal of Legal and Political
           Sociology,* II(1943), 30-51.
1944a   Contributing Editor to Henry Pratt Fairchild, ed., *Dictionary of Sociology.* New
           York: Philosophical Library, 1944.-"Consciousness," 61-62; "discontinuity," 95;
           "feeling, collective," 119; "feeling, we-," 119; "jurisprudence," 165; "patterns, sym-
           bolic," 216; "patterns, technical," 216; "Physiocrats," 220; "pluralism," 222;
           "pluralism, jural," 222-223; "pluralism, political," 223; "pluralism, philosophical,"
           223; "pluralism, sociological," 223; "sociability," 275; "social cause," 277; "socialism,
           guild-," 297; "sovereignty," 304; "syndicalism," 315; "syndicalism, revolutionary,"
           315.
1944b   *La Déclaration des Droits Sociaux.* New York: Editions de la Maison Francaise, Inc.,
           1944.
1944c(*)   *(Main Editor:) Russian-English Military Dictionary.*
1945a   "Draft of a Bill of Social Rights," *Journal of Legal and Political Sociology,* III(1945),
           79-94.
1945b   *"Review:* Paul Vignaux, *Traditionalisme et Syndicalisme. Essai d'Histoire Sociale
           (1884-1941),* in-12, pp. 193, $1.25, Collection 'Civilisation', Edition de la Maison
           Francaise, New York, 1943," *Renaissance,* II-III(1944-1945), 483-485.
1945c   *(Ed.:) Twentieth Century Sociology.* Edited by Georges Gurvitch and Wilbert E.
           Moore. New York: The Philosophical Library, 1945.-Gurvitch wrote "Social
           Control," pp. 267-296 and, together with W. E. Moore, "Preface," [pp. i-iii].
1946a   *The Bill of Social Rights.* New York: International Universities Press, 1946.-Slightly
           different from the original French edition of 1944..
1946b   *Déclaration des Droits Sociaux.* Paris: Librairie Philosophique J. Vrin, 1946.-Slightly
           different from the original French edition of 1944.
1946c   "Au Pays de la Bonne Volonté," *Esprit,* 15 (Novembre 1946), 702-708.
1946d   "La Réprésentation Ouvrière et le Problème des Nationalisations-'Conseils de Con-
           trôle' et 'Conseils de Gestion'", *Esprit,* (1er Janvier 1946), 107-112.
1946e   "Vers l'Unité Ouvrière," *Esprit,* 14(1er Février 1946), 270-279.
1946f   "La Vocation Actuelle de la Sociologie," *Cahiers Internationaux de Sociologie,*
           I(1946), 3-22.

1947a (*Discussion:*) Pp. 69-71 in Jean Wahl, *Petite Histoire de "l'Existentialisme"*. *Suivie de Kafka et Kierkegaard. Commentaires.* Paris: Editions Club Maintenant, 1947.

1947b "Microsociologie et Sociométrie," *Cahiers Internationaux de Sociologie,* III(1947), 24-67.

1947c "*Reviews:* MacIver (Robert M.), *Social Causation,* New York, Ginn et Co, 1942 et Sorokin (Pitirim), *Sociocultural Causality, Space, Time,* Durham, Duke University Press, 1943," *Cahiers Internationaux de Sociologie,* II(1947), 172-182.

1947d (*Ed:*) *La Sociologie au XXe Siècle,* I-II. Publié sous la Direction de Georges Gurvitch. En Collaboration avec Wilbert E. Moore. Paris: P.U.F., 1947.-Translation of the original English edition with an added one-page "Avertissement," p. vii, for French readers.

1948a *Initiation aux Recherches sur la Sociologie de la Connaissance. Fascicule 1.* Paris: C.D.U., 1948.

1948b *Morale Théorique et Science des Moeurs.* Deuxième Edition Revue et Corrigée. Paris: P.U.F., 1948.

1948c "La Philosophie Sociale de Bergson," *Revue de Métaphysique et de Morale,* 53(1948), 294-306.

1948d "La Sociologie du Jeune Marx," *Cahiers Internationaux de Sociologie,* VII(1949), 3-42.

1949a "Groupement Sociale et Classe Sociale," *Cahiers Internationaux de Sociologie,* VII(1949), 3-42.

1949b (*Ed.:*) *Industrialisation et Technocratie.* Exposés de M. Byé *et al.* Recueil Publié sous la Direction de Georges Gurvitch. Introduction de Lucien Febvre. Paris: Librairie Armand Colin, 1949.-Gurvitch contributed the article "La Technocratie Est-Elle un Effet Inévitable de l'Industrialisation?" pp. 179-199, and to the discussion on pp. 33, 95-97, 158-159, 164-165, 209-211.

1949c "*Reviews: Sociologie de la Connaissance et Psychologie Collective.*-Sorokin (Pitirim).-*Social and Cultural Dynamics,* vol. I-IV.-New York, 1937-1941.-Znaniecki (Florian).-*The Social Role of the Man of Knowledge.*-New York, 1940, Columbia University Press. De Gre (Girard).-*Society and Ideology. An Inquiry into Sociology of Knowledge.*-New York, 1943.-Merton (Robert K.).-*Sociology of Knowledge* dans *Twentieth Century Sociology.*-New York, 1945, sous la Direction de G. Gurvitch et W.E. Moore. Traduction Francaise, Paris, I, p. 376-416.-Wilson (Logan).-*The Academic Man.*-New York, 1942.-Bernal (J.D.).-*The Social Function of Science.*-Londres, 1939.-Meyerson (Ignace).-*Les Fonctions Psychologiques et les OEuvres.*-Paris, 1948.-Mead (Georges H.).-*Mind, Self and Society,* 4e éd. 1944.-Leenhardt (Maurice).- *Do Kamo.*-Paris, 1947.-Chapple (E.D.) and Coon (C.S.).-*Principles of Anthropology.*-New York, 1944," *Année Sociologique,* (1940-1948), I, 463-486.

1949d Editor of *Sociometry,* Nos. 1-3, Vol. XII, February-August 1949.-This number which contains a translation of "Microsociologie et Sociometrie" from 1947 and a brief "Editorial," p. vii, by Gurvitch, was republished in 1950 by Beacon House as *Sociometry in France and the United States-A Symposium.*

1950a "Avertissement," pp. vii-viii in Marcel Mauss, *Sociologie et Anthropologie,* Précedé d'une Introduction à l'OEuvre de Marcel Mauss par Claude Lévi-Strauss. Paris: P.U.F., 1950.

1950b "Nécrologie: Marcel Mauss (1873-1950)," *Revue de Métaphysique et de Morale,* 55(1950), 223.

1950c "*Review:* Jean Lacroix: *Marxisme, Existentialisme, Personnalisme,* Paris, P.U.F., 1950," *Cahiers Internationaux de Sociologie,* X(1951), 186-187.

1950d "A Sociological Analysis of International Tensions," pp. 243-256 in Hadley Cantril, ed., *Tensions That Cause War. Common Statement and Individual Papers by a Group of Social Scientists Brought Together by UNESCO.* Urbana: University of Illinois Press, 1950.-Gurvitch also signed the "Common Statement," pp. 17-21.

1950e *La Vocation Actuelle de la Sociologie. Vers une Sociologie Différentielle.* Paris: P.U.F., 1950.

1951a   "Les Degrés de la Liberté Humaine," *Cahiers Internationaux de Sociologie,* XI(1951), 3-20.

1951b   "Die Gegenwártige Lage der Soziologie und ihre Aufgaben," pp. 10-14 in Karl Gustav Specht, ed., *Soziologische Forschung in Unserer Zeit-Ein Sammelwerk Leopold von Wiese zum 75. Geburtstag.* Köln und Opladen: Westdeutscher Verlag, 1951.

1951c   (*Main Editor:*) "Psychologie Collective et Psychologie de la Connaissance," *Année Sociologique,* 1951(1948-1949), 171-212.-"Avant-Propos," 171-175 written by Gurvitch.

1951d   "Le Pluralisme de la Fonction Symbolique," *Année Psychologique,* LI 1949 (1951), 547-549.

1952a   (*Main Editor:*) "Psychologie Collective et Sociologie de la Connaissance," *Année Sociologique,* 1952 (1949-1950), 203-244.

1952b   "Réponse à une Critique. Lettre Ouverte au Professeur Léopold von Wiese," *Kölner Zeitschrift für Soziologie,* 5(1952/53), 98-103.-Reprinted in *Cahiers Internationaux de Sociologie,* XIII(1952), 94-104.

1952c   "*Review:* Michel Gordey: *Visa pour Moscou.* Paris, 1951. Gallimard," *Cahiers Internationaux de Sociologie,* XIII(1952), 189.

1953a(*)   (*Discussion:*) Georges Friedmann, ed., *Villes et Campagnes. Civilisation Urbaine et Civilisation Rurale en France.* Paris: A. Colin, 1953. Pp. 118-121, 133, 148-150.

1953b   "Hyper-Empirisme Dialectique. Ses Applications en Sociologie," *Cahiers Internationaux de Sociologie,* XV(1953), 3-33.

1953c   (*Main Editor:*) "Psychologie Collective et Sociologie de la Connaissance," *Année Sociologique,* 1953(1951), 151-188.

1953d   "Les Voies de la Démocratisation Industrielle," *Esprit,* Juin 1953, 964-972.

1954a   *Le Concept de Classes Sociales de Marx à Nos Jours.* Paris: C.D.U., 1954.

1955a   "Le Concept de Classes: *un Dialogue entre Georges Gurvitch et Henri Lefebvre,*" *Critique,* XI(1955), 558-569.

1955b   "Le Concept de Structure Sociale," *Cahiers Internationaux de Sociologie,* XIX(1955), 3-44.

1955c   *Déterminismes Sociaux et Liberté Humaine-Vers l'Etude Sociologique des Cheminements de la Liberté.* Paris: P.U.F., 1955.

1955d   *Les Fondateurs Français de la Sociologie Contemporaine.II. P.J. Proudhon.* Paris: C.D.U., 1955.

1955e   *Les Fondateurs Français de la Sociologie Contemporaine.I-Saint-Simon: Sociologue.* Paris: C.D.U., 1955.

1955f   (*Main Editor:*) "Psychologie Collective et Sociologie de la Connaissance," *Année Sociologique,* 1955(1952), 251-304.

1955g   "On Some Deviations in the Interpretation of the Concept of Social Structure," *Sociometry,* XVIII(1955), 501-518.

1956a   "Les Caractères Cardinaux des Classes Sociales," *Archiv für Rechts- und Socialphilosophie,* XLII (1956), 153-170.

1956b   "La Crise de l'Explication en Sociologie," *Cahiers Internationaux de Sociologie,* XXI(1956), 3-18.

1956c   "Le Dynamisme des Classes Sociales," pp. 285-290 in *Transactions of the Third World Congress of Sociology. (Koninklijk Instituut voor de Tropen, Amsterdam, 22-29 August, 1956),* Volume III. London: International Sociological Association, 1956.

1956d   "Les Phenomènes Sociaux Totaux et la Science de l'Homme," *Esprit,* 24(Mars 1956), 390-397.

1956e   "Sociologie du Théâtre," *Lettres Nouvelles,* Nº 35(Février 1956), 196-210.

1957a(*)   *Combat,* January 23, 1957.

1957b   "Continuité et Discontinuité en Histoire et en Sociologie," *Annales. Economies. Sociétés. Civilisations,* 12(1957), 73-84.

1957c   "Philosophie et Sociologie," *Encyclopédie Francaise,* XIX(1957), 19.26-15 - 19.28-4.

1957d(*)   *Pour le Centenaire de la Mort d'Auguste Comte (1857-1957). Trois Chapitres d'Histoire de la Sociologie: Auguste Comte-Karl Marx-Herbert Spencer.* Paris: C.D.U., 1957.

1957e   "Le Problème de la Sociologie de la Connaissance-A la Mémoire de Lucien Lévy-Bruhl," *Revue Philosophique de la France et de l'Etranger,* CXLVII(1957), 494-502.

1957f   "Réflexions sur les Rapports entre Philosophie et Sociologie," *Cahiers Internationaux de Sociologie,* XXII(1957), 3-14.

1957g   *"Review:* Gottfried Eisermann, *Die Grundlage des Historismus in der Deutschen National-Ökonomie,* Stuttgart, 1956, Enke," *Cahiers Internationaux de Sociologie, XXIII(1957), 175-176.*

1957h   "Une Source Oubliée des Concepts de 'Structure Sociale,' 'Fonction Social' et 'Institution': Herbert Spencer," *Cahiers Internationaux de Sociologie,* XXIII(1957), 111-121.

1957i   "Structures Sociales et Systèmes de Connaissances," pp. 291-307 in *XXᵉ Sémaine de Synthèse. Notion de Structure et Structure de la Connaissance, 18-27 Avril 1956.* Paris: Editions Albin Michel, 1957.-Followed by a discussion, pp. 308-342, of Gurvitch's contribution by Gurvitch, Perelman, Leroy, Eggers, Jones, Davy, and Rueff.

1957j   "Three Paths to Self-Management," pp. 20-28 in Branko Horvat *et al,* eds., *Self-Governing Socialism. A Reader. Volume Two. Sociology and Politics, Economics.* New York: International Arts and Sciences Press, Inc., 1975.-Originally written in 1957.

1957k   *La Vocation Actuelle de la Sociologie. Tome Premier. Vers la Sociologie Différentielle.* Deuxième Edition Refondue et Augmentée. Paris: P.U.F., 1957.

1958a   "Mon Itinéraire Intellectuel," *Lettres Nouvelles,* 6(Juillet-Août 1958), 65-83.-Republished with editorial comment on 1958-1965 in *L'Homme et la Société,* 1(1966), 3-12.

1958b(*) *La Multiplicité des Temps Sociaux.* Paris: C.D.U., 1958.

1958c   "Le Problème de la Sociologie de la Connaissance," *Revue Philosophique de la France et de l'Etranger,* CXLVIII(1958), 438-451.

1958d   "Rechtssoziologie" and "Wissenssoziologie," pp. 182-234 and 408-452 in Gottfried Eisermann, ed., *Die Lehre von der Gesellschaft.* Stuttgart: Ferdinand Enke Verlag, 1958.

1958e   "Réflexions sur la Sociologie de la Vie Morale," *Cahiers Internationaux de Sociologie,* XXIV (1958), 3-17.

1958f   "(Séance du 29 Novembre 1958 Rapportée au 31 Janvier 1959:) Structures Sociales et Multiplicité des Temps," *Bulletin de la Société Francaise de Philosophie,* 52(1958), 99-142.

1958g   (*Ed*:) *Traité de Sociologie,* publié sous la Direction de Georges Gurvitch. Tome Premier. Paris: P.U.F., 1958.-Gurvitch contributed the following articles: "Avant-Propos," p. vii; "Objet et Méthode de la Sociologie," pp. 3-27; "Brève Esquisse de l'Histoire de Sociologie," pp. 28-64; "Problèmes de Sociologie Générale," pp. 155-251.

1958h(*) "Workers' Councils," *Pregled,* 1958, 99-107. (In Yugoslavian.)

1959a   "Conclusion: Les Cadres Sociaux de la Connaissance Sociologique," *Cahiers Internationaux de Sociologie,* XXVI (1959), 165-172.-Gurvitch gave this speech at the second meeting of *l'Association Internationale des Sociologues de Langue Francaise,* held in Royaumont 18-20 March, 1959. Gurvitch's contribution to the discussions of the speeches by Raymond Aron, Charles Perelman and Albert Memmi can be found on pp. 71-73, 129-130, 161.

1959b   "Entretien avec Georges Gurvitch" par Jean Duvignaud, *Lettres Nouvelles,* 1ᵉʳ Avril, 1959, 23-25.

1959c   "Pour le Centenaire de Durkheim," *Cahiers Internationaux de Sociologie,* XXVII(1959), 3-10.

1959d   "Préface," pp. 3-5 in Pitirim Sorokin, *Tendances et Déboires de la Sociologie Américaine.* Traduction de Cyrille Arnavon. Paris: Aubier, 1959.

1959e   "Le Problème de la Sociologie de la Connaissance, III," *Revue Philosophique de la France et de l'Etranger,* CXLIX(1959), 145-168.

1959f(*) *La Sociologie de Karl Marx.* Paris: C.D.U., 1959.

1960a   "Commémoration du Centenaire de la Naissance d'Emile Durkheim: Allocution de M. Georges Gurvitch," *Annales de l'Université de Paris,* 30(1960), 38-40.

1960b   "Deux Aspects de la Philosophie de Bergson: Temps et Liberté," *Revue de Métaphys-*

ique et de Morale, 65(1960), 307-316.

1960c "Enquête Sociologique sur la Connaissance d'Autrui: Avant-Propos," *Cahiers Internationaux de Sociologie,* XXIX(1960), 137-138.

1960d "Pour le Deuxième Centenaire de Saint-Simon (1760-1960)," *Cahiers Internationaux de Sociologie,* XXIX(1960), 3-13.

1960e "Saint-Simon et Karl Marx," *Revue Internationale de Philosophie,* 14(1960), 399-416.

1960f (*Ed.*:) *Traité de Sociologie,* Publié sous la Direction de Georges Gurvitch. Tome Second. Paris: P.U.F., 1960.-Gurvitch contributed the following articles: "Avant-Propos," p. [1]; "Problèmes de la Sociologie de la Connaissance," pp. 103-136; "Problèmes de la Sociologie de la Vie Morale," pp. 137-172; "Problèmes de Sociologie de Droit," pp. 173-206; "Introduction: Note sur les Phenomènes Psychiques Totaux," pp. 333-338.

1961a "Conclusions Générales (du IIIᵉ Colloque de l'Association Internationale des Sociologues de Langue Francaise, Genève, 2-4 Mai, 1960): Les OEuvres de la Civilisation et les Structures Sociales Sont-Elles Menacées par le Dechaînement Actuelle des Techniques?" *Revue de l'Institut de Sociologie,* 1961 1/2, 277-288.

1961b "Dialectique et Sociologie selon Jean-Paul Sartre," *Cahiers Internationaux de Sociologie,* XXXI(1961), 113-128.

1961c *Morale Théorique et Science des Moeurs. Leurs Possibilités-Leurs Conditions.* Troisième Edition Revue et Corrigé. Paris: P.U.F., 1961.

1961d(*) *La Multiplicité des Temps Sociaux.* Deuxième Edition. Paris: C.D.U., 1961.

1961e "(Perspectives du Socialisme:) Le Sort des Structures Sociales Actuelles," pp. 151-160 in *Quel Avenir Attend L'Homme?-Rencontre Internationale de Royaumont (17-20 Mai 1961).* Paris: P.U.F., 1961.-Followed by a discussion of Gurvitch's article, pp. 160-176.

1961f(*) *La Sociologie de Karl Marx.* Deuxième Edition. Paris: C.D.U., 1961.

1962a *Dialectique et Sociologie.* Paris: Flammarion, Editeur, 1962.

1962b "L'Effendrement d'un Mythe Politique: Joseph Staline," *Cahiers Internationaux de Sociologie,* XXXIII(1962), 5-18.

1963a *Déterminismes Sociaux et Liberté Humaine-Vers l'Etude Sociologique des Cheminements de la Liberté.* Deuxième Edition Revue et Completée. Paris: P.U.F., 1963.

1963b(*) "Préface" to George Herbert Mead, *L'Esprit, le Soi et la Société.* Traduit de l'Anglais par Jean Cazeneuve, Eugene Kalein et Georges Thibault. Paris: P.U.F., 1963.

1963c "Social Structure and the Multiplicity of Times," pp. 171-184 in Edward A. Tiryakian, ed., *Sociological Theory, Values, and Sociocultural Change.* Glencoe and London: The Free Press and Collier-Macmillan Ltd., 1963.

1963d(*) (*Ed.*:) *Traité de Sociologie.* Publié sous la Direction de Georges Gurvitch. Tome Second. Seconde Edition Corrigée.-Gurvitch published the same articles in this edition as in the first edition (1958).

1963e(*) (*Ed.*:) *Traité de Sociologie.* Publié sous la Direction de Georges Gurvitch. Tome Second. Seconde Edition Corrigée. Paris: P.U.F., 1963.-Gurvitch published the same articles in this edition as in the first edition (1960).

1963f *La Vocation Actuelle de la Sociologie. Tome Premier. Vers la Sociologie Différentielle.* Troisième Edition Revue. Paris: P.U.F., 1963.

1963g *La Vocation Actuelle de la Sociologie. Tome Second. Antécédents et Perspectives.* Deuxième Edition Refondue et Augmentée. Paris: P.U.F., 1963.

1964a "Dialectique et Explication en Sociologie," pp. 232-240 in *Mélanges Alexandre Koyré-Publiés à l'Occasion de Son Soixante-Dixième Anniversaire. II. L'Aventure de l'Esprit.* Introduction de Fernand Braudel. Paris: Hermann, 1964.

1964b *Pour le Centenaire de la Mort de Pierre-Joseph Proudhon. Proudhon et Marx: Une Confrontation.* Paris: C.D.U., 1964.

1964c "Sociologie de la Connaissance et Epistémologie," pp. 193-207 in Volume IV of *Transactions of the Fifth World Congress (Washington D.C., 2-8 September, 1962).* Louvain: International Sociological Association, 1962.

1964d "Les Variations des Perceptions Collectives des Etendues," *Cahiers Internationaux de*

Sociologie, XXXVII(1964), 79-106.

1965a   *(Ed.:)* C.-H. de Saint-Simon, *La Physiologie Sociale. OEuvres Choisies avec Introduction et Notes de Georges Gurvitch.* Paris: P.U.F., 1965.

1965b   *Proudhon. Sa Vie, Son OEuvre Avec un Exposé de Sa Philosophie.* Paris: P.U.F., 1965.

1965c   "(Les Classes Sociales dans le Monde d'Aujourd'hui-Ve Colloque de l'Association Internationale des Sociologues de Langue Francaise, 29 Septembre-4 Octobre 1964:) Avant-Propos," *Cahiers Internationaux de Sociologie,* XXXVIII(1965), 3-8.

1965d   "La Sociologie de la Connaissance," *Revue de L'Enseignement Supérieur,* Nos 1-2(Janvier-Juin 1965), 43-53.

1966a   *Les Cadres Sociaux de la Connaissance.* Paris: P.U.F., 1966.-This and the following works were published posthumously.

1966b   *Etudes sur les Classes Sociales.* Paris: Editions Gonthier, 1966.

1966c   "Proudhon et Marx," *Cahiers Internationaux de Sociologie,* XL(1966), 7-16.-Reprinted, pp. 89-97, in *L'Actualité de Proudhon. Colloque des 24 et 25 Novembre 1965.* Bruxelles: Editions de l'Institut de Sociologie de l'Université de Bruxelles, 1967. Followed by a discussion, pp. 98-114, by Delsinne, Goriely, De Smet, Bartier. Interventions by Gurvitch on pp. 45-47, 130-139.

1966d   "Société, Technique et Civilisation," *Cahiers Internationaux de Sociologie,* XLV(1966), 5-16.

1967a   *Sociologie de la "Construction Nationale" dans les Noveaux Etats. VIe Colloque de l'Association Internationale de Langue Francaise. Royaumont 28-29-30 Octobre, 1965:* "Conclusions Générales," *Revue de l'Institut de Sociologie,* 1967-2/3, 561-562.-Gurvitch also contributed to the discussion (pp. 277-281, 543, 556, 558).

1969a   "Mikrosoziologie" and "Tiefensoziologie," pp. 692-695 and 1162-1167 in Wilhelm Bernsdorf, ed., *Wörterbuch der Soziologie.* Zweite, Neuberabeitete Ausgabe. Stuttgart: Ferdinand Enke Verlag, 1969.

Works by Gurvitch Available in English

Works that were originally published in English are not included here. For those, see the main bibliography, 1930-1935, 1939-1946, 1949, 1950, 1955, 1957, 1963. For a broad introduction to Gurvitch's work, see "The Works of Gurvitch-Extracts," pp. 40-110 in Georges Balandier, ed., *Gurvitch,* trans. Margaret A. Thompson and Kenneth Thompson (New York: Harper & Row, 1974). The parentheses denote the year when the work originally appeared.

(1956)   "The Sociology of the Theatre," pp. 78-81 in Elizabeth and Tom Burns, eds., *Sociology of Literature and Drama-Selected Readings.* Middlesex, England: Penguin Modern Sociology Readings, 1973.

(1958)   "My Intellectual Itinerary or 'Excluded From The Horde'", *Sociological Abstracts,* 17/2 (April 1969), i-xiii.

(1958)   *The Spectrum of Social Time.* Translated and Edited by Myrtle Korenbaum, Assisted by Phillip Bosserman. Dordrecht, Holland: D. Reidel Publishing Company, 1964.

(1966)   *The Social Frameworks of Knowledge.* Translated from the French by Margaret A. Thompson and Kenneth A. Thompson. Oxford: Basil Blackwell, 1971.

Index

Abbagnano, Nicola, 181-2 (n. 151)
Adler, Max, 121
Adorno, Theodor W., 83
Aillet, Georges, 43, 161 (n. 71)
Alexander I, 17
Althusser, Louis, 119-20
Anderson, Perry, 116
Ansart, Pierre, 182 (n. 172)
Arendt, Hannah, 82
Aron, Raymond, 119, 134, 140-1, 183 (n. 192, 194)
Association Internationale des Sociologues de Langue Française, 128
Autogestion, 123, 178 (n. 77)

Bakunin, Michael, 16
Balandier, Georges, 83, 174 (n. 137), 180 (n. 116-7), 181 (n. 126, 128), 195
Baritz, Loren, 76
Bastide, Roger, 181 (n. 123)
Bauer, Ileana, 183 (n. 195)
Beauvoir, Simone de, 96-8, 146
Belinsky, Vissarion, 16
Bell, Daniel, 71, 124
Berdiaev, Nicholas, 33
Bergson, Henri, 8-10, 163 (n. 3), 170 (n. 7), 190-1, 193-4
Bernsdorf, Wilhelm, 195
Bernstein, Eduard, 137
Bibliothèque de Sociologie Contemporaine, 100
Blanc, Louis, 41
Blumer, Herbert, 75
Bonald, Louis de, 38, 41
Bosserman, Phillip, 66, 162 (n. 86), 168 (n. 118), 173 (n. 106), 181 (n. 127), 195
Bottigelli, E., 183 (n. 196)
Bottomore, T. B., 133, 182 (n. 152)
Bouglé, Celéstin, 57, 59, 100
Bourdet, Yvon, 123, 179 (n. 78)
Bourgeois, Léon, 38, 42
Bourricaud, François, 179 (n. 96)
Braudel, Fernand, 111-2, 124-5, 194
Brunschvicg, Léon, 68, 186
Bukharin, Nikolai, 112, 137
Burgess, Ernest W., 74-5, 77-8
Burnham, James, 95, 109-12

Cahiers Internationaux de Sociologie, 100, 109, 119
Cantril, Hadley, 76, 191
Casanova, Laurent, 94
Cazeneuve, Jean, 131, 185
Centre d'Etudes Sociologiques, 100
Chiaromonte, Nicola, 169 (n. 129)
Chicherin, Boris, 45, 185-6
Clark, Terry Nichols, 3
class concept, 2-3, 5-6, 21-2, 106, 113, 137-8, 140-1, 146, 149, 191-2, 195
Claudin, Fernando, 93
"collective effervescence," 63-4, 108, 174 (n. 121)
Colletti, Lucio, 56, 62
Comité de Forges, 81
community, 11-3, 18, 27, 29, 33, 37-8, 41-2, 47-8, 57-8, 61, 64-7, 73, 77, 79, 105-6, 124, 147, 189
Comte, Auguste, 41, 134, 192
conflict theory, 118, 129, 133
"conscience collective," 57, 60-1, 63, 189
Cooley, Charles H., 79
creativity, 29
Croix de Feu, 81
Cuvillier, Armand, 100, 111-2, 181 (n. 144)

Damascius, 138
Davis, Kingsley, 118
Davy, Georges, 100, 131
De Gaulle, Charles, 91, 117
De Queiroz, Maria Isaura, 179-80 (n. 96)
democracy, 163 (n. 5), 186, 189
"depth sociology," 9, 11, 53, 63-8, 81, 104-5, 126, 195
Derathé, R., 166 (n. 78)
determinism, 7-11, 13, 18, 63-4, 108-9, 115, 126, 132-4, 192, 194
dialectic, 24-5, 30, 33-4, 63, 121, 129, 138-40, 145, 183 (n. 195), 192, 194
Duguit, Léon, 42
Durkheim, Emile, 2-3, 56-68, 75, 78-9, 81, 100, 103, 108, 113, 134, 147, 182 (n. 161), 189, 193
Durry, Marcel, 155 (n. 3)
Duvignaud, Jean, 37, 83, 120, 122-3, 132-3, 140-1, 181 (n. 126, 128), 184 (n. 199), 193

Ecole Libre des Hautes Etudes, 169 (n. 122)
economics, 109
Eisermann, Gottfried, 193
Eisner, Kurt, 56
empiricism, 78, 80, 92, 127-8
Engels, Friedrich, 43-4, 121, 137
epistemology, 20-2, 30, 32; *see also* sociology
    of knowledge
equality, 12, 19, 44-5
Esprit, 102, 122
ethics, 20, 22-3, 26-9, 126-7, 189-90, 193-4;
    see also values vs. facts
existentialism, 96-9, 107-9, 133-4, 186, 191

facts: *see* values vs. facts
Fajon, Etienne, 102
Fanon, Frans, 122
Faris, Ellsworth, 74
Faris, Robert E. L., 75, 78
fascism, 20, 34-5, 50, 69-70, 81-2, 109-10,
    122, 125, 128, 139, 167 (n. 107)
Fauconnet, Paul, 59, 68
Febvre, Lucien, 191
Fernandez, Ramon, 178 (n. 66), 187
Fichte, Johann Gottlieb, 8, 10-1, 20-36, 42,
    47, 138-9, 183 (n. 185), 185-7
Ford, Joseph B., 179 (n. 85)
formalism in sociology, 56, 67, 106-7, 124
Foucault, Michel, 119-20
Fougeyrollas, Pierre, 111-2, 183 (n. 195)
Fouillée, Alfred, 58
Fourier, Charles, 41
Frank, Simon, 8, 32-3
French Communist Party, 92-6, 102-3, 117
French society, 47, 57-8, 80-1, 89-94, 117
freedom, 44-5, 98, 108-9, 128, 132-4, 192, 194
Friedmann, Georges, 95, 112, 119
functionalism, 88-9, 118, 130-1

Garaudy, Roger, 94, 122, 140-1, 184 (n. 197)
Gierke, Otto von, 38, 42, 47, 185
Giraud, Henri, 91
Giustizia e Libertà, 70, 163 (n. 8)
Glazer, Nathan, 71
"global societies," 64, 67, 106-7, 124-5, 162
    (n. 86)
Goethe, Johann Wolfgang, 150
Goldmann, Lucien, 1-4, 6-7, 13, 21-2, 100-1,
    111, 113, 120-1, 131, 145, 148 (note), 149
Gorz, André, 120-1

Gradovsky, A. D., 186
Gramsci, Antonio, 13, 70, 88-9
Granger, Gilles, 131
Grotius, Hugo, 10-1, 41, 186
group, 64-5, 67, 105-6
Gucinski, Adolf, 183 (n. 195)
Guérin, Daniel, 178 (n. 75)
Gueroult, Martial, 154 (n. 33, 35), 187
Guild Socialism, 39, 190

Gurvitch, Georges: ideas on sociology, 11,
    35, 50-145; in France, 47, 100-1, 172 (n.
    77, 79); in Prague, 20; political activities,
    19, 46, 70, 155 (n. 60), 155 (n. 3), 157 (n.
    54), 163 (n. 8); political ideas, 8-11, 82-6,
    101-3, 116, 122-4, 132, 158 (n. 3) 161 (n.
    75); professional activities, 37, 69, 100,
    115-6, 128, 169 (n. 122), 172 (n. 77, 79),
    178 (n. 73), 185

WORKS:
*Bill of Social Rights (Déclaration des
    Droits Sociaux),* 69, 82-7, 101-2, 163 (n.
    4), 190
Le Concept de Classes Sociales, 115-6,
    134, 137-8, 140-1, 192
*Déterminismes Sociaux et Liberté Hu-
    maine,* 115, 124, 126-7, 132-4, 177 (n.
    122), 192, 194
Dialectique et Sociologie, 115-6, 129,
    138-40, 194
Essais de Sociologie, 11, 53, 60-2, 67-8,
    70, 80, 83, 104-5, 163 (n. 2), 189
L'Expérience Juridique, 37, 49-50, 188
Fichtes System der Konkreten Ethik, 11,
    20-34, 183 (n. 185), 185
Les Fondateurs Français, 115, 192
L'Idée du Droit Social, 11, 20, 35-44,
    46-7, 50-3, 59, 63, 65, 67, 69, 82-3, 135,
    146, 155 (n. 11), 163 (n. 2, 4), 186
Morale Théorique et Science des Moeurs,
    29, 60, 62, 67-8, 162 (n. 84), 163 (n. 2),
    189, 191, 194
"My Intellectual Itinerary" (*Mon Itinéraire
    Intellectuel*), 7-10, 101, 193, 195
"La Réprésentation Ouvrière," 101-2, 190
Rousseau and the Declaration of Rights,
    7, 11-3, 185
*Social Frameworks of Knowledge (Les
    Cadres Sociaux de la Connaissance),* 115,

124, 127, 134, 195
"The Social Structure of Pre-War
    France," 80-1, 190
"A Sociological Analysis of International
    Tensions," 106-7, 191
La Sociologie de Karl Marx, 115, 134,
    193-4
*Sociology of Law (Eléments de Sociologie
    Juridique),* 51, 53, 60, 67-9, 80, 83, 104,
    106, 125, 163 (n. 2, 3)
*Spectrum of Social Time (La Multiplicité
    des Temps Sociaux),* 126, 129, 193-5
*"La Technocratie est-elle un Effet
    Inévitable de L'Industrialisation?,"*
    109-11, 191
Le Temps Présent, 36-7, 47-9, 187
*Les Tendances Actuelles de la Philosophie
    Allemande,* 29-30, 186
Traité de Sociologie, 115, 134, 193-4
The Truth of the Monarch's Will, 7, 185
Twentieth Century Sociology, 37, 69,
    72-3, 77-9, 100, 104, 167 (n. 95), 190-1
"Vers l'Unité Ouvrière," 101-3, 190
La Vocation Actuelle de la Sociologie, 90,
    103-8, 111-3, 115, 124, 128-9, 146, 170 (n.
    7), 191, 193-4
*"Les Voies de la Démocratisation In-
    dustrielle,"* 122-3, 192

Halbwachs, Maurice, 57, 59, 137-8
Hartmann, Nikolai, 186
Hauriou, Maurice, 39, 42, 186
Hauser, Philip M., 75
Hegel, G. W. F., 1, 7-10, 24-6, 30-1, 36,
    42, 109, 112, 134, 138-9
Heidegger, Martin, 186
Herzen, Alexander, 16, 33
Hessen, W. M., 45
Hessen, Sergius, 46, 156 (n. 22), 185
Hobbes, Thomas, 6
Holmes, Oliver Wendell, 42
Homans, George C., 71
Hoover, Herbert, 73
Horkheimer, Max, 107
Hughes, Everett C., 75-6
Hughes, H. Stuart, 82
Husserl, Edmund, 25, 63

"ideal type," 55-6
idealism, 1, 20-34, 45-6, 59, 67

ideal-realism, 23-6, 33, 40
ideology, 6
individualism, 8, 10-3, 18-9, 27-8, 32, 37-8,
    41-2, 57-8, 61, 73-4, 77, 79, 104, 147
industrial democracy: *see* workers' control
international law, 47-9
intuition, 8, 25-6, 30-1
irrationalism, 25-7, 29-31, 33-4, 55-6, 129

Janne, Henri, 128
Jaurès, Jean, 57
Johnson, Alvin, 69
Jonas, Serge, 175 (n. 7)
Jouhaux, Léon, 39
Journal of Legal and Political Sociology, 169
    (n. 122)
"juristic socialism," 43-4, 46-7
justice, 40, 49-50, 97-8, 157 (n. 56), 186, 189;
    see also law

Kahn, Paul, 172 (n. 80), 174 (n. 137)
Kanapa, Jean, 94, 140
Kant, Immanuel, 8-9, 21-2, 27-9, 41, 47, 138-
    9, 185
Kaskell, Walter, 48
Kautsky, Karl, 7, 10, 137
Kierkegaard, Soren, 8-9
Kistiakovsky, 186
König, René, 140, 183 (n. 192)
Kolko, Gabriel, 77, 89, 92-3, 116
Kolko, Joyce, 116
Korenbaum, Myrtle, 157 (n. 54), 178 (n. 61)
    180 (n. 110), 195
Korkunov, N. M., 186-7
Koyré, Alexandre, 194
Krause, Karl Christian Friedrich, 42, 186-7
Kriegel, Annie, 120, 178 (n. 59)

labor law, 48
Lafargue, Paul, 92
Lapierre, J. W., 111, 175 (n. 146)
Lask, Emil, 8, 23, 31, 186
Laski, Harold, 42, 49
Lasalle, Ferdinand, 36
Lavrov, Peter, 16
law, 8-9, 11-3, 35-50, 67, 86-7, 161 (n. 75),
    189-90, 193-4; *see also* natural law and
    "social law"
Lazarsfeld, Paul F., 76, 92
Le Fur, Louis, 42, 156 (n. 22), 186

League of Nations, 48-9
Lebensphilosophie, 24-5, 27-8, 30
Ledrut, Raymond, 181 (n. 125)
Lefebvre, Henri, 70, 95, 109, 116, 119-23,
    131-3, 140-5, 149 (note), 177 (n. 43), 178
    (n. 75), 183 (n. 195), 192
Leibniz, Gottfried Wilhelm, 41
Lenin, V. I., 7, 10, 14-5, 17-8, 22, 31-2, 36,
    43, 54, 70, 95, 103, 112, 137, 150
Leroy, Maxime, 48, 187
Lévi-Strauss, Claude, 77-8, 119-20, 125, 130,
    161-2 (n. 80), 179 (n. 88), 181 (n. 134),
    191
Lévy, Emmanuel, 187
Lévy-Bruhl, Lucien, 3, 57, 61-2, 103, 189, 193
liberal bourgeoisie, 32, 47, 51-68, 147-8
Lichtheim, George, 183 (n. 195)
Lipset, Seymour Martin, 71
liberty, 12-3, 19, 132-4, 192-4
Lossky, Nicholas, 8, 29, 32-3
Lukács, Georg, 2, 34, 36, 50, 55, 76, 137, 148
    (note), 149
Lukes, Steven, 179 (n. 84)
Lyashchenko, Peter I., 15

MacIver, Robert M., 89
magic, 189-90
Maistre, Joseph de, 41
Mallet, Serge, 120-1
Mannheim, Karl, 6, 83-4, 169 (n. 124)
Martin, John Vincent, 161-2 (n. 80), 164
    (n. 22), 173 (n. 106), 179 (n. 89), 182 (n.
    155)
Martindale, Don, 1
Marx, Karl, 3, 6-9, 20-3, 38, 41, 43-4, 70-1,
    78, 102-3, 107, 109-10, 112-6, 121, 124,
    134-45, 148, 182 (n. 169), 191-5
Marxism: and sociological theory, 1-7, 71, 78,
    95, 112, 118-24, 140-5; in France, 70,
    94-5, 120-2, 140-4; in Russia, 7-8, 16-7,
    31-2, 45, 54; in the U.S., 71
Maunier, René, 161 (n. 171)
Mauss, Marcel, 3, 57, 59, 67, 105, 191
Mead, George Herbert, 194
Menger, Anton, 187
Merleau-Ponty, Maurice, 94-9, 103, 121,
    124, 141
Merton, Robert K., 76-8
Michels, Robert, 71
Mikhailovsky, Nicholas M., 53-4, 147

Mitzman, Arthur, 2
Mommsen, Wolfgang, 55
Montesquieu, 134, 189
Moore, Wilbert E., 77, 79, 190-1
morality: see values vs. facts, and ethics
Moreno, Jacob L., 112
Morin, Edgar, 94, 120
Morin, Gaston, 48
Mounier, Emmanuel, 102
Mullins, Carolyn J., 2
Mullins, Nicholas S., 2
Myrdal, Gunnar, 76

natural law, 12, 45, 187-8
neo-Kantianism, 8-9, 23-5, 31, 33-4, 45
Nichols, Larry, 157 (n. 45)
Nietzsche, Friedrich, 34
Nizan, Paul, 68, 70
Nolte, Ernst, 82
Nowgorodzeff, Paul, 45

Ogburn, William F., 76-7

Pannekoek, Anton, 83-4
Pareto, Vilfredo, 71, 77, 137-8
Park, Robert E., 74-5
Parsons, Talcott, 77-8, 88, 125, 130, 179
    (n. 88, 89)
Pascal, Blaise, 2, 4
Pavlov, Ivan, 54
Petrazhitsky, Lev, 40, 45-6, 53, 186-8
phenomenology, 25, 33-4, 71-2
Physiocrats, 41
philosophy of law: see law, natural law,
    "social law"
Piaget, Jean, 131
Plato, 138
Plekhanov, G., 7, 10, 18
Plotinus, 138
pluralism, 11, 38-9, 45, 48, 61, 135-6, 190
Politzer, Georges, 70
positivism, 31, 46, 53, 61-2, 79, 119-20, 124-5
    127-8, 133, 145
progress, 74, 78
Prokopovich, Theophan, 185
Proudhon, P.-J., 8-11, 39, 41-2, 46-7, 53, 59,
    84, 86, 111, 115-6, 124, 134-6, 138-9,
    144-5, 157 (n. 56), 160 (n. 40), 182 (n.
    169), 185-6, 192, 194-5
Pseudo-Dionysius, 138-9

Puchta, Georg Friedrich, 42
Pugachev rebellion, 14

Racine, Jean, 4
Radbruch, Gustav, 187
Rankovic, Miodrag, 178 (n. 73)
Razin, Stenka, 14
reason, 24-5, 30, 33
"reciprocity of perspectives," 60, 161-2
    (n. 80)
Renard, R. G., 156 (n. 22)
Rickert, Heinrich, 23, 25, 31, 189
Rodinson, Maxime, 179 (n. 84)
Roman law, 37-9
Roosevelt, Franklin Delano, 86
Ross, E. A., 72-4, 79
Rousseau, Jean Jacques, 6-8, 10-3, 41, 185
Russian society, 13-8
Russian intelligentsia, 13, 16-8, 31-3, 44-7,
    147, 152-3 (n. 55)
Russian revolution, 9, 18-9

Saint-Simon, Comte H. de, 8, 38, 41, 52, 59,
    115, 134-5, 144, 192, 194-5
Saleilles, Raymond, 42
Salomon, Albert, 77
Sartre, Jean-Paul, 94, 96-9, 111, 113, 120-2,
    133-41, 194
Savigny, Friedrich Karl von, 42
Scheler, Max, 55-6, 64, 186
Schelling, Friedrich Wilhelm Joseph von, 23
Schmoller, Gustav, 137
Scheuner, Ulrich, 156 (n. 22)
Schul, Pierre-Maxime, 181 (n. 147)
Schumpeter, Joseph, 137-8
Schwendinger, Herman, 73
Schwendinger, Julia R., 73
Secrétan, Charles, 38, 186
Selznick, Philip, 71
Simiand, François, 59
Simirenko, Alex, 183-4 (n. 196)
Sinzheimer, Hugo, 48, 156 (n. 24), 161 (n.
    71)
Small, Albion W., 72-4, 147
Smith, Dusky Lee, 73
social control, 73-4, 77, 79-80
"social law," 9, 11, 35-43, 46-7, 155-6 (n. 14)
    163 (n. 2, 4), 186-7, 189
social structure, 80, 119, 130-2, 190, 192-4
social theory, 5-7, 146-50

socialism: see workers' control
sociality, 53, 64-6, 105, 162 (n. 86), 188-9
sociological theory, 1-4, 146-50,
sociology: in general, 50-145; in France, 52,
    57-9, 68, 118-22; in Germany, 52-3, 55-6;
    in North America, 71-82, 117-8; in
    Russia, 53-5
sociology of knowledge, 1-4, 127, 191-5
sociology of law: see law and "social law"
sociometry, 81, 105, 191
Solidarity movement, 38, 42, 47, 49, 57-8,
    158 (n. 67)
Solovyev, Vladimir, 45-6, 185
Sorokin, Pitirim A., 1, 54-5, 78, 137-8, 159
    (n. 19), 179 (n. 85), 179-80 (n. 96), 180 (n.
    114), 181 (n. 127), 193
sources of law, 47-8, 187-8
Specht, Karl Gustav, 192
Spencer, Herbert, 74, 134, 182 (n. 161), 192-
    3
spontaneity, 63, 108, 129-30; see also "collec-
    tive effervescence"
Stack, Georges C., 182 (n. 155, 156)
Stalin, Joseph, 35, 70, 93, 112, 117, 121, 140
    178 (n. 65), 194
state, the, 8-11, 38-9, 41, 45, 61
Stirner, Max, 8-10
strategy, 5-7, 21-2, 52, 146-50
structuralism, 118-21, 130-1
Struve, Peter, 31
Subjectivist School, 53-4
symbols, 192
syndicalism: see workers' control
Szalai, Alexander, 107

Taranowsky, F. W., 45, 185
technocracy, 107-11, 123-4, 128, 179 (n. 79),
    191
theatre, 192, 195
Thompson, Kenneth A., 164 (n. 22), 195
Thompson, Margaret A., 195
Timasheff, Nicholas S., 1, 43, 53-4, 164 (n.
    22), 172 (n. 82)
time, 126, 193-5
Tiryakian, Edward A., 194
Tito, Marshal, 93-4
Tkachev, Peter, 16-7
Tocqueville, Alexis de, 134
Tönnies, Ferdinand, 64
"total social phenomenon," 57, 59, 67, 105,

183 (n. 193), 192, 194
totality, 41, 183 (n. 193)
Toulemont, René, 168-9 (n. 118)
Tran-Duc-Thao, 96
Treves, Renato, 161 (n. 75), 163 (n. 3)
Trotsky, Lev (Leon), 17, 35, 68
Tumanov, V. A., 156 (n. 27)

United States, 70-1, 88-9, 91

values vs. facts, 21-2, 27-8, 39-40, 50, 52-5,
    58-60, 62, 69, 71-2, 74-6, 82, 86, 103,
    109-10, 120-1, 145, 147-8, 161 (n. 75), 162
    (n. 84), 168 (n. 117), 175 (n. 146), 189
Vekhi, 18, 31-3
"Verstehen," 55
voluntarism, 10, 13, 18, 32-3, 63, 65, 100,
    102-3, 147
Vranicki, Predrag, 122

Wahl, Jean, 191
Ward, Lester F., 72-4
Weber, Max, 55-6, 58-9, 67, 71, 79, 81, 103,
    110, 113, 137
"we": *see* community
Wiese, Leopold von, 55-6, 65, 175 (n. 143),
    192
Wirth, Louis, 75
Wisscheslawzeff, 23
workers' control, 9, 19, 37-9, 46, 48-9, 69,
    82-6, 90-2, 101-2, 110, 117, 121-5, 128,
    135, 145, 177 (n. 52), 178 (n. 73), 178 (n.
    77), 179 (n. 78), 192-3

Zhadanov, Andrei, 93-4
Znaniecki, Florian, 3, 77-8